Isabella

Power, Glory
and Dust

To
BERNICE
With all my best
Adrian Coort de Leija

Isabella

Power, Glory and Dust

Jaime de Soussa

Pentland Press, Inc.
www.pentlandpressusa.com

PUBLISHED BY PENTLAND PRESS, INC.
5122 Bur Oak Circle, Raleigh, North Carolina 27612
United States of America
919-782-0281

ISBN 1-57197-223-4
Library of Congress Control Number: 00-130510

Printed in the United States of America

Very humbly, very tenderly, this book is dedicated to Spain, my country, and to Andalusia, my home, whose history has truly become a part of me.

And to Trudy, my gentle and wonderful wife, without whom the English version of this book would not have been possible.

Table of Contents

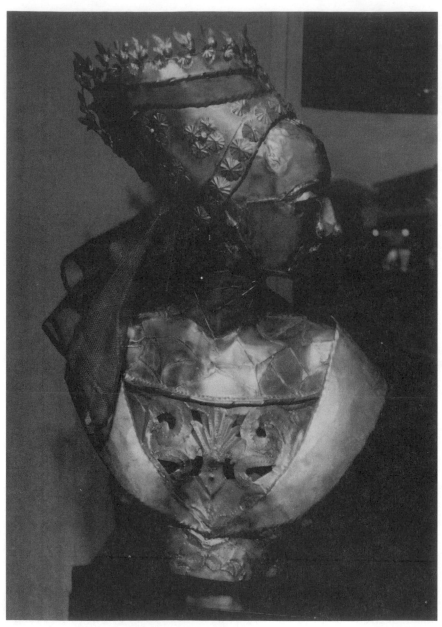

Isabella
Metal Sculpture by Lee Menichetti
1992 Palm Beach, Florida

To the Readers

Isabella is an authentic epic—historically correct, but written in novel style to avoid the cold, impersonal presentation of a history textbook. The names and facts are historically real and authentic.

Based on the author's own original research into documents hidden for some 500 years by the Spanish Inquisition, it revolutionizes our understanding of Ferdinand and Isabella, their Jewish ancestry, and the origins of anti-Semitism in Europe with the beginning of the Diaspora in Spain in 1492, contemporaneous with the first voyage of Christopher Columbus to the Americas. Of course, this collection of historical facts is in opposition with the "official history" of Spain. But the official history of Spain had been written and enforced for centuries, by the monarchy, under the "dictates" of the church and the Inquisition Holy Office.

The timeliness of the revision of traditional concepts of Spanish history imposed by the Inquisition is highlighted by the documents issued by the Vatican.

Historically the Spanish Inquisition was a period marked by the forced conversion of Jews and the persecution of heretics that the Pope seemed to be evoking when he spoke in his letter today of "acquiescence given, especially in certain centuries, to intolerance and even the use of violence in the service of truth." The Pope said historical circumstances did "not exonerate the church from the obligation to express profound regret for the weakness of so many of her sons and daughters who sullied her face."

Rome
November 14, 1994

The book is an English translation from the original text which is written in French and Spanish.

Author's Note

This partly fictionalized account of one of the most critical and probably one of the most important periods of Spanish history was born of simple curiosity.

I was brought up in France, and so my knowledge of the history of my own country tends to be very academic: thorough, but somewhat banal and orthodox, not making a lot of sense to me. The country was a kingdom with a vacant throne, a legal fiction that General Franco maintained throughout his own "reign." I wanted to find out more about the realities of Spain's historic past.

I followed this idea and began my research. It became an extraordinary voyage of discovery in a half-hidden world, frozen in time and hidden away in old books and ancient leather chests containing documents which seemed to have been hidden, undisturbed for one, two, or even three centuries.

This was the starting point for the book.

Much later, I came to understand that the bureaucracy, and even more, the all-powerful Inquisition, had held on to this rich mine of information, keeping it out of the "official" version of history. Then the idea of translating the book into English took shape in my mind.

But the creating force behind the birth of this translation was Trudy, my wife, before we were even married. Her belief in me and her continuing support enabled me to bring together the people who would make it happen . . . particularly John Lea, whose translation showed a clear and intelligent understanding of the work: without him, we would never have arrived at a text in which my own thoughts were accurately represented in the English language. His culture and his skills helped me to bring the work to the stage of its publication.

Prologue

In the middle of the fifteenth century, the word *Spain* did not mean the same thing as the political and geographic entity of today. In 1450 the Iberian peninsula was divided into a multitude of small kingdoms: from north to south they were Galicia, the kingdoms of Castile and Leon, Navarre, and Aragon; then came Catalonia, Valencia, and Murcia; and in the far south the Muslim kingdom of Granada. The peninsula evolved along lines that led to this cluster of minor realms.

Before the Christian era, Roman legions occupied much of the land. They brought with them slaves and free Roman citizens, mostly of Jewish or Latin origin, although some came from North Africa. But at the beginning of the sixth century, the Roman Empire fell when all of Europe was invaded by the barbarian tribes of the north, principally the Visigoths. These alien hordes occupied the whole peninsula, leaving no trace of Roman civilization for centuries, submerging entirely the magnificent culture of antiquity. Their rude, uncivilized way of life heralded the period that has become known as the Middle Ages—or, more accurately, the Dark Ages—which held sway between 500 and 711.

In 711 the most important event in European history took place, an event that, sad to say, has either been neglected or its importance minimized by history. It was the year when Muslim tribes from the whole southern Mediterranean seaboard, from Damascus westward, set out to overrun Europe. History reveals that the Islamic invasion, which was launched in 711, took control of territory as far as the very gates of Paris. Subsequently, these occupying forces gradually withdrew southward.

By 1450, after 750 years of Muslim occupation in part of Spain, a *convencencia*—a spirit of assimilation, of agreement, of consensus—was established between the original population and the invaders. This period is now known in Spain as the 'Golden Age.' Islamic culture blended with the best of Jewish civilization, as well as with the lifestyle of the Christians of Visigoth ancestry who had been transformed into Gentiles. These very different peoples became closely interwoven with each other, living together more or less harmoniously for years.

The various Christian kingdoms continued to wage war on each other for centuries, each seeking supremacy over its neighbors. Nevertheless, in spite of this internecine fighting, they were linked loosely by what has been called "the spirit of reconquest," an old myth that was born in the darkness of the Middle Ages. These Christians aspired to reconquer, slowly but surely, the territories occupied by the Muslims.

The Kingdoms of Castile and Leon covered the greatest geographic area, occupying the whole central part of Spain and sharing a common frontier with the Muslim world in the form of the Sultanate of Granada. The Kingdoms' neighbor—sometimes enemy, sometimes friend—was the feudal and poverty-stricken Kingdom of Aragon. The King of Aragon, Juan II, was a ruler of mean and ignoble spirit. He had a son, Ferdinand, who was part Jewish on his mother's side. The kingdoms of Castile, Leon, and Aragon should, in theory, have been able to forge an alliance between them that would have increased and consolidated their power, but perpetual feuding came between them.

In 1450 the ruler of the kingdom of Castile and Leon was Henry IV, a monarch whose reign was marred by an uneasy lope between insanity and death. In 1451 dona Isabella, his half-sister, was born. She was destined to grow up under very difficult circumstances. Isabella was of Visigoth ancestry, but she also inherited Jewish blood from her mother's side of the family. Portraits of the period depict her as being of medium height, with ash-blond hair and gray-green eyes.

The sixteenth-century Spain of Charles V created the most powerful empire the world had ever seen. Its simple beginnings can be traced back to a winter evening in the Castilian highlands, in a country racked by civil war.

On that cold night, two royal adolescents kissed. These first tentative caresses of the royal heirs, Isabella and Ferdinand, took place in a time of war, misery, and darkness. They were very poor. They had friends, however, and a fervent, youthful belief in the destiny of their great but divided land: Spain.

When they kissed, Spain was already feeling the breath of spring. Hopes for a peaceful, united land were in the air. The long winter was ending. In the streets of Madrid, children sang:

All the flowers of Aragon and Castile are in bloom . . .

Isabella and Ferdinand did not know it at the time, but eventually they would rebuild their country and wrest Granada from the Moorish King Boabdil. They would open up the golden sea-lanes to Columbus's *caravels* and influence the future of the world in ways in which they could not even dream.

The Catholic Monarchs were a fiercely tight-knit family. This unity would be challenged by the terrifying fires of the Inquisition, flaring up in the Jewish quarters of Toledo and Seville. A young Jew, David Ezra, "the shield of Israel," would seek revenge for the wrongs done to his people. The shadow of heresy and of sin would darken their reign, dedicated to God. . . .

The old social order, built over many centuries, had seen Christians, Moors, and Jews living in peaceful coexistence; it was swept away by Ferdinand's deliberate policies. With it vanished all human values, for the sake of a superficial national unity.

It is helpful to note some specific dates. Isabella lived from 1451 to 1504; Ferdinand from 1452 to 1516. Isabella married Ferdinand in 1469 at the age of eighteen. They reigned together from 1474 until her death; he continued to rule until 1516. It is important to bear in mind that in 1469, at the time of their union, Christopher Columbus was only an obscure merchant and sailor. He was from an old Jewish family that had converted to Christianity. He was born in the little village of Felanitch, in Majorca, and emigrated to Genoa, Italy, to avoid being caught up in the toils of the Inquisition.

Our principal actors have now taken their places before the glorious red-and-gold flag of Spain. Let the curtain be raised, and the play begin.

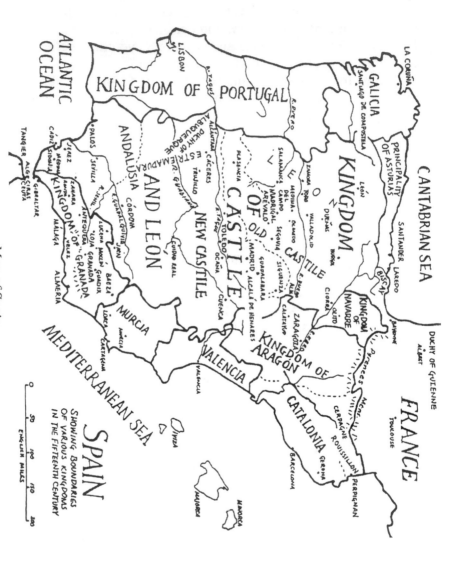

Map of Spain

1

Kingdom Without a King

"One more story, dona Albonza. Just one. After that, you can go to sleep."

The old *duenna* sighed, lifted her plump hand smeared with a perfumed cream that flaked off the wrinkled skin, and let it gently fall back on Isabella's head.

"Which story would you like to hear? The legend of Saint Casilda?"

At the sound of that name, Isabella could imagine herself breathing the odor of the crypt, seeing the yellowing bones of the saints behind the reliquaries' small window. She had outgrown these legends; they gave her only slight pleasure, and no longer thrilled her at all. She shook her head.

"No, dona Albonza. Instead, tell me the story of the seven children of Lara."

"Oh, my Lord! You've heard it at least twenty times. What do you like so much about that story?"

Isabella shrugged. She wasn't about to admit—even to the old duenna, who would listen to anything—that each time she heard the names "Almanzour" and "Lara" some magic spell took her into a world of violence where she breathed more freely, where her heart beat faster. In her mind's eye, she could see the severed heads of the seven children in a line on the low Granada wall, smell the pungent vapor of the flowing blood.

The duenna tilted her head back just a little and lowered the lids over her blind eyes, reddened with inflammation. The fingers of her left hand tapped rhythmically but gently on the back of Isabella's neck.

"Once upon a time in the lands of the south there reigned a king—the Moorish King Almanzour. He was cruel, wealthy, and powerful. His palace and his gardens . . ."

Isabella always loved to wile away the time with dona Albonza in talk of Almanzour's palace and gardens, to breathe in the smell of the roses and the orange trees; but the duenna would be hurrying to the foothills of the jagged mountains. Instead of roses and orange trees, scrubby clumps of pines; instead of mosaic floors, shiny under a fine spray of water, wild ramblas of dry streams; instead of pets, wild goats and bears.

Following their horses, the seven Lara children made their way down a stony track. Right at the end of the path, where the highest olive trees grew, a party of Moors was waiting for them. "They attacked at the hottest time of day . . ."

Isabella was only half listening. The first words of the story were enough. The rest she knew by heart. Occasionally she became aware of the warm voice of the duenna, the words again sparking her imagination.

More than anything else, Isabella was fascinated with the scenery, the backdrop. The lands of the South, the kingdom of Granada where the last of the Moors clung, behind their mountains, to their dry-blood–colored fortresses . . . She had dreamed of all this from her earliest years. In contrast, the unending plains of Castile, the chalky tablelands, made her feel sick. Yet she loved the kingdom of Castile, which, since the dawn of the reconquest of the country from the Moors seven centuries earlier, crept with glacial slowness toward the southern valleys, battle by battle.

But she felt impatient at the way the Castilian nobles took care of their own selfish interests rather than those of the kingdom. As for King Henry, her brother, he deserved only too well the title imposed on him by the opposition cliques: Henry the Powerless. He had failed to make his wife, Queen Joan the Portuguese, lead a decent life; how could he enforce even minimal discipline on this unruly bunch of peacocks who treated the court as either a birdhouse or a battlefield?

Despite these problems, the time was ripe to move against the Moors. The Kingdom of Granada was no stronger than the strength of its citadels. The Moorish princelings fought between themselves, tore each other away from the towns, and—convinced of the Christian princes' apathy—planned to insist on their upkeep by those very princes.

The towering figures of the reconquest had not been much use: El Cid Campeador, Saint Fernando, and so many others whose powers had been greatly overestimated. Their tombs were marvels of fine stone and elegant sculpture, but even if brought back to life their limited soldering skills would not have contributed much to the present need.

The age of the great commanders seemed to be over. If tomorrow the Muslim hordes, flying the green flag of the Prophet, were to sweep across Spain from the margin of the African deserts, again the Christian princes would retreat toward Asturias like a herd of goats.

"When Lord Lara arrived in the Emir's Alcazar and saw the severed heads of his seven sons, it . . ." The *duenna's* voice weakened as she grew sleepy. Isabella heard her murmur, but what she saw was the severed heads, set up in line like so many melons on the low brick wall, bleeding in the sun.

Lord Lara let out a cry. Suddenly the heads seemed to come back to life, the limbs to be torn like roots from the hard stone, the bodies to revive, while the breath of God passed over the Granada plain, quieter but deeper than the noise of a thousand war drums.

The seven children climbed off the wall, charged as one through the Alcazar's rooms, massacred the Moorish warriors and, covered with blood, came back to kneel before their father and to return to him the keys of the town.

Isabella's vision was not quite the same as the legend, but she was happy with her version. A fierce shudder of fire ran from her shoulders to her temples when the cry of old Lord Lara rang out, a cry that would never again be heard in Spain, a cry whose deep meaning was no longer understood by anyone, a cry heralding a secret power that now would only be laughed at.

A gentle snore woke Isabella from her dream. She opened her eyes and freed her sticky hands from the armchair's polished wood. Knees painful with cramp, she rose.

Dona Albonza was asleep.

⚜

The morning's commotion was over. The huge red-brick fortress of Medina del Campo was sleeping under the scorching July sun. As she crossed the highest gallery in the central courtyard, for a moment Isabella had the impression that she alone remembered her brother . . . the brother whose corpse would probably be brought home in a few days.

The news of his death came as no surprise to Isabella; what was more, she felt no emotion. He had been leading a *camarilla*, a clique of high Castilian noblemen, to lay siege to the citadel of his own brother, don Henry. One mouthful of poison, and Alfonso was no more than a memory! In the Castilian Court's games of intrigue—plots hatched, plots thwarted—his death was part of a macabre routine. Poison had come to be looked upon as a fair weapon.

Alfonso had moved on Medina with a double objective: to capture the citadel of his brother, the king, and to force his brother to name him successor to the throne in the place of Queen Joan, who had managed to drag a promise of succession out of the sick king. Riding through the red dust of the Castilian highlands, how many times had Alfonso thought about the queen in agony, blue-faced from the effects of poison? The queen had foreseen his plan. Instead, it was Alfonso who died, in the shade of a clump of juniper, facing Medina.

Alfonso . . . so difficult to love. Isabella had almost forgotten her brother's personality. She only remembered that he was like Henry: the same mask, but modeled from too soft a clay, the lines marked by impotence, cruelty, boredom.

Neither one of them had been capable of governing alone, or even of governing himself. They were weak. Their actions, particularly Henry's, were often taken against the dictates of their own wills. Contradictory decisions issued by the chancellery were inspired by the queen's favorite, Beltran de la Cueva; by Juan de Villena, doyen of the great noblemen of Castile; and by the ambassadors of Louis XI, King of France, and of King John of Aragon.

What's the point of talking about which favorite, which king, which slim-hipped adolescent he will sell his power to? Isabella mused. Whose sword will he choose to rely on? That's the question.

From where she stood in the corner of the gallery, Isabella could make out the windows of the royal bedchamber, the curtains drawn. As soon as he'd learned of his brother's death, King Henry had taken to his bed. He was in poor health, subject to periods of agonizing depression. . . . The Jewish doctors had given up trying to get him out of them. During these times, he lay prostrate, blind, deaf, only reviving to scream abuse and blasphemies or to moan and groan. Finally he would emerge slowly from this night of the soul, this silence pierced by flashes of madness.

Isabella felt that the day was near when Henry would fail to climb out of this pit. And the uneasy balance of Castile's government, with its opposing forces, would lead to anarchy and to war.

The queen was not capable of keeping control; her wild behavior would automatically keep her out of the running. The *Hermandades*, associations of great and greedy noblemen, would come into play. The *picaros*, the highwaymen, would come into the open. The winds of rebellion would blow in the church and monastery. The most obscure of noblemen, no matter how little blessed with wealth, would feel impelled to drastic action, eager to unsheathe his sword. Law and order would disintegrate into confusion.

Before recognizing that his end was near, King Henry had to decide of his own free will—and of his will alone—to exercise his authority and choose a successor. It was time to get rid of the problems, the violence that surrounded the Castilian Court. Castile had to be born from a union of serenity and of power, for such was its destiny. Spain's harmony could only come from uniting Castile, Navarre, Aragon, the Barcelona region, and the Moorish kingdom of Granada. Grouped together under the banner of Spain, they could rebuild—as did the Lara children around their father—a unique power.

"Isabella? Where are you? Why have you left me alone?"

Dona Albonza. The *duenna* groped her way toward Isabella.

"You're going to the king? You shouldn't. I'm sure the queen is with him—she will send you packing."

"The queen has no reason to send me packing—I'm coming to get news of my brother. You exaggerate, dona Albonza!"

"You know very well that's not so! Be careful, Isabella. With Alfonso gone, you'll again find yourself in competition with her for succession to the throne, and she will stop at nothing to take your place . . . nothing, not even murder. She killed your brother Alfonso. She will kill you as well. She's a wicked woman."

Isabella shrugged. "You're not telling me anything new, dona Albonza. The king supports the queen and his daughter, Jeanne."

The duenna's pudgy hand tightened on Isabella's arm. "You know very well that Jeanne isn't his daughter!" Isabella turned her head away from the *duenna's* sickly breath, its loathsome warmth on her ear. "The court is fully aware of it, Isabella. Jeanne is la Beltraneja, daughter of Beltran de la Cueva and the queen. A child of adultery. Once, before my eyesight became so bad, I leaned over her cradle. Jeanne already had Beltran's features—red eyebrows, strong nose, stony gaze. . . . If at some future time this girl should reign over Castile, God will have turned away from our people."

"Dona Albonza!"

The Princess began to walk along the gallery to the courtyard, warmly redolent of orange blossom.

"Excuse me, Isabella." She saw the king's doctor, the Jew, Salomon Ezra, about to leave the royal chamber. She joined him as he stepped out into the burning heat of the patio.

"How is my brother?"

The old doctor stroked his mud-colored beard. "I've done all I can, your Highness, but nothing has worked. Would you like my very honest opinion? The king has lost the desire to get better. This happens every time some difficulty lays him low. It's his way to escape, to abandon his responsibilities. He's like an ostrich, plunging his head in the sand to avoid seeing danger."

"May I talk with my brother?"

"You may." The voice was not Salomon Ezra's.

Isabella swung round. "Don Beltran—I thought you were . . . out hunting?"

"One must abandon pleasure when matters of state require. I heard that your brother was ill. So here I am." Don Beltran de Cueva moved away from the column against which he had been leaning, signaling with his glove that the doctor should go away.

"What will the king decide?" Don Beltran whispered to Isabella.

"Have you any doubt?" she asked sharply. "He will hold to his decision. If the queen is not called upon to take the throne, then Jeanne will be."

Don Beltran's glance at the girl was an expression of doubt. "Do you really believe what you're saying?"

Isabella looked scornfully at the queen's favorite.

"I beg your pardon," he said. He smoothed his red eyebrows with his forefinger, bowed his head abjectly, and sat down on the low wall surrounding the courtyard, his back to the sun.

"How good it is to hear you say that, Isabella! I can't tell you how much I'm upset by the . . . gossip about Joan's birth . . . but praise the Lord!—don't believe a word of it. How can the pure and faithful friendship I have for the queen be so distorted . . . so misrepresented? Me—with my spotless life, smooth and straight as this sword?"

Slanderers attacked Don Beltran like a swarm of wasps. He was criticized for his wealth, his privilege, and for holding the office of Grand Master of the Order of Santiago, which the queen had bestowed on him. He had even been criticized for taking advantage of the king's supposed impotence to arouse guilty passions in the queen's heart. Impotent, the king? That wasn't the opinion of his favorite, dona Guiomar!

He broke off. His hand, which has been gesturing to emphasize his points, stopped in full flight. He turned his gaze toward the king's door, which had just opened.

The Villena Marquis de Villena, his brother Pedro Giron, the Archbishop of Toledo, Monsignor Carillo, and the Marquis of Santillane, came toward them.

Isabella inclined her head before leaving them to enter the king's chamber.

The queen struggled to raise her heavy eyelids, blue with fatigue and powder, as Princess Isabella bowed before her. Dona Guiomar, the king's favorite, quickly turned away, hiding her dark face behind a lace handkerchief.

King Henry of Castile seemed to be sleeping. Filtering through the silken drapes, the light of two candles on the headboard gave the sick man's features an unexpected appearance of gentleness and peace. The relaxation of this feigned slumber revealed the king's true personality. He was not fundamentally bad; Isabella had some fond memories of their childhood together. Weakness was his downfall. Betrayals, desertions, cowardice, all sprang from that one fatal flaw. Henry had stopped believing in his kingly mission years before. Indeed, he hardly believed in his own existence. His lack of steadfastness was the cause of his wrongdoing and his unfaithfulness.

Isabella was sure that her brother the king was only pretending to be asleep, and that he sensed her presence, even with his eyes closed. What was the point of this childish play-acting?

Henry was mimicking death. Isabella thought of Alfonso's real death—Alfonso laid out on a makeshift litter between two horses, his face uncovered as tradition demanded. The dust of the *meseta*, kicked up by the horses on the rough trails of Old Castile between Segovia and Medina del Campo, settled back on that face.

Isabella was aware that the king was prepared to let her leave without having uttered a single word. She had hoped that he would make some sign of understanding, some secret indication that brother and sister were united in purpose. But no. Not even that.

She felt a surge of rising anger. She had to hold back a wild desire to tear apart this staged tragedy, to pull her brother out of bed, to beat out of him just one moan, one word, one plea.

She spun round on her heel. The queen rose in her path.

"I don't want to leave you with any false hope," she said. "The king has made his choice. Our daughter, Jeanne, will succeed him."

"Don't worry about that. I have no intention of going against my brother's wishes."

"I want to believe what you say. You should know that the king called for Jeanne this morning, and kissed her in front of everyone."

"That may be sufficient indication for you," said Isabella, "but before jumping to conclusions about the succession, you should wait for a more definite decision."

A shadow crossed the queen's face. The fleshy folds of her neck trembled under the heavy choker. "The future is mine, Isabella. You will never be Queen of Castile. As soon as the king is able to make decisions, he will name a husband for you."

"That will be the fourth nomination. I will only marry a man if it pleases me to do so."

The queen tapped her foot on the floor. Her bosom quivered under a lace blouse. "When I was sixteen I would never have dared talk back like that—my father would have whipped me. I'm only too well aware of the husband you're looking for: Prince Ferdinand of Aragon, son of that ambitious old King John, who has the idea that he's going to unite the two kingdoms for his own benefit. But to give yourself to Ferdinand would be tantamount to giving him Castile. Those Aragon dogs think that they can get away with anything. At least you don't want to marry the Jew, David Ezra . . . you love him, though, don't you?"

A shadow loomed against the wall.

"Your Highness," said the chaplain. "Please keep your voice down, or you will wake the king."

The dry heat of the courtyard helped restore Isabella's peace of mind. As evening drew near, the heavy perfume of orange blossom became more noticeable. Someone called her to her room, and she made her way there.

It was Cabrera, one of the most important people in all Castile, head of the king's household.

"Andres," said Isabella, "the king has chosen. Jeanne, my niece, is to be queen."

"No," replied Andres. "I was in the king's room this morning. The queen brought his daughter to him, and he kissed her. That doesn't mean a thing. Don't despair, Isabella."

꧁⚜꧂

Isabella's room, deep in shadow, was almost cold. She stretched out on her bed, played briefly with the fringe of the four-poster's drapes. Ferdinand, David . . . David, Ferdinand. Did she love Ferdinand? She hardly knew him, but she was sure that he was the one she would marry. He was young, sturdy, tanned, thin-lipped—suited more for command than for love. "He already loves you," Andres Cabrera had assured her. Isabella doubted it; she had been told the same about other suitors. But she knew that she had to marry Ferdinand of Aragon. That was the price to be paid for the unity of Spain.

Isabella buried her face in a cushion and breathed in the fragrance of times past. Eyes closed, she conjured up the image of a face she would have adored to see as a suitor—that of David Ezra, son of the king's old doctor.

She loved David with a love that was sufficient unto itself, a love with no future, a love with no hope. David was Jewish, and even though Jews were accepted at court, people would have reacted strongly against any romance—no matter how chaste—between the princess and a heretic.

So chaste this love had remained, in a court that did not allow asceticism to impede its propensity for sin. The king's erratic rule spawned a torrent of depravity, but Isabella and David kept alive their doomed vision of innocence and purity.

David—his colossal build, his cat-like movements, his finely-chiseled features below a shock of curly red hair. She tried to dismiss the thought of him. There was only Ferdinand for her. Where was he, what was he doing now? Was he thinking of her?

꧁⚜꧂

Ferdinand was at Gerona, in the north of Spain, besieged by the French. The same heat that scorched the south bore down on the old fortress.

Ferdinand recognized each room, each staircase, each corridor. He could walk for hours from one end of the fortress to the other, eyes closed. He could stop anywhere at random, eyes still closed, describe exactly where he was, and give an accurate count of the towers and turrets, steeples and pinnacles, that sprang from the unbelievable chaos of timeworn, sun-beaten roofs descending in russet waves to the green Onar.

He had already noticed an ordinary bunch of startlingly yellow wild stocks. Even after so many years away, he found that things were the same. The besiegers bathed in the waters of the river, as in the olden days. Then, the Catalans; now, the French, men of John of Armagnac and Ferry of Lorraine. Just like the olden days . . .

"Ferdinand!"

The call hit the Prince of Aragon like a stone hitting the back of his neck. He turned, breathless, a name on his lips: "Mother." His eyesight, blurred by fatigue and by the intense glare of the stones, could only make out a vague shape. It was not his mother approaching him, but his private tutor, Juan Margarit. The prelate's voice was gently scolding: "I thought you were in your room, but here you are running all over the place, exposed to gunfire. When will you become more sensible? Come with me! Father Rocaberti would like to see you. Tell me: Why did you turn round so sharply? You looked like a hunted animal."

"It was six years ago, your Grace, six exactly. Shot was raining down on Gerona. There was famine. Our soldiers fought among themselves for a handful of beans. My mother and Captain Luis Despuig were alone in putting up a fight against the Catalans, while waiting for Aragon's troops to arrive."

"I shall never forget, sir, the taste of those moldy beans as they softened in my mouth. Nor shall I forget the soldier, his head taken off by a cannonball, who went on running until he fell near me. Nor my mother's cries when she thought I was in danger."

"It was her voice I seemed to hear when you called me. In my sleep, I heard her cry for many weeks after the siege had ended."

"How did even one stone remain standing in Gerona? To what miracle do I owe my life? I've even forgotten why we were fighting . . ."

"Don't stay in the sun, child," chastened his tutor.

"Do I know why we're fighting today? When I'm too troubled by these questions, when I'm not even sure of the cause we uphold,

I tell myself that God has chosen me and that my ignorance is simply another sign of his trust."

The tutor replied, "Can we ever know what causes the Divine Will to choose to reject us? You fight for a just cause. The cause of Aragon, and, even more important, the cause of Spain. Never forget that."

⁂

A Gerona crowd was packed into the cathedral. People overflowed down the steps and into the square, pressing into the shadow of Charlemagne's Tower and around the statues of the Apostles.

"Of course," pursued Ferdinand in a bass voice. "That is what always happens at the beginning of a siege. Fear and dread drives the crowds into the basilicas. They seek answers from God—but only men respond." As a ready answer, the voice of Vicar General Alfonsella, with its harsh Aragon accent, thundered beneath the vaulted roof.

Prince Ferdinand and the tutor, Juan Margrit, made their way along a narrow alley like a mountain pass under the plain dark walls of the Bishop's palace. From the chilly interior of a store festooned with white earthenware pots a gentle singing could be heard. Ferdinand took heart from that voice.

Father de Rocaberti was waiting for Ferdinand, surrounded by his staff—with scruffy beards and stooped backs.

"We need you here," he said. "We are at a critical juncture. If we try to resist, there will be a massacre. The French have just mounted a heavy gun attack to try to destroy the walls. The people of Gerona will not hold up under bombardment. If we negotiate, though, we might buy enough time for King John to arrive. What's your view?"

Ferdinand took off his felt hat and sat down on the Captain's right. Everyone's gaze was upon him.

"We must stand firm," he said. "Gerona did not surrender to the Catalan guns six years ago. French guns won't worry us."

Rocaberti chewed on his lips through white whiskers. His dry fingers, adorned with heavy rings, drummed on the edge of the table.

"You think the people of Gerona will hold out under fire?"

"I've seen them battered by ferocious attacks, pushed like animals into the flames. If they cannot hold out, then there is no fortress in Aragon that can. Think what my father's answer would be. . . ."

King John II of Aragon had never given way to the weariness and indifference that were characteristic of Father de Rocaberti. As far back as he could remember, Ferdinand had always known the king to be driven by cold, remorseless determination. He could envisage him now in Sargasso, shut into his study, bent over his maps and papers, his fox-like face in deep profile in the candlelight, offering a thin cheek for his son's kiss.

Ferdinand had for a long time believed his father to be incapable of showing affection—his functions were those of a well-oiled watch, and worked on automatic reflex—but he had soon changed his mind. This harsh, unemotional seriousness was but one aspect of his personality, the aspect he found most difficult to conceal. Even though his higher feelings remained hidden, they were the wellspring of his actions, entirely devoted to restoring the glory of Spain.

Navarre dozed in the imagined security of its mountains, Castile's blood unresistingly drained away in its civil wars, while the Moorish kingdom of Granada held out against the rest of the Iberian peninsula. This was the state of things as John dreamed of unification, traveled the rough mountain tracks, and—in spite of the opposition of France, England, and Italy—led a party that, even in the face of setbacks, would allow for no withdrawal. He called himself "the soldier of unity."

Ferdinand did not like him, but nobody liked King John; and he in turn despised everyone else. But he admired him so much that he couldn't conceive of devoting himself to any cause other than that championed by his father.

At the same time that Ferdinand was bolstering the morale of Gerona's defenders, and as French soldiers marched through the fields of the Guer and the Onar, King John was on his way through the Ter valley, swept clear by the swords of Captain Verntallat and his formidable alpine infantry.

"We must defend ourselves at all costs," said Ferdinand. "The king will be here in less than a week."

Three days later, the king's pennants could be seen fluttering on the horizon.

"Step forward, Ferdinand," said the king.

The lad was gripped by a dry hand that started to feel his own. The king was purblind: he had always postponed being treated for the cataracts from which he suffered. Ferdinand heard a short asthmatic wheeze whistle through the king's yellow teeth.

"It's not you, Ferdinand. No! I don't recognize you any more. . . . My son never used to dress like this. Silk—ermine—gold everywhere . . . haven't I told you to dress more simply when you meet me? Don't you know that jewels and costly garments grow on us like leprosy, and eat into us, body and soul?"

"I wanted to show my respect, Father," stammered Ferdinand.

"Address me as 'your Majesty' when we are not alone. You will show more respect by not dressing like the dandies who drag their swords around the Court of Castile. They make me sick. . . ."

"You have come from Castile, your Majesty?"

King John nodded.

"I spent two weeks at Medina del Campo. I had heard that King Henry has a Jewish doctor famed throughout Castile: Salomon Ezra. God knows I hate doctors—especially Jewish doctors. But it's as easy for me to tell the face of an enemy from that of a friend as it is to see the difference between night and day. Do you know what I said to this Jew? Let him wait! The word I hate most."

The king leaned back, head sunk between his protruding shoulders. He mumbled a few incoherent sentences, and again clutched the prince's arm.

"I've got more news for you—I've decided to marry you off."

Ferdinand was amazed at this unexpected turn of events. He was not too greatly surprised at the news itself—he knew that the king has been thinking about it for a long time, but the tactlessness of the way it was announced stunned him. He wondered if he would ever get used to this crude frankness . . . and to this abuse of authority.

"What do you say to that, Ferdinand?"

"What can I say, your Majesty?"

The king smiled, cracking his fingers as he rubbed his hands together. "You're not even curious. Don't you care who is going to be your bride?"

"Who have you chosen, your Majesty?" asked Ferdinand, in a tone-less voice.

"The Princess of Castile: Isabella."

Ferdinand was heartened by this piece of news. Who knew what ugly woman the king might have selected? He couldn't remember exactly when he had met Isabella for the first time. But he did recall his father and Isabella's brother Henry seated at a great table in a medieval hall hung with great Arab tapestries.

Ferdinand and Isabella had looked sideways at each other. He was still a small, timid boy; she was a fresh, rosy-cheeked blonde girl with a direct gaze. He remembered wanting to tug her pigtails so she wouldn't mistake his shy manner for stupidity.

Subsequently the two youngsters came together again. Ferdinand still wanted to pull her blonde plaits, this time to show how much he liked her, and to express the unspoken affinity that he felt between them. The desire to tug that fair hair became an obsession with him. Suddenly one morning he decided to go ahead and do it, to break the ice between them. Then just as suddenly he dismissed the idea.

As time went by, Ferdinand's thoughts of Isabella became pleasant but without passion. Gradually, even the memory of her face faded away, and he was left with just a vague impression of the young Castilian girl's bright liveliness.

"I hope you understand how important this choice is," said the king. "I am convinced that one day soon Isabella will rule Castile. I will do everything I can to make sure that happens."

Again he leaned back in his chair. His violet-colored lips broke into a twisted smile.

"You, King of Aragon, and she, Queen of Castile. Great things would come of such a union."

Ferdinand solemnly nodded his head. Then he blurted out unthinkingly: "When can I see my betrothed?"

A fit of coughing and wheezing threw the king forward. His face took on the yellowish color of old wax.

"How stupid you are!" he screamed. "I said that I've decided to get you married. The problem is that at present we are the only ones who are in agreement about it. It might take a revolution, a war even, before this marriage can take place. Tomorrow, we could be overtaken by events, making me change my mind. Get out of here, before I give you the back of my hand!"

Humiliated, Ferdinand spun on his heel. He was on his way out the door when the king called him back.

"I beg your pardon," he said. The king stretched out his hand to be kissed.

⁂

The king treated me like the lowest of his servants—me, Prince of Aragon! Ferdinand was thinking about his encounter with his father as he walked along the covered way. The village seemed to whisper as evenings shadows fell. A water-carrier sang a sad song in an alleyway by the Bishop's palace. A donkey loaded with fish climbed toward the castle, stumbling on the uneven surface.

Ferdinand's thoughts were of Isabella as he watched the sun glinting on distant stubbled hills. He dreamed of her for a few moments, but his dream was distracted by the sight of eel fishers busy on the dusk-darkened waters of the Onar.

If only the Princess of Castile looked like Maria, how he would love her! He would take the Medina road, scale the castle walls, fight his way, sword in hand, past the guards, to smash down the princess's door and carry her off in his arms.

The thought of Maria was very sweet. He ran down the steps of the fortress four at a time; the guards saw his violet cape flying across the courtyards. He plunged into the shadow of the cathedral, passing the *callejons* where children sprang from the doors like jack-in-the-boxes.

Maria lived at the far end of a court, near the Arab baths. She would probably be alone. Maria was waiting for Ferdinand. She had put a carnation in her brown hair.

Isabella blushed slightly when she looked at herself in the mirror above the old Andalusian chest of drawers. The carnation she had tucked over her left ear complimented her like a poppy in a field of wheat. It would be wonderful if Ferdinand thought so too. But she pulled the flower from her hair brusquely. Such flirtatiousness would not befit the dignity of Castile's future Queen. She studied herself full face, and then in half-profile . . . she could detect in that face an indication of majesty, the renowned majesty of the ancient Trastatamare family.

Three days earlier, Isabella heard that she was to become Queen of Castile. Her brother had made his choice. He had finally realized that Afonso's death could only have been instigated by Queen Joan. She, in turn, had been influenced by her favorite, Beltran de la Cueva, and by several other lords in the inner circle that hovered around the queen. He had scarcely been able to sit upright in his chair when making the announcement, but his voice had been firm and clear.

His choice had thrown Medina del Campo into confusion. The queen decided to leave. No longer could she tolerate these constant changes of mind, the permanent air of suspicion, these statements followed always by denials. She would return to Portugal, to her brother, King Afonso the African.

Her packing cases and chests were piled up in the courtyard; coaches and wagons rattled over the drawbridge. She would take with her little Jeanne, some of the young people fussing around her, her domestic staff, and her lovebirds.

Beltran de la Cueva hesitated before leaving with her. He caught the last coach as it was moving.

Seated near her brother, Isabella had seen the dust cloud raised by the queen's passage fade on the horizon, revealing a copse of cypress trees standing like so many vertical black swords.

"We will have to fight," said Isabella. "The queen is bound to retaliate for having been made to look so ridiculous. Portugal has a powerful army. There is no love lost between Afonso and you. . . ."

The king said nothing. A tear coursed down his thin cheek. "Don't leave me, Isabella. Now I have only you to lean on." He took hold of her hand and caressed it frantically.

"Have I ever mentioned leaving you?"

"You all have! You're all leaving, one after the other. What do you care about my suffering? What do you care even if this suffering brings me to death's door?"

"You're not being fair."

"Maybe not, but I'm thinking clearly. Even you—you'll leave one day. You'll marry the Duke of Guyenne, and then you'll wait patiently for the news of my death before showing up for your share of the spoils."

"The Duke of Guyenne? You know very well that he's not the one I'm going to marry, whatever you might have promised him. My future husband's name is Ferdinand. One day he'll be King of Aragon. And with him I will build a new Spain."

❦

The king went to bed that evening half crazy with anger and distress. Sleep still evaded him when he saw an auburn beard and a pair of fiery eyes leaning over his bedhead.

"Villena! What do you want? Leave me alone. I am the unhappiest man alive. The queen betrays me, the princess rebels against my wishes."

"There's nothing worse than a sickness for which there is no cure, your Majesty," said Villena. "I remember the days when you had no time for despair. You used to say to me: 'Villena, I need to take my mind off things this evening,' and on the spur of the moment I would arrange some entertainment. Are you less of a player now than you were then?"

"Who really understands me, Villena? My country no longer has a king, my body is no longer alive. What entertainment could possibly take my mind off this state of affairs? The humblest mule-drivers are happier than I . . . sometimes I hear them singing as they go along their way."

"What a pity!" sighed Villena. "This very evening a troupe of actors is stopping in Medina. A dozen slim-hipped and supple boys and girls. The pleasures of the Orient are at your door. Aren't you going to allow them in?"

The king brightened. He stroked his face with his old man's hand, pretending to groan. "Villena, you are my damned soul. I'm indebted to you for most of my private hell. Help me get up. . . ."

The king would give in. He was not one to cling stubbornly to his decisions for long. He knew men other than the Duke of Guyenne who would make a good match for his sister. Isabella had never seen the duke—but then, she had never seen most of her other suitors either. She envisaged them as having fox's snouts, pointed ears, slavering lips, and goat's beards.

Only Ferdinand of Aragon found favor in her eyes. She had met him previously, but couldn't remember when or where. The fact that they were the same age had given rise to rumors about the possibility of their being united in marriage. He hadn't displeased her, though he'd seemed a bit too timid.

Ferdinand combined toughness with sensitivity, marks of good breeding. It hadn't taken Isabella long to find out that the Prince of Aragon's reserved manner was due more to pride than to timidity. She had also discovered that he was dreaming of pulling her braids and inviting her to go riding with him.

Among her innumerable suitors, Ferdinand was the only one who made any impression on Isabella. Usually they made their approach through an ambassador, who would lay down certain conditions. The king would give his approval and fix a date for the engagement. Then suddenly there would be an international crisis in Europe. Treaties would be torn up, signatures declared void. Her brother would send Isabella back to her palace-prison, where the unchanging scenery was seen only through protected windows. Meanwhile her suitors would vanish into the dust of their chancelleries.

Only Ferdinand, it seemed to her, was in any way human.

Looming behind the princess was the shadow of King John. Crafty, stubborn, cruel, King John of Aragon had but one thought in his head: the unity of Spain. Isabella would have liked to know him better, to see this incarnation of an ideal. He was said to be small and ugly, but she imagined him to be very appealing. He was described as being morally despicable, but to her he was good, open, and brave.

⚜

"Andres, what was going on in Villena's rooms tonight?" Isabella asked.

"The duke was comforting your brother in his usual way. I was there when the orgy began, but it sickened me and I left. Your brother, on the other hand, seemed to be quite revived by it. Villena knows his weaknesses, and the king swears by him."

"I'm anxious to get away from this place. Wherever I go, I seem to be rubbing shoulders with monsters, to be living at the edge of hell. At times I persuade myself that this castle is nothing but a stage set, that all these dukes, marquises, and captains are but actors in a revolting comedy, and that it will all fade away at dawn. I wake up—and nothing has changed. If only I could meet Ferdinand of Aragon, talk with him. Do you think that's possible, Andres?"

Andres Calebra shook his head like a faithful dog.

"No, your Highness, it's not possible. You're going to need a lot of patience. I know King John: what he wants, he gets. For your part, you must do everything in your power to help him. Are you sure you are doing everything?"

"What are you trying to say?"

"I'm going to be frank, because you have done me the honor of confiding in me. You saw David again last week. . . ."

Isabella turned away quickly, to hide her sudden blushes. "I saw David, that's true. But I didn't see how that can hinder the plans of the King of Spain. David is my best friend—he'd be my only friend if it weren't for you, Andres. Must I give up seeing him?"

"Yes, your Highness."

Isabella faltered. "I can't. You know what he means to me. I owe him the best times of my life. He's been more than a companion . . ."

"I know, your Highness. You love him."

Isabella made no reply.

"As queen," Andres continued, "affairs of state will leave no room for love in your life. The less you love the Jew, the more love you will have for the Prince of Aragon. Will you be able to live with that?"

"I don't know," said Isabella. She added in a lower voice: "But what does Ferdinand think about our marriage? You met Peralta, the envoy from Aragon, last night. What did he tell you?"

"That Ferdinand is an obedient son."

"Obedient! That's just what I was afraid of."

"Don't jump to conclusions. Ferdinand can't be in love with you—he hardly knows you. But I asked Peralta to take back to the prince the medallion with your portrait, the one you asked me to look after for you."

"A medallion!" Isabella's voice was bitter. "You think that's enough?"

"I almost forgot," said Andres Cabrera with a sly smile. "Before he left, Peralta gave me this to pass on to you. It's a medal with an engraving of the Prince of Aragon. Apparently it's a good likeness. What do you think of it?"

"Ferdinand. . . ." murmured Isabella.

⁂

The black domes of the Seo of Saragossa were outlined against a flaming sky. Ferdinand gazed at the scene with a bored yawn. Fortunately, the meeting with the king was over. Ferdinand stood up, pulled Peralta's sleeve, and indicated that he should follow. They went into an adjoining office where the candles had not yet been lit. Night had almost fallen.

"Peralta," said Ferdinand, "far be it from me to argue about the importance of my marriage to the Princess of Castile. I will soon be King of Aragon, and I already know that a king is called upon to sacrifice his own interests to those of his country. But, by God, I had no idea that I would be deprived of my liberty so soon."

His pompous speech amused the constable, who nodded gravely. Small king-in-the-making, he thought to himself. Little embryo! You're already puffing out your chest!

Much needed to be done before the royal image that Ferdinand tried to present to the world would be complete. He needed to be prompted about the requirements of protocol, and had not yet carried his sword into battle. But he had the one essential quality: pride. That would save him. In a few years' time it would not be a good idea to cross swords with this young cock.

Ferdinand bit his lip. He had shown enough greatness of spirit, of self-sacrifice, to be permitted one guilty little thought. "Tell me, Peralta—what's Isabella like?"

He added—perhaps a little too quickly— "Not that such details matter to me, of course, but, well . . . you know what I mean, Peralta."

"I understand," breathed Peralta. Looking puzzled, he clapped his hands behind his back, and swayed back and forth.

Ferdinand's face was a picture of uncertainty. "Is she . . . ugly?"

He shivered slightly when he saw that the constable looked unexcited, and replied only after hesitating. "She's not in the least ugly."

"But. . . ?

"For my taste, her beauty is somewhat severe, cold—formal. But you should congratulate yourself. I believe that she will make a most acceptable queen."

"Yes, of course," said Ferdinand, unconvinced.

"A queen who is too radiantly beautiful can cause problems for a monarch. Take, for example, Juana, the King of Castile's wife. Beautiful—and flirtatious. Those two words are made to go together."

"That's true," sighed Ferdinand. "As for an ugly queen. . . ."

"Did I say that Isabella was ugly?"

A smile that disappeared as quickly as it came lit up the prince's face.

"No," continued Peralta, "Isabella is one of those women who are unconscious of their own beauty. They need some external influence to make them realize it—a passionate love affair, for instance. I'm sure that love would make Isabella more than pretty—she would become beautiful. It would bring light to her eyes, warmth to her complexion, self-confidence to her walk."

With scarcely concealed terror, Ferdinand saw in his mind's eye an adolescent girl with dull eyes, lifeless skin, lanky physique. This image looked the same as the girls presented at court by the barons from the highlands of Aragon, nobles come like horse-traders to sell their fillies. Isabella was an ugly girl, he felt sure. Peralta's reservations spoke volumes. He was suddenly unhappy.

Peralta understood. He put his hand on the prince's shoulder. "Now, now, don't fret. Just to tease you, I painted a picture darker than the reality. You will be pleased with Isabella, I'm quite certain. She's blonde, with blue-green eyes. If her brother, King Henry, let her have more money, she would rival the countesses of Lerida and Catalayud with her glamour."

Ferdinand's face clouded over. He turned his back to the window, the better to make out Peralta's expression.

"At what point were you making fun of me? When you implied that Isabella is ugly? Or when you compared her to the Countess of Lerida?"

"All I wanted to do was to warn you about the two disappointments you might come up against. Let us just say that Isabella is as beautiful as the Countess of Lerida . . . but less flirtatious."

Ferdinand shrugged and turned to face the window again. The domes of the Seo were now no more than shadows brushed by a fiery cloud. "I've heard that she's a religious bigot. True, Peralta?"

"She is pious."

"It's said that her morals are too strict!"

"She takes life seriously."

"Have you ever seen her laugh?"

"I've seen her smile very prettily, Ferdinand."

"Will she be stupid?"

"She has the innocence of those who spend a lot of time waiting for the future to arrive."

"One last question, Peralta. In the name of the friendship you have for me, I ask you to be very candid in your reply. Do you believe that I could love this princess?"

Little embryo king, thought Peralta, attached to happiness like a fetus to his umbilical cord. He smiled. "If you believe that happiness is important to a sovereign then, yes, Ferdinand, I'm convinced that you could live happily with Isabella."

"When can I meet her?"

"What impatience! I believe that you will have to wait for the right time."

"How long is that?" Ferdinand spoke thoughtlessly.

Peralta put his left hand on his chest and felt the outline of something in his pocket—the medallion Cabrera had passed on to him. Isabella's portrait emphasized the wonderful delicacy of her features.

When he had left Saragossa for Castile to have his conversation with King Henry and Isabella, King John had presented him with a small medal bearing an engraving of the prince in a rather surly way. "You will give this piece of jewelry to the silly goose as if it had come from Ferdinand himself."

"How forgetful I am!" Peralta exclaimed. "I have a gift for you, passed on to me by the Princess of Castile."

Too abruptly, Ferdinand grabbed the medallion on the end of its fine chain as the constable handed it to him.

"Beautiful Valladolid workmanship, Ferdinand! Just look at the fineness of the features, the delicacy of the colors. . . ."

In a choking voice, Ferdinand said: "Peralta, light this candle, I beg of you."

⁂

The flame of the candle the maid had just lit illuminated the big golden-barred cage where a small monkey sat shivering. He was dressed in a red jerkin decorated with silver braid. His watery eyes blinked sorrowfully.

Poor animal! thought Isabella. He wouldn't survive long in the icy cold of the palace of Madrid. Already, in spite of the brazier glowing near him in the gloom, he seemed close to death.

"He's called Jacinto," said a voice from the far end of the room. Isabella gave a start. "Who are you?"

The Marquis of the Villena stood up and walked slowly toward Isabella.

"I hope that this simple little gift will be acceptable to you. King Afonso of Portugal keeps many of them. Since his wife died, he has transferred his affections to his animals. What a strange but lovable man. If you could only see his castle in Lisbon! Some of the rooms swarm with parrots, monkeys, with wild animals of every sort. He brought them back from his African expeditions, along with Negroes and remarkable carvings in costly wood."

Villena leaned forward to the monkey and tried to tease him, without success. "King Afonso commanded me to pay you his respects. He is very fond of you. What he has learned about your Highness sends him into raptures. He is desperately anxious to make your acquaintance, and . . ."

"You're wasting your time! When you see King Afonso's ambassador next, assure him of the enormous sympathy and respect that I have for his master, and ask him to convey my thanks. But be sure he understands that each new attempt will be foredoomed to failure. I will not marry that old fool."

Villena was unable to disguise an expression of dismay. Usually, Isabella was very restrained in revealing her desires. This unexpected air of authority, this liveliness, which contrasted with the spirit of acceptance urged upon her in the prayers and verses of the Gospels, this fierceness . . . all these things amazed him.

"King Afonso is very young in appearance. He would make an excellent match—not to mention that such a marriage would guarantee the unity of Spain and Portugal. You are too well informed not to be aware of that."

"The unity of Spain is my great concern, Marquis de Villena. Bringing together the kingdoms of Castile and Aragon will be the starting point for that to take place."

"Your brother is opposed to such a union, and you know why: it would put the wolf together with the lamb, the wolf being Aragon."

"I am quite capable of defending my country."

The marquis hid a smile behind his beard. To hear Isabella talk, one would believe Castile's destiny to already be in her hands. But not even he could be certain who would succeed King Henry, who could very easily go back on his word, as he usually did.

"That's a line of reasoning you will have to pursue with your brother when the time comes. But I doubt if he'll be receptive."

"I'll go to him at once."

"Be very careful! The king is resting—he's not at all well."

"I heard that he'd been injured yesterday in some disreputable establishment in Madrid. So what you say is true."

"It was nothing serious—just a knife wound in the fleshy part of his shoulder."

"He's visiting brothels now—you with him, when you're not ahead of him! His mistresses and his favorites aren't enough for him any more."

The Marquis of Villena sighed. "The king finds relaxation only in his pleasures. He claims they are his best armor against death, the very thought of which is mental agony for him. But he quickly grows weary, and he gives me the responsibility of finding new amusements to keep the idea of mortality away from his tormented spirit. As a faithful servant, I obey."

" . . . and you have him at your mercy. You put into his head the ridiculous notion that I should marry that old character. With me in Portugal, you would be free to maneuver. It wouldn't be long before Queen Joan and her daughter were back in the palace. He would never have been capable of putting together such a plan!"

The little monkey whined and covered his head with his two front paws.

"All your scheming is too late, marquis! In the last few weeks, my brother has given me too much liberty for me not to make use of it."

⚜

There was an atmosphere of conspiracy in the small, bare-walled room in the north wing of the palace. Outside a dark garden could be seen, overrun with wild grass. Light from the heavy bronze chandeliers fell on the faces of prelates and other influential people: Isabella's friends, her supporters, those who believed that her accession to the throne would herald a golden age for Castile and for Spain.

"The document is ready," said the chamberlain. "It needs only your signature, your Highness."

"For safety's sake, read it once more before you sign," said a fat, red-faced prelate—Monsignor Carillo, Bishop of Toledo.

A chair was brought forward, and Isabella sat down at the enormous antique table. She read it over again, slowly, in a loud voice.

The draft marriage contract was exactly what the princess had wished it to be. Its terms were perfectly clear. Isabella and Ferdinand undertook to serve and to honor King Henry until the end of his reign, and to acknowledge him as King of Castile. Ferdinand would respect Isabella's rights when she became Queen, as well as the laws and privileges of all Castilians. He promised to have Isabella's name beside his own on all public proclamations.

"There is nothing to be added or erased," said the princess.

She sensed a murmur of satisfaction. Having signed the document with an air of authority, she turned to Andres Cabrera.

"This letter must be with the Chancellery of Aragon in four days. Time is short. Ferdinand and the king must reply within two weeks. You know the pressure I'm under to accept King Afonso of Portugal. I am afraid that my brother the king might resort to drastic measures—violent ones, even—to persuade me of that. And the only weapon I have against those measures is quiet resistance."

"We will make haste," said Andres.

Gradually, the room emptied. Isabella stopped the Papal Legate, Cardinal Antonio de Veneris, as he was about to leave.

"I sense that this contract did not have your total support. Please be good enough to tell me what you disagree with."

The cardinal placed his icy hand on the princess's.

"I couldn't bear to disappoint you," he said. "You are so enthusiastic about implementing your plans! I truly hope they succeed—if not, would I have been here today?"

"But you must be aware, my child, that your marriage can only take place with a dispensation from Saint Peter, bearing in mind your close family relationship with Ferdinand of Aragon. I fear you might have to wait a long time for such dispensation."

"I can't wait," said Isabella, without emotion. "This dispensation would be welcome, but if necessary we'll have to make do without it."

"You wouldn't dare!"

"Circumstances will force me to."

"There is only one way to give a semblance of Christian legality to this union . . ."

". . . and that is to produce a forged Papal Bull. I understand that fully, cardinal. And that's just what I'm expecting you to do."

The Legate's hand tightened on hers. She saw a flash of lightning in his piercing gaze.

"What you are asking me is . . ." he said.

"Let me have your decision tomorrow. God is with me. I will pay back His support a hundredfold."

⚜

Isabella spent the rest of the night tossing and turning in her bed. As soon as sleep overtook her, she was again caught up with thoughts of Ferdinand. She opened her eyes, and saw the sky of dying summer glowing through the open window.

In the small hours, numbed with the early morning chill flowing in from the garden, she got up, groped her way to the window, and leaned on the sill. First light was beginning to flood into the eastern sky. A gentle breeze played around the sloping rooftops.

She was about to close the window when she caught a glimpse of a moving shadow at the end of the courtyard. It was a horseman. He got as far as the kitchen, where there was already a fire burning in the hearth, and dismounted.

Isabella saw that it was David Ezra. She quickly closed the window and leaned back against it, her heart beating wildly. She had sworn to put him out of her life—but here he was, looming out of the night-darkened, sleeping town.

His sudden appearance unleashed in Isabella such a flood of memories that she could not prevent herself from dreaming of him. She went back to sleep with his name on her lips.

⚜

The four mule-drivers left Saragossa in the early hours of the morning.

They were wrapped up to their eyes with blankets, and underneath they wore woolen clothes. In spite of this, the biting gusts of wind off the *meseta* of La Muela chilled them to the bone. Day had just dawned when they arrived at the first village, guided there by faint lights in the distance and by columns of white smoke rising in the clear, metallic air.

The narrow valley was flanked by steep slopes scarred with deep crevices and crested with a few sparse stands of olive trees. While they were in its shelter the wind did not greatly slow them down. But when they came out into the *meseta* it started blowing with such force that the four men had to dismount and tug at the mules laden with chestnuts, olives, and salted meat.

At La Almunia they stopped and munched a few olives in the shelter of an oil press. A mouthful of Carinena wine gulped from the flask, and the four *muleteers* braced themselves to face the high wind. It was then that they saw coming toward them two soldiers accompanied by a troop of ragged *muchachos*. The soldiers were muffled in furs; from afar they could have been taken for bears had it not been for the spears they leaned on as they struggled along.

The four men glanced surreptitiously at each other. The youngest of them stood up, letting his blanket fall back on his shoulders. His face, half-hidden though it was under his gray woolen hat, was not that of a mule-driver.

"Who are you?" asked one of the soldiers gruffly.

Judging by the expression on his face, he would much sooner have been in front of a fire in the warmth of the guardhouse.

The young mule-driver moved closer to him, half-opened his leather tunic, and pulled out a sheet of parchment to which was attached a wax seal.

"You can't stay here," said the soldier, "so press on as far as the castle."

He pointed out a small red *castillo* nestling on a cold and barren hillside. The young man nodded.

"What can I do to help you?" the soldier continued.

"Stop the wind, if you can. We'll take care of everything else."

The four *muleteers* got to their feet and untied their animals.

"Don't say a word about this meeting," said the young man. "If you do, I'll easily find you again—and I'll make sure you swing for it."

The mule-drivers edged out into the howling wind. The second soldier came up to the one who had been speaking.

"Why are you letting them go? They could be highwaymen or spies."

"Idiot!" said the first. "Didn't you recognize Prince Ferdinand?"

⚜

Mateo de Moncado was very familiar with this part of the country. They had taken his advice when he assured them that it was better to go through the valley of the river Jalon and to cross the Virgin Range, whose jagged, snow-covered ridges stood out against the March sky.

Ferdinand agreed with Mateo. He had seen this range long ago, one spring evening when the scent of mountain grass was in the air. The same sparkling snow, the same sawtooth profile against the southern sky.

He had been traveling back with King John of Aranda de Duero, far to the west in Castile territory, and Isabella had been much on his mind. Seeing the Virgin Range, he had been reminded of the princess. Now he thought of her again as his small band tackled the frozen banks of the Jalon.

Valley after valley, forest after forest. The wind whistled off the slopes, raising snow flurries, blowing eddying gaps in the scrub. Mateo had made a good choice: The track was passable. That night they slept on last year's straw in a shepherd's hut.

In the middle of the night Ferdinand got up without disturbing his companions, wrapped himself in his thick blanket, and sat on the doorstep, where he was sheltered from the wind. The moon was just rising behind the mountains. It climbed slowly into a crystal-clear sky, empty but for one little white cloud. A few minutes later, the mountain peaks shook off the darkness, their jagged outline sharply etched against the moonlight.

The virgin, murmured Ferdinand. He closed his eyes, and saw Isabella as though his eyelids held her image, identical to the portrait on the medal he wore around his neck.

Ferdinand was going to Isabella by the solitary way of the mountains, like a thief in the night. In order to present himself at the palace of Valladolid he only took his three companions mounted on mules laden with bags—which might be stolen by highwaymen. For clothes, he had old rags that smelt of the sweat and grime of the previous owner. But Isabella would recognize him at first glance.

"Go, my son," Mossen Garparo Ferreres, King John's confessor, had told him. "May God take care of you on your travels."

Ferdinand feared no highwaymen nor Castilian soldiers, neither fatigue nor cold. He had been afraid only that Isabella might not return his love.

Now, he knew. Isabella was like this mountain—pure and beautiful. So close to heaven that the grace of God enfolded all.

A hand rested on the royal shoulder. He saw Rocaberti's white beard furrowed by a smile.

"You're not being very sensible, my boy. Come back inside. Tomorrow will be a long day."

Ferdinand sneezed. Rocaberti scolded him like an angry cat. "You see, dimwit! Do you want to arrive in Valladolid with a fever, red nose, hoarse voice?"

"I don't care, provided I arrive . . ."

⚜

"I must get back to Toledo," said David Ezra. "I have business to attend to. I'll spend the rest of the winter in my castle in the

Guadarrama highlands hunting wolves if this snow keeps on for a few more weeks."

He stood up and slowly walked around the room. Isabella longed to see him sit down. He never stayed in one place for long—not in a town, not even in his chair. He had a dynamic, mobile personality. Sometimes, when circumstances forced him to be still, Isabella smiled inwardly to see him wanting so much to move that she thought he would burst.

Do I really love him? she asked herself.

For nearly a month he had been staying with his father, the king's doctor, in the Madrid palace. She had been able to see him almost every day, but never on a regular basis. He would appear without warning and then, however much Isabella wanted to be with him, he would not be there. Sometimes he would be out hunting, or he'd be with some important individual in Madrid's Jewish quarter.

All this gave the princess an opportunity to assess how important he was to her; an importance she argued about with him, but which she could not deny.

She had received him coolly, but he wasn't offended by her distant manner. When she happened to come across him in some palace corridor, with his tall, rather cat-like frame, his untidy mop of hair, his perpetual smile, when he would try to take her in his arms and whisper tender words in her ear, she stiffened and refused to return his kiss.

One day she told him: "I no longer have the right to see you, David. For me, the very sight of you is a blasphemy. I am to marry the Prince of Aragon."

David's smile quickly faded. The Jew had been gone for several days before coming back. She caught sight of him one morning, stretched out on the lawn in the warm autumn sun, watching her window. He had waved to her, and then disappeared once more.

"Please understand what I'm telling you," she said to him again. "Our love threatens to jeopardize my forthcoming marriage. And that marriage must take place."

The word love made David smile. He could not take so seriously these secretive meetings, these long discussions about trivia, these embraces that were hardly less innocent than those between a brother and sister.

"I understand," David sighed. "I must leave you since you're taking your love away from me."

"No! Stay. . . ."

She made no objection when he drew her to him and passionately kissed her.

"When will you be mine, Isabella?"

"Never, David!" But even as she spoke, she doubted her own words.

She would never be David's. Perhaps she would never be Ferdinand's, either. The Prince of Aragon had left her without a word. She watched anxiously for Peralta's return, but the constable seemed to have given up the idea of coming back to Castile.

Relations between the two kingdoms were strained. King Henry had learned of certain initiatives taken by his cousin of Aragon: As a result, he kept the frontiers under close surveillance.

Isabella was aware of all this, but she had hoped that Ferdinand might find some way to be with her. Either he lacked imagination or he had given her up.

David placed himself in front of Isabella. "You shouldn't stay in Madrid," he said. "You are surrounded by enemies. Sooner or later, your brother will put you under guard. Come with me to Toledo."

Isabella shook her head. "Of course I've thought about leaving—but not with you, and not to Toledo. I know that I'm not safe here. Would I be safe in Valladolid? Andres Cabrera thinks so. He is an excellent advisor."

David knelt down, took her hands, and pressed them to his lips. He reached out for her, held her tight, and kissed her with a desperate longing. She stayed motionless in his arms for a few moments of eternity.

"God protect you," she said.

"Will we see each other again soon?"

"Who knows, David."

Isabella's departure took on the appearance of a flight. A few leagues out of Madrid, she joined up with Andres Cabrera at the head of some fifty lancers, trustworthy men.

At Valladolid she felt safe, but it wasn't long before the news from Madrid became alarming. The king had reacted sharply against what he called her "running away." He ordered her to return. But for her to return would have meant acceptance of luxurious imprisonment in the palace.

One morning, Andres went into the princess's study, his face haggard.

"We must leave Valladolid. Villena has just set out with two hundred lancers. We are no longer safe in this town."

Isabella's face remained calm. "We will stay here. I won't fight, and I won't run away. If . . ."

"Isabella!"

The princess fixed Cabrera with an astonished stare. He never called her by her first name. He began again: "Your Highness, answer me, I beg of you. Why are you giving up?"

"Why should I stubbornly go on? I believe that the Aragon Court has forgotten me, and that even Ferdinand thinks of me no more. Their silence speaks louder than words, Andres. Besides, taking everything into account, this marriage no longer seems so desirable to me. There will soon be a war between Castile and Aragon, and King John will not be able to hold out. I had a wonderful dream . . . but it meant no more than any other dream. I would be foolish to attach any great importance to it." Isabella looked away from him. Tears shone in her eyes.

"I refuse to believe that all is lost, your Highness. Your brother will think twice before becoming involved in a conflict. You know very well that he has a horror of war."

"If only it were just him! But Villena is the real king. He will stop at nothing."

"Wait for another week or two. I am convinced that the king will back off, faced with your opposition."

Isabella banged her hands down on the table." You want me to wait! Six months ago, Peralta showered me with promises. Since then—nothing. I'm weary, Andres, wearier than you can possibly imagine."

❧

If only David were there! But where was he? He had sent her a bracelet from Toledo, a bouquet of heather from his Guadarrama castillo. Perhaps one day soon he would suddenly appear, coming from who knows where—Granada, perhaps, or Salamanca. With David, one never knew.

Isabella spent the next two days in a foul mood. Anything, she felt, would be better than the uncertainty she was experiencing. Far from confirming her decision to give up, the knowledge that Villena and his troops were on the way only gave force to her unacknowledged desire to flee. Every hour that went by added another stone, another bar to the prison she felt being built around her.

Her need to react against the feeling that she was allowing herself to be enslaved was at times overwhelming. So much so that she made wild use of the days of liberty that were left to her. She had her mare saddled up, put on her riding clothes, and rode off alone into the cold north wind, not caring where she was headed. She rode wherever the wind went, driving into its invisible resistance, which she loved to feel beating against her face and tugging at her horse.

She had been galloping for a long time and the mare was showing signs of fatigue, shaking its neck irritably in the wind. She pulled on the bridle, and the animal came to a standstill, champing at the bit and spitting out flecks of foam.

Isabella was still surrounded by the same monotonous landscape. Fields of wheat and oats stretched as far as the eye could see. Chalky outcrops seemed blue in the full light of day; furrowed spurs of rock thrust high above the small groups of sheep and goats.

She stayed motionless for several minutes, stroking the mare's shiny neck. She feasted her eyes on the vast expanses of wheat already green, on the sky already a deep azure blue. She knew that by the time the early reapers cut the first ears of wheat, her destiny would be engraved in stone.

A little click of the tongue, a touch of the whip. She pulled the horse around on the path back to Valladolid.

On one such evening she lost her way. A hill hid the town from her, and she went round in circles before reaching the top of a rocky mound from where she could at last see the cathedral and the city walls of Valladolid in the violet haze of dusk. And none too soon. A band of highwaymen was hurtling down the slopes of the other side of the valley, heading directly for her. They did not give up the chase until she crossed the Great Bridge over the River Pisuerga.

It wasn't until she got to the other side of the river that she realized she hadn't been in the least afraid. In fact, she had actually enjoyed the pursuit. That evening she asked Cabrera to take her to Duenas under cover of darkness.

Villena came closer. His vanguard reached the palace and took control of the city. Cabrera was held in custody in his suite. The only companion allowed the princess was her *duenna*, dona Albonza.

One morning, Isabella was preparing to leave the palace on her mare. A sergeant ordered her to dismount, and to hand the horse over to him. She slapped his face; the man merely smiled.

That evening, two guards were posted on every palace gate.

Villena was expected to arrive early the next day.

The Governor of Duenas Castle was a good man. He kept slapping his stomach, encircled by a red belt that hung down to the ground. "You've been lucky," he said. "But what if you'd fallen into the hands of the king's supporters, eh?"

Ferdinand opened the front of his cape to reveal a belt so heavy with knives, daggers, and *navajas* that it would have been difficult to add so much as a toothpick. "And we have other weapons as well," said Ferdinand. He went to one of the mules, plunged his hand into a sack of sunflower seeds, and pulled out several pieces of gold.

"That's as may be," said the governor, "but let me proceed. I have ways of getting into the palace of Valladolid. Once inside, I ask to see the governor and hand him a letter from Villena, requesting that he give Isabella into my safekeeping. And I bring you back the little goose . . ." He gave his belly a friendly slap.

"That's all very well," said Rocaberti, "but you've forgotten Villena's seal. I presume that he won't send it to you?"

"I have so many seals in my office that any time I wish I can throw all the great families of this kingdom into total confusion."

"You stole them?" asked Monsada.

"Do I look like a thief? No, sir. Let's just say that I have a taste for copying jewelry of this type . . . and a certain amount of skill."

"You are a dangerous man," said Ferdinand.

"Even more so than you might think, your Highness. I will make you a seal of my own design while you're eating. Benito! Get busy with their lordships' mules, and saddle my horse."

Isabella hardly spoke three words during the entire meal. The passages were busy with strange comings and goings. Isabella's hand toyed with Ferdinand's medallion . . . even now, she was still reluctant to throw it out the window or give it to a servant.

Once the meal was over, the commotion seemed to diminish, and when the bugle sounded curfew it ceased altogether. Dim torchlights traversed the courtyard. A candle sputtered on its ring as it went out.

Isabella knelt at her *prie-Dieu,* facing a little Virgin encircled with roses past their prime. Their petals were falling slow and silent, like snowflakes. She makes up her mind to spend half the night praying, the other half keeping watch. She was in the middle of her third rosary when a hand lightly touched her shoulder.

"Your Highness," said the servant, "in the next room there is a nobleman who wants to see you. He is here on behalf of the Marquis of Villena."

It took a long moment for Isabella to come back to reality . . . her present situation . . . the marquis's power. . . .

"The marquis could not proceed any further," said the nobleman. "He has a fever, and has taken to his bed in my retreat in Duenas. He requests that you go to see him without delay. Here is his letter."

Isabella ran her eye over the sheet of parchment, then looked at the man. He was smiling, his hands on the front of his red belt.

"Fine," said Isabella. "I'll have my bags packed."

⚜

Ferdinand threw a few pieces of charcoal on the glowing embers. He pressed his forehcad against the window bars as if he could see what was happening, despite the darkness, despite the rain that had fallen since the governor left. Rocaberti, Mateo, and the Count of Prado were snoring on their blankets, stretched out on the bare wooden floor.

The prince could not keep still. His distress increased with every second that went by. He had gone some way along the Valladolid road, but had fallen back, defeated by the cold and the night. Or perhaps a trap had been set for them.

Villena's men, he felt sure, were going to break into the castle. He imagined he could hear their footsteps, see their shadows. A large Madrid clock sounded the hour like a gong, and all became silent once more.

Ferdinand was freezing cold. But then a sudden warmth flooded over him. He opened the window onto the night and the rain, and closed it again. He banged his head on the lintel of the low door. He felt lost—empty . . . then all at once a wave of happiness brought him peace. Softly he spoke the princess's name: "Isabella . . ."

⚜

Isabella looked at the four men standing around the huge table. None dared say the first word. Cardenas, who was accompanying the princess, pointed to Ferdinand: "There he is, your Highness."

Ferdinand saw that the governor, hands on his stomach, was beaming at the small group of faceless men gathered around his enormous gray robe. He still couldn't bring himself to believe that this was Isabella. He stepped forward uncertainly, as if treading in a swamp, bent forward. "You're Isabella?"

"And you're Ferdinand?"

They smiled at each other, shyly touched hands, and shyly kissed. Ferdinand breathed in a fragrance compounded of rain and youth. He helped her off with her cloak, took her arm, and led her to the glowing brazier.

By its light, Ferdinand saw her put her hands out to the fire. He did the same, but quickly pulled his hands back; he was ashamed of his cracked skin and dirty fingernails. His hands were painful—not because of the cracks, but because he was overwhelmed by a feeling of emptiness in the palms, a crushing desire to hold something or someone.

He took a step back, overcome with emotion. He wanted to be a hundred leagues from Duenas, to ride through the *meseta* until his horse fell exhausted.

I must say something to him—it doesn't matter what, thought Isabella. Poor Ferdinand! He's been waiting for me for so long, and all I can do is sit here, stiff and silent, concerned only to warm my frozen hands.

The warmth and comfort were making her drowsy, dulling her hearing. Something inside her refused to believe that she was really at Duenas and that Ferdinand was with her. On the way there, the governor had explained to her that her life would truly begin when she arrived at this fortress, which he pointed out profiled against the inky-black sky. She thought she'd been drinking.

I like him in these old mule-driver's clothes. Isabella had only needed a few moments, taking in every detail of his face, to be sure that she would love him. Not just for his chestnut hair curling down to his neck, his bright eyes, his tanned complexion, his slim figure. Rather it was his shyness, which somehow brought him closer to her.

If only she would smile, thought Ferdinand. I would make a vow to love her for the rest of my life. He didn't much care for the rather severe blonde tresses, which reminded him of the little girl he had known. He sensed her steely toughness. Would the fire's heat put some warmth into those wide blue-green eyes? Perhaps her somewhat fixed expression would take on more life when the warmth made itself felt. He watched her intently, and wanted to touch her as one would lightly touch a too-perfect statue, to see it if were real.

He spoke very quickly: "Do you feel better? Would you like some warm wine?"

Isabella shook her head, and her braids moved as if alive on her breasts. The others looked at her in silence, a silence that reminded her of the hush that comes over a crowd at a moment of high drama between matador and bull. She quickly dismissed that uncomfortable idea from her mind.

"I have had a bed made up for you, your Highness," said the governor. "My house is not a palace, but you will be safe here."

"I will follow you," said Isabella.

⚜

Isabella and Ferdinand opened their window shutters at almost the same moment. They waved to each other before hurrying to dress for dinner.

The weather had cleared, and the plateau was like a dazzling sea stretching to the horizon. Strong gusts of wind swept the ramparts and seemed to strike a note from an invisible crystal bell in the sky.

The prince and princess sat down at the table. Steaming bowls of hot goat's milk were set before them. The previous day's worries vanished like rain clouds after a summer storm.

Isabella and Ferdinand listened to Andres Cabrera, at the top of his brilliant conversational form, and smiled at each other. When Isabella rested her hand on the table, Ferdinand's eyes lingered on it. When Ferdinand gripped a knife to cut the rye bread loaf, Isabella followed his movements with her eyes. Both of them were quickly discovering new things about each other, as though turning the pages of a book.

"We cannot stay here," said Andres. "In a few hours, the trick will be discovered. Villena will scour the countryside, and we will have two hundred landers at our gates, not to mention the artillery the marquis will bring to bear as his way of welcoming us."

Isabella swallowed her last mouthful of milk. "You're right, Andres. We must leave Duena, and set out for Valladolid."

Ferdinand dropped his knife. Cabrera was rooted to the spot in amazement. "For Valladolid! But surely we'll run into Villena on the way?"

"I'm certain we will. You may think that would be walking into the lion's den, but I believe not. Can you seriously imagine the marquis would put irons on the feet of the Prince of Aragon and the Princess of Castile?"

Ferdinand and Cabrera exchanged quick glances. Ferdinand shut his knife-blade with an audible snap. "I believe," he said, "that you are right, Isabella. Speaking for myself, I don't like running away."

⚜

They encountered Villena just outside Valladolid. A cluster of lances could be seen moving against the background of the poplars on the banks of the Pisuerga.

Ferdinand sped up his horse to draw alongside Isabella, so he could feel her thigh against his own. He held out his hand, and Isabella's nestled in it like a bird.

"Courage!" he said.

"I don't need courage. I'm not afraid of the Marquis of Villena. He's the person I most despise in the world."

Ferdinand's hand squeezed Isabella's. "What do I have to offer you?" he asked. "Nothing—or nearly nothing. I'm king only of a pathetic little place—Sicily. Hope is the one thing I have plenty of. But I'm certain that together we can achieve great things."

"With God's help," Isabella replied, "within a month we will be married in Valladolid, where many people are still loyal to me. This town is all I can offer you. I'm poor, Ferdinand, the poorest princess that Castile has ever known. But after we're married there will no longer be a frontier between your country and mine. There will simply be Spain, and one day we will reign over it."

Isabella and Ferdinand rode on in the high wind. They could see the outline of Valladolid's white cathedral in the far distance. In front of them, the Castilian lancers redeployed into a fan-like formation, the terrible marquis at the pivotal point. Ferdinand continued to hold Isabella's hand.

Villena rode forward from his soldiers. He wore the white cape of the Grand Master of Santiago, emblazoned with a red cross. A gold chain encircled his chest. When he was a few feet in front of the royal pair, he stopped, switching his gaze from one to the other. He was so baffled and confused that he forgot to take off his helmet.

"Pull yourself together," said Isabella. "I would like to present my fiancé, don Ferdinand of Aragon. It's very good of you to come to meet us with such an impressive escort."

The old marquis removed his helmet bad-temperedly, bowed curtly, and said before dismounting: "I am your servant, your Highness."

⁂

Valladolid expected one prisoner; instead a betrothed couple arrived. Villena led the small party. His expression was so gloomy that it was he who seemed to be the prisoner.

Before leaving, he had ordered all the professional rabble-rousers to be gathered with the object of whipping up mass hatred against his prisoner. Instead, his horse pushed its way through a silent and confused throng. No angry cries were heard. The prince and princess needed no protection against threatening gestures.

No sooner had the doors of the palace closed on the procession than Valladolid brought out its festive flags and carpets. Musicians and singers wandered up and down, even into the Moorish and Jewish sections, linking in song the names of Isabella and Ferdinand, of Castile and Aragon. Kindling was piled up for bonfires of joy, and innkeepers hung garlands of bottles in their arcades.

⁂

A few days later, as Isabella was quiet, alone, in her large room, she saw coming into the far end of the room the Grand Master of Santiago, booted and spurred. Isabella confronted him.

"You're surely not leaving us already, Marquis? Why are you in such a hurry to get back to Madrid?"

"The king has recalled me, your Highness. I've already stayed too long."

"Your report was not very acceptable, I imagine. What are you going to tell the king, Marquis! 'Assert your authority, Sire! Declare Isabella a harmful sister! Act at once, or your throne could be in danger!' your Highness!"

"You need only talk, and the king will act. He hears only you."

She crumpled her handkerchief into a ball, and went on in a less-excited voice: "You don't like me, I know, and nothing could make you believe that I wish you well. Our disagreements go back so far into the past that I can no longer find the energy to work out how they started in the first place. In fact, with your help I would find it very easy to forget them."

Villena stood up very straight. His sword clinked against his thigh armor. "I obey the king, your Highness. His wish is mine."

"Those are just words. I was hoping for a different reply."

"There is no different reply, your Highness."

"So—it's war?"

"It will be whatever the king wishes."

"Tell him clearly that I will marry Ferdinand of Aragon, and nobody else. Regardless of him, regardless of you."

"You will need a dispensation from Saint Peter."

"Already arranged."

"Who will pay for the expense of the wedding? You haven't even enough money to buy yourself a respectable robe."

"The Jews have offered us money."

"You have no army. The king pays your guards. How can you hold out against him?"

"Every town we enter will be another town on our side. Spain already loves us. She has been waiting hundreds of years for us. The names of Isabella and Ferdinand are already being whispered throughout Castile. "Make sure my brother understands that I will never conspire against the Crown . . . but if he gets in our way, he should know nothing will change my decision!"

※

Noblemen arrived from everywhere. All those whom the king thought of as his enemies gathered at Valladolid around the prince and the princess.

Among the first to arrive was the Duke of Medina-Sidonia. He carried greetings from Andalusia to the betrothed couple. The reconquest of Moorish Granada was too dear to his heart to miss any opportunity of helping bring it to a successful conclusion.

The Grand Admiral of Aragon, don Fadrique Enriquez, came the next day. Ferdinand's grandfather on his mother's side was a tough old man, worn out by ceaseless battles at sea and on land.

The Jewish bankers came up with less money than they had promised. King John of Aragon, who had promised nothing, sent his blessing, but not a single penny. A reply had been expected from King Henry of Castile. None came.

※

In spite of the fur cloak over her shoulders, Isabella almost froze to death in the icy chill of Valladolid's basilica. Monsignor Carillo's sermon was long, pompous, and boring.

Someone had to shake the Admiral Enriquez by the shoulder; he had fallen asleep, legs stretched out across the aisle, tears of cold running down his thin cheeks.

In the cold north wind of October, the crowd stamped their feet on the ground. Nothing was distributed to the milling children and beggars except smiles. The band wouldn't play until the very last moment; they hadn't been paid in advance.

Enthusiasm and belief were both missing from the crowd's emotions. Ironic overtones were easy to detect in their cheers of "king" and "queen." King and queen, Ferdinand and Isabella certainly were, but of what kingdom? Sicily! Their bid for greatness was more the stuff of dreams than of reality, of legend more than history. Tomorrow they would waken with no wealth other than the love they shared, in a ruined palace full of silent servants and sad crows. As for their borrowed clothes, their costume jewelry—the Jews would be coming to take them back.

What was left for them? The dream of a love! If it could really happen. They were still not fully aware of the breadth and depth of their love. They would go through many trials and tribulations together before that partial awareness would become certainty. They hardly knew each other. Only on very rare occasions had they found an opportunity to see and talk to each other in private, without being surrounded by Medina-Sidonia, Enriquez, Carillo, and all the others.

✦

Ferdinand sat on a divan, both hands dangling between his knees, in the small study of the residence that John de Rivero, lord of Valladolid, had put at his disposal. This dead time between the ceremony and the wedding reception disconcerted him. He was cold. He'd been cold, it seemed, as long as they'd known each other.

Without being helped, Isabella managed to get her wind-blown hair back into some sort of order. She came and sat beside him, resting her head on his shoulder. She also was cold; even wrapping her hands in her fox-fur muff didn't warm them.

"Ferdinand," she said, "what's troubling you? I was watching you during the service: you didn't smile at me once. Don't you have any feelings for me any more?"

He leaned his head on the back of the divan. "I'm sorry. I think I'm tired."

He was not about to let her know that he was bored to death. A consuming need to see Saragossa once more was breaking his heart. He would have traded all today's promises to spend a few hours roaming the gray streets where the wind from the *llanos* and the *meseta* blustered wildly, and to wander through the palace corridors, wondering which of his lovers he might find: Leanor, Micia, or Sancha. It was enough for him to knock on any door at random. He admitted to himself that he would prefer Sancha, whose husband had left for Rosas. He could walk along a deserted passageway, knock at a door . . .

"Ferdinand! I sometimes have the idea that you don't love me, that I'm as much as a stranger to you as I was a few weeks ago."

"No," he said, "it's not that. I just feel uneasy . . . uncomfortable. Nothing around us rings true. This house is not ours. The Jews paid for our wedding reception. Are we truly wed? Everyone knows that the papal dispensation is a forgery. We have no kingdom, no army, no way of supporting ourselves. Ambition, and ambition alone, is what inspires those who put their trust in us. I fear that exile might be our only real choice. I like clear-cut situations, Isabella. And this one is far from clear-cut."

He put his hands flat on his knees. Isabella knelt on the bare floor and put her icy hands into Ferdinand's.

"Have faith, my Ferdinand. Be patient. God has blessed our union. All around us may be mere deception, but our love makes everything fine and true. And Spain needs this love."

In saying "God" and "Spain," thought Ferdinand, she says it all.

He was going to push her away when their eyes met. Her gaze was of such frankness, such purity, that it made her face shine. He saw her in a new light. Had he underestimated her beauty? Had he ever come across such symmetric features, such lovely coloring, lips as warm and inviting—with no artifice?

A wave of silky hair gave a wider appearance to the gentle curve of her brow, rose-tinted from the cold. He realized that he had not kissed her, that he had failed to pay her even this simplest compliment. He sought her lips. She leaned toward him.

"Forgive me," he whispered. "I'd almost forgotten that you are my wife, and that you will remain my wife in the face of all opposition."

"Yes, Ferdinand, I am your wife. God . . ."

He pulled her to him and smothered the next words with another kiss. She slid her cold hands under his red jacket, seeking the warmth of his body. Ferdinand trembled. His hands urgently caressed her in a rougher, more unmistakable embrace. "No, Ferdinand. Tonight . . ."

2

Two Kings Without a Kingdom

The vixen was still alive. The trap's iron teeth held her paw only by its nerve; the flesh had already torn away. As the hunter approached, she let out a croaking bark, her back hunched up, and she closed her eyes as if refusing to look at the weapon that would finish her off.

Ferdinand was about to draw his hunting knife when he heard the sound of a galloping horse. A rider appeared on the far side of the river. He waved his arms wildly, and Ferdinand heard him shout: "Come back quickly, your Highness!"

Before Ferdinand had time to ask what was going on, the horseman pulled his horse around and galloped back in the direction of Duenas. Ferdinand jumped into the saddle, and then was struck by an afterthought. He went back to the vixen, which had started whining again, and crushed her head under his heel. Then he threw the still-quivering body onto his horse and forded the river in a great spray of water.

"Don't go too far," Isabella had begged him when he left to go hunting. "I'm afraid that today might be the day."

The birth would be within a few days of the first anniversary of their marriage. Ferdinand no longer wanted to believe it. It was more than a week since Isabella had felt that she was near her term, that pains were going through her like a thousand needles.

Ferdinand made all speed, conscious of a growing anxiety. He went through the main gate of Duenas at a demonic pace, caused great alarm to several black pigs, swept into the castle courtyard, and threw the reins to a groom.

Ferdinand's blood turned to ice as he entered Isabella's room. She was stretched out on the bed, unmoving, hands flat on her belly. Her face was covered with a white sheet. Dead? Impossible. Scarcely two hours ago she had stood in front of him, she was talking, she . . .

Someone caught hold of his arm in a rough grip. He heard a voice from what seemed to be very faraway. "Don't stay here, sir. The child will be born at any moment."

Ferdinand, deathly pale, turned to the midwife. "So she's not dead?"

"Dead, her? Poor girl!"

"But why the sheet?"

"One of her little ideas. She doesn't want anyone to see her in pain. She talks of 'dignity.'"

Ferdinand kissed the fat woman on both cheeks, and left the room unsteadily to sit in the hallway. He sat slumped in a darkness where he imagined firebirds flying around him, and only roused himself when a hand touched his shoulder.

"Your Highness—it's a girl! See how pink, beautiful, and plump she is. A shining little watermelon."

"Isabel!" Ferdinand murmured.

He snatched the baby from the midwife's arms, and would have taken her to show to his grandfather Fadrique, to Monsignor Carililo, to Buendia, had not the fat woman stopped him in time.

Ferdinand went into Isabella's room, kissed her brow, and walked around her bed before the grumbling of the maidservants made it evident that he was not wanted. He was unaware of the servants passing him in the corridors. His expression was distant as the Governor rudely collided with him. His heart was filled with a deep joy. His body felt light as a feather; he bumped into chests, doors, walls, without paying attention. He needed movement and altitude. After walking for a long time, he reached the top of the castle keep, out of breath and running with sweat. He rested to let his frantic heartbeat calm down.

This great happiness was vital to him; he could not have borne it if some accident had taken it away from him. That would have been the last straw after all the ordeals that he and Isabella had been through, and after all the love they shared, which had helped them in their times of trial. Ordeals? They would encounter more of them in the future, but from now on they would be better prepared to deal with them.

Ferdinand decided that he would wait not a day, not an hour even, to get the news to his brother-in-law, King Henry of Castile, and to his father, King John of Aragon. He felt impelled to tell the whole world, so that his great joy would shine forth to the most distant courts of Europe, even as far as the frontiers of the Barbary Coast and of Russia. In the next few weeks, all Spain would know of Elisabeth's arrival. But the first to know would be King Henry.

Where was he? What was he doing? He had replied to none of Isabella's letters asking him to acknowledge their marriage—to legitimize it, as it were. He wouldn't even meet her. Why?

Ferdinand could only conjecture what lay behind their silence. The kingdom had become one great battlefield. There was fighting in the counties of Benavente, Biscaya, Andalusia. The Hermandades of Castile had split in two, and the nobles who were its backbone were shirking their duty, which was to keep order through force of arms. They were using those arms now to settle their own quarrels.

Only Villena was on top of the situation. It was easy to see his hand in each of these brief wars. As payment for mediating between opponents, he would extract from one, a town, from another, a title. He was the evil spirit of anarchy. His goatee could be seen wherever the sword's gleam became a flame.

As for the king, he seemed oblivious to all this turmoil, and to the invidious position in which Isabella and Ferdinand found themselves. Make them submit? Hunt them down? Had it been only a question of doing what he wanted, he wouldn't have waited for long; but his armies were at a standstill in all corners of his kingdom. True, he still had his Moorish guards, but he was reluctant to throw the white *jellabas* of his cavalry into such bloody chaos.

King Henry still delayed making a public disavowal of Isabella. Before doing that, he wanted more definite news that La Beltraneja, his supposed daughter, had married someone who would be able to ensure Castile's future after his own death: Charles de Guyenne, nephew of King Louis XI of France.

The King had failed in his attempt to have Isabella accept Charles. So he had offered him to young Jeanne, who cared for him even less than her mother liked "Uncle" Beltran, so generous with dolls from Seville and with sugar-coated pastries.

Already envoys from the French Court haunted the palace of Segovia and pressed King Henry for a decision. But Henry would not make that decision. He played with his favorites, threw pieces of gold at his jesters, and said, "Tomorrow. . ."

Now and again he saw Monsignor Carillo, Bishop of Toledo, appear at court—sword clinking on his armor, red face creased with worry lines. The prelate had withdrawn his support for the union of Isabella and Ferdinand.

"They want to do just as they please," the monsignor commented gruffly. "Ferdinand replies to my advice: 'I will not be ordered about by you or by anyone else.' He dared to give me that reply."

Henry hid a smile behind his handkerchief. "Be that as it may, how are you going to help bring them together?"

Monsignor Carillo had not yet openly declared himself for Henry and against Isabella. He was waiting for the right moment. Isabella, the silly little goose, had just given birth to a baby. That could change the course of events.

⚜

"This must change," Ferdinand murmured.

He lifted up his head again, as he stood atop Duenas' watch-tower. What would happen? He knew nothing any more, but felt sure that events were about to take a new turn. He and Isabella faced an embattled future, but anything would be better than being mired in their present uncertainty and misery.

Isabella did not seem to be affected by their problems: she mastered them. It wasn't the same way for Ferdinand—his feet were held fast by the soil of this land of their exile. He looked at the holes in his stockings, his creased and crumpled coats, his threadbare doublets. He would again have to ask the Jews for charity. He couldn't take a single step, in Duenas or elsewhere, without encountering the arrogant stares of an Isaac or an Abner.

What good was the Inquisition? he whispered to himself. He clenched his fists and dreamed of the stake.

The bells of Duenas rang out to acclaim the birth of Elisabeth. The very air around Ferdinand vibrated. He leaned forward into an arrow slit: below was the red soil of the countryside. Shadows of clouds full of rain passed across the landscape, under the October sky.

A horseman had just pulled up in the castle courtyard. Ferdinand could only make out the fair curly hair, the powerful shoulders, but he knew at once that it was David Ezra. Another Jew!

Where had he come from? One never knew. His father owned property all over Castile, and David traveled from one place to the other. Wherever Isabella and Ferdinand found themselves, David would appear, and Isabella would drop everything to greet him.

His previous visit lasted nearly a week. Ferdinand had stayed close to Isabella. From the moment David Ezra arrived, her face shone like the *meseta* after rain.

Does she still love him? Ferdinand wondered. He got no answer, except for the happiness Isabella radiated whenever the Jew appeared.

King Henry took little Jeanne by the hand. They left the chapel of the Papular monastery, eyes dazzled by the translucent mauve colors shimmering on the new marble *reredos*, bathed in the light of the spring morning. They walked all around the cloisters, where they could hear the music of water leaping down from the Guadarrama mountains. The air was redolent of lilacs and of snow.

"So I won't be seeing my fiancé?" asked Jeanne.

Henry broke off a small lilac branch and smelled it, his eyes half closed. They were going ahead with a betrothal ceremony—a symbolic one only, in the absence of the fiancé, Charles de Guyenne. He would be represented by some important people: the Cardinal of Albi, the Count of Boulogne. It was the third time that little Jeanne had asked the same question since she and the queen had returned from Portugal, and the third time he had avoided answering.

They left the cloisters in a crowd of courtiers and fine ladies. The princess mounted a silver-caparisoned chestnut mule that was doing a little dance in the dust: the king, a chestnut horse whose gold-faced clothes reached to the ground.

They came to the river flats which ran the Lozoya.

The gleam of helmets, the excited noise of the crowd, the multicolored clothing of the captains and the wealthy, the page boys, and the ladies of the court. Brass bands massed beside a little grove playing thunderous music. Opposite them was a platform decorated with dark red velvet and surrounded by the king's Moorish guards—everything fascinated the young girl. She couldn't believe that all this was in her honor, that the miserable exile in Portugal was over, that the king—her father—had decided to make her his heiress, and to disavow Isabella.

Seated on a canopied throne, she was amused for a moment by the shadows of the canopy's gold fringes playing over her shoes. "Stand up, sit down, salute!" the Archbishop of Segovia, Monsignor Arias, kept repeating, and soon the performance began to bore her.

But the music was soon struck up once more. When Jeanne closed her eyes she felt that the sun on her skin and the mountain wind in her hair were like a different kind of music, played on thousands of little gold and silver bells.

The golden crown was in the form of a garland, but Jeanne didn't have time to see it placed on her head. She tried very hard to pay attention to the speech of Professor Antonio Nunez of Ciudad-Rodrigo. She heard him proclaim Isabella's disinheritance, but his voice was so monotonous that she felt she might fall asleep.

Seeing the king and queen right in front of her shook her out of her doze. She straightened her back and put on a serious expression to listen to them swearing that she was their legitimate daughter. Watching them, she remembered that the queen had promised her dolls from Segovia, and that Uncle don Beltran would bring them for her.

Now the crowd was shouting its excitement. Jeanne was astonished to realize that all the great and the good of Castile were stepping up to kiss her hand—the lords of Arevalo, of Valencia, of Benavente, of Miranda, of Seville. She was greatly pleased by this—so much so that she made a mental note to tell her confessor that very evening, as she felt that sinful pride played a large part in that pleasure. She wanted to call out to the queen and ask her, "Your Majesty, will I always be known as 'La Beltraneja'?"

❧

"Quiet," Isabella whispered. "You'll wake Isabel."

Ferdinand swore under his breath, and went on walking heavily across the room.

"This can't go on, Isabella, can you understand that? I know your brother won't leave us alone—we have no choice other than prison or exile."

King Henry was winning easily. He had taken the town and the fortress of Medina del Campo. A week later, it had been Valladolid. Ferdinand had only just escaped from that city under cover of night, through the cellars and alleyways of the Jewish quarter until reaching the river, which he hurriedly crossed. Hardly had two weeks gone by when it was announced that Villena was prancing around before Avila.

Then there had been the absurd pantomime of an engagement ceremony at Papular for La Beltraneja and Charles de Guyenne, and the solemn declaration that Jeanne was now the appointed successor to the throne of Castile.

"I can't go on, Isabella. If we don't take refuge with my father we will be captured."

"Henry is trying to force the pace. If we give up now, we'll simply help him achieve his aims."

"We will also help him by doing nothing."

"Our side is growing stronger every day. Monsignor Carillo has not yet committed himself, proof that he is not at all certain of my brother's ultimate victory. The Parliament secretly supports us—and you know the power of the assemblies. The people keep quiet, but they are for us."

Ferdinand kneaded his hands; Isabella heard the joints crack. He gave a great sigh. "I sometimes have the feeling of being lowered inch by inch to the bottom of a well, and every day losing more light, warmth, and air."

His footsteps sounded again in the room. "And the gold that we owe to all those Jews," he went on. "How are we ever going to pay it back? I don't like being in debt, particularly to Jews. When I come across them, they adopt an overbearing manner. God forgive me, but I believe that I could kill them with an easy conscience."

"God would not forgive you," Isabella said, gently.

"Jeanne! Jeanne! Do you hear me?"

"Yes, Mother."

"Why do you spend all your time by that window?"

"I'm waiting for my fiancé, Mother. This is the direction from which he'll come. Why is he so late? Guyenne isn't that far from Segovia. Why doesn't he write? It's months now since we were betrothed, and he hasn't sent me a letter or a present."

"Listen, and promise not to cry. Your fiancé isn't coming. He's at Bordeaux, at death's door, Juanita! Now—you promised me not to cry."

"It's nothing, Mother. I will remain a maiden. Am I so ugly that no one wants me?"

"You are pretty, Juanita, and one day a man will fall in love with you. Do you know that there's a possibility that you might marry the king of Portugal's son? Why don't you answer me?"

"Mother?"

"My child?"

"Why is there always snow on the mountains?"

Ferdinand felt suffocated in Duenas. The summer was tropically hot. The Pisuerga was nothing but a river of pebbles. Only occasionally, when there was a storm in the mountains to the north, did a trickle of rust-colored water run through it. Soon the wheat would be harvested, wheat bearing little grain. The cisterns sounded empty, and water had to be brought in by mule from out-of-the-way valleys.

Little Elisabeth fell ill. Cases of plague had been reported from Medina del Campo and Valladolid, and Isabella and Ferdinand were very afraid. The baby was slow to recover: her skin was pallid, and she had to be nursed day and night. Most of the domestic staff had fled from the castle, so Isabella had to cope with the infant on her own.

Horsemen could often be seen coming out of the distant haze. They would come as close as the moat, close enough that the links in their chain mail could be seen. They would shout insults and sing obscene songs. Then they would disappear back into the dazzling glare of the plain, brandishing their lances as they went.

Ferdinand and Isabella had not taken seriously the proposed wedding between La Beltraneja and the Duke of Guyenne, any more than the plan to marry her off to the prince of Portugal, a scheme that had been no more than a momentary thought.

The rumors that were rife about the betrothal of Princess Jeanne-la-Beltraneja to an Aragon Grandee, the Duke of Segorbe, seemed to have more substance. The duke was King John's nephew, and the king held him in high regard. Villena had taken the matter into his own hands, and appeared to want to bring the matter to a successful conclusion in as short a time as possible.

Ferdinand didn't believe it at first, and threw out the Dominican friar who told him the news while playing with his rosary beads and drinking a goblet of beer. If these rumors had been founded on truth, surely King John would have warned him.

"I must leave," said Ferdinand. "This business is getting too serious. I will be back in a few weeks."

Isabella shook her head. She couldn't stop thinking about the cavalrymen who came to hurl their insults at the walls of Duenas, about the bogus monks who might get into the fortress and attempt to poison or kidnap her. As if he already understood her fears, Ferdinand added, "My mind is made easier by the fact that last week Medina-Sidonia sent an army to our rescue. And, besides, the fortress is strong enough to withstand a siege."

Isabella was convinced that the opposite was true. Many of her servants and officers were in the pay of Grand Master Villena.

Duenas wouldn't hold out for three days. Isabella guessed that she would be tried and condemned, while, back in Aragon, Ferdinand would find his old lovers and then lead a life of fighting and fleeing.

"Leave," she said. "But hurry back if you want to find us alive, Elisabeth and me."

"If you only knew how much I love you."

There was almost no one Isabella could rely on, apart from the Duke of Medina-Sidonia. He would not betray her. They were linked by two emotions: hatred of Villena, and the desire to reconquer the southern kingdoms, an ambition that had already swallowed up a large part of the duke's wealth. They often talked about it: in fact, it was the main topic of their conversation.

They were not driven by nostalgia for a lost cause, but by a longing for the struggle that would lead to victory in this last and most difficult stage of seven centuries of Reconquest.

Tears welled in Isabella's eyes when Medina-Sidonia reminded her of Granada's rich river valleys, the gardens of Almeria and Malaga, the prosperous orchards of the Levant coast, the white and gold splendor of the Moorish palaces set against the tawny brown of the mountains.

Medina stayed on. Isabella shared her misery with him just as she had with Ferdinand. Without him, who would be left to say that she hadn't given up the exhausting fight?

For Villena allowed her no rest.

Duenas was no more than a memory. The same went for Olemdo and Arevalo. At dawn, she had a clear picture of these abandoned towns in her mind, after a night of little sleep and too-real dreams.

Elisabeth cried in her arms under the rough woolen cloak and wouldn't go back to sleep unless rocked by the movement of the horse. They followed goat-tracks across mountains in the gray light of dawn, across windy and rainswept plains. Winter was as harsh as summer had been scorching. As the proverb had it, "Nine months of winter, three months of hell."

As far as Isabella was concerned, it was always hell. The ranks of the army that trudged behind her—badly equipped, underfed, ill-paid—dwindled as time wore on. Ferdinand rarely sent news, and even when he did, it was long delayed in reaching her. David Ezra hadn't been heard from for some weeks, and Isabella hungered in vain for news of him.

One day they arrived before the old Arab walls of Torrelaguna, having spent the night under leaden skies plodding through the Guadarrama snows. Isabella decided to wait for Ferdinand there.

It was getting near Christmas. One morning, on the ramparts with the duke, Isabella saw a group of wretched-looking horsemen coming toward them from the west. She felt a surge of excitement: She had recognized Ferdinand. She leapt on her unsaddled horse and raced to meet him. So tightly did he embrace her that Isabella felt she was being crushed.

"How's Elisabeth?" was his first question.

"She's in good health."

"I bring good news. Cardinal Borgia, the Papal Legate, has received the Holy Father's dispensation for our marriage. There is no longer a cloud over our union. The cardinal asked me to bring you this ivory crucifix."

They came to the bridge. "What did King John have to say?" asked Isabella.

"He was not at all pleased to see me. According to him, the planned marriage of the Duke of Segorbe is no more than a fairy story. Yet Segorbe was to come to Madrid for a meeting with King Henry. Things are moving very quickly. And my father turns a deaf ear!"

"I believe that he secretly supports his nephew, the Duke of Segorbe."

Ferdinand froze, taking his hand from Isabella's arm and looking at her with affection and fear. "That is a thought so terrible that it's never as much as crossed my mind."

"Mother, why is my fiancé, the Duke of Segorbe, so late in arriving?"

"He's very sick, Jeanne, and I've told you already."

"The same as Charles de Guyenne?"

"Yes, the same as him."

"Is he going to die as well?"

"Perhaps."

"Then why was he in Requena last week?"

"Who told you that lie?"

". . . and why didn't he come through Segovia? I want to be married, Mother, you know that very well. I can do nothing against Isabella without a husband to act for me."

"I wanted to keep it from you, but since you know it already. . . the Duke of Segorbe is the most conceited and stupidest person you can imagine. It's true that the Grand Master met him in Requena. But do you know what Segorbe had the nerve to do? He offered his hand to be kissed by all the great people of Spain who were there. Mendoza took his hand and made fun of him—he said. . . 'Truly, my lord, you have a ravishingly beautiful hand.' Did you know that as well, Juanita?"

"No, I did not. Mother, the season's nearly over. Look at this rosebud—it's fading even before it has opened."

Ferdinand had to go to Aragon once more. King John was in Perpignan, besieged by twenty-thousand French troops commanded by Philippe de Bresse. Seventy-six years old, the king fought like an old lion, and he would eat nothing except the mule-meat and rancid chestnuts that were the everyday fare of his soldiers.

Ferdinand raised regiments in Navarre, Aragon, and Barcelona, and swept down on the Roussilon. Just in time: everywhere they were at the limit of their strength.

King John and Ferdinand embraced in front of the table where the truce had just been signed, and went back together to Barcelona. A string of bonfires was lit from Aragon to Sicily. In the Balearic Islands, the king of France was burned in effigy. Services of thanksgiving made the rafters ring in the Palma cathedral.

Isabella was in Torrelaguna when she heard the news. She spent the night giving thanks to the Virgin. The following day, she heard more news: Monsignor Carillo, Archbishop of Toledo, had asked to see her. He was engaged once more with the king's advisers concerning some obscure business about a cardinal's hat, which he was expecting, but which had not yet been placed on his head.

Booted and spurred, Carillo again appeared before Isabella. He offered her troops, eternal friendship, gold, and prayers. Above all, he brought with him a gleam of hope. Following his quarrels with Segorbe, Villena had taken a small group and left Madrid, heading for a stronghold deep in the mountains—Penafiel.

This joyful news was almost too much after the recent dreadful swings between hope and despair. Isabella was overwhelmed by it. She took to her bed, and stayed there for several days. Borgia's ivory figure of Christ hung on the wall opposite her, so that she could see it throughout the day—and the night as well, by the dim light of the little Jewish lamp that David had brought her and that was always with her.

As she dozed, Isabella was aware of this light even when her eyes were closed. She sensed in it the promise of a new dawn, a light that would illuminate her whole existence with ever-growing power and clarity. And she dreamed a dream . . .

She saw herself opening the gates of the towns from which she had fled in the half-light of morning, standing on the towers of cathedrals flaunting the banners of Castile. On the hilltops were regiments of soldiers shouting her name and Ferdinand's, lances and helmets shimmering in the sunlight. Crowds of black-robed students, schoolbags on their arms, were parading in front of the palace walls, praising in song the deeds of the young hero of Perpignan.

She saw herself leaving the palace to acknowledge her subjects. King Henry was waiting for her. She mounted her ceremonial horse, caparisoned in gold-brocaded velvet and looking like some beautiful ship. The king led her by the steed's bridle through the streets of the city . . .

Next morning, Carillo's fist hammered on the door. This was no time for sleeping. All Castile was clamoring for Isabella; the towns were ready to fall like ripe fruit.

"Shouldn't I wait for Ferdinand, Monsignor?"

The Archbishop's spurs clinked against the foot of the bed. His ruddy face wrinkled. Isabella must act as quickly as possible. How surprised Ferdinand would be when, coming back through Castile, he found all the conquered cities retaken!

This last comment of the Archbishop's made up Isabella's mind. She blew out the Jewish lamp, rummaged in her chests to find the least worn—and also the least feminine—of her clothes. After all, she was setting out on a way of conquest.

Little Elisabeth watched her mother dress, sucking her thumb and shrinking back, wondering what was happening. The sword with its damascene sheath that the queen fastened to her leather belt held a particular fascination for her. Elisabeth tried to grab it, but the coldness of the metal made her cry.

First, Isabella took her daughter to a very dear friend, Beatrix de Babadilla, Andres Cabrera's wife. They swore never again to leave each other.

Isabella arrived unheralded at Aranda de Duero, and tore into Queen Joan's suite. She had expected to find the queen at home, but found nothing except an unmade bed and, hanging over a chair, a belt bearing the arms of Beltran de la Cueva. In the adjoining room were spread out the remnants of a feast: wine-stained tablecloths, overturned armchairs, burned-out candles in the chandeliers. The servants, hardly awake, confirmed that the queen had fled to Madrid at the king's side.

"To Madrid!" cried Isabella.

Carillo had to restrain her excitement; it was still too soon. He talked of Madrigal, where Isabella had been born; of Medina del Campo, where she liked to live; of Valladolid, where she had married Ferdinand. This touched a raw nerve in Isabella. So many memories had been stolen from her—she was now going to reclaim them at swordpoint.

✥

While Isabella was leading her troops from one town to the next, Borgia was explaining to the old Marquis of Villena just what advantages he could gain by siding with her. Andres Cabrera was in Madrid attempting to influence the king to be more kindly disposed toward his sister. Villena turned a deaf ear. King Henry proudly spoke of "honor," had he not, two years ago, chosen little Jeanne to succeed him? Then first one and then the other bent with the wind.

Dressing her dolls, la Beltraneja waited for the arrival of the fiancé of which she dreamed. In Madrid, the king's wife found young lovers to replace the aging don Beltran.

Isabella was reunited with Ferdinand in Aranda. They looked at each other for a few moments before throwing themselves into each other's arms.

"Look what I've brought you," said Ferdinand.

A valet came forward bearing a leather casket adorned with silver hinges. Ferdinand opened it and brought out a solid gold diadem studded with precious stones, resting on a small cushion of crimson velvet. The arms of Castile and of Aragon were emblazoned on the front.

"It is a gift from my father. He hopes that you will be wearing it in the near future."

"And I—what have I to give you?" Isabella spoke sadly.

"You bring me a kingdom, and your love, Isabella."

✥

During the long months of the summer they had been running all over Castile. It was not a real war but worse than that— permanent small battles, each one with its loss of wounded or dead companions. Isabella and Ferdinand were always with their soldiers, living that exhausting life. Then came the last days of the Castilian autumn, a period of mellow fruitfulness. Isabella and Ferdinand savored every moment of being together.

Waking one morning, they saw that the first snows had fallen on the mountains, and that the reddish sediment of winter was appearing in the Duero. The end of the year was drawing close, and Isabella had not yet been crowned with King John's diadem. But her face was blissful, wearing that rarest of crowns: happiness.

Some time later, on a morning just three days before Christmas, the noise of a cavalcade filled the courtyard. A lady accompanied by a few horsemen swept into the castle stairway, and asked to speak with Isabella—still asleep, even though the hour was late.

"Beatrix! It's you!"

Beatrix pushed back her hood and made a perfunctory curtsey. Her face was shiny from the cold. "Madame," she said, struggling with her emotions. "Madame, King Henry waits for you in Segovia."

3

The Bells of Segovia

King Henry, just back from the hunt, hadn't had time to change his clothes. His boots were dirty with mud and slush.

He had been told of Isabella's arrival while he was tracking down a herd of wild boar in the Balsain forest, near the monastery of St. Ildefonse. He often came back to hunt in these parts. The thrill of the chase re-energized him, the contact with trees and animals gave him new vigor, made the blood run quicker through his veins.

Isabella had been awaiting him for several hours in the room that had been set aside for her in the Alcazar of Segovia. When the king came in and pushed back his small gray cap, Isabella hardly recognized him. His gait was still elegant, his bearing noble; but his face was emaciated and weak. His gaze was still alert, but heavy and swollen eyelids gave no hint of liveliness. His shoulders were stooped, and his hair, although curly still, was white at the temples.

The king smiled as soon as he saw his sister. She rose to greet him. He walked toward her slowly, eyes blinking as though against bright sunlight. With his sleeve, he wiped away a tear caused by the cold, and said simply: "I'm glad to see you, Isabella."

She bowed curtly.

"I can't see you very well," he continued. "Come closer."

He took her hand and led her close to a window that overlooked the ravine through which ran the river Eresma. He examined Isabella in silence, holding her hand up with his as if they were going to dance. He nodded his head gravely.

"You are very beautiful. And what self-confidence, what majesty! You will be the finest jewel in the crown of the Trastamare family. As far as I can remember, you are twenty years old."

Isabella corrected him. "Twenty-four."

"I beg your pardon—my memory isn't as good as it used to be. Where is Ferdinand?"

"At Turegano. He had a problem to resolve with the count."

Isabella was keeping the truth from her brother. Ferdinand was waiting for a signal from her before showing his face in Segovia. He wanted to be sure the king's invitation was not a hidden trap.

"I hope that at least you brought my niece, Elisabeth?"

"I left her in Aranda. I'm concerned about her health. She would have found the journey too trying."

The King's face seemed to darken. He let go of Isabella's hand, and turned his back on her. "You're afraid I'm luring you into a trap, is that the case? You don't trust your own brother. Do you take me for a monster?"

"Dona Beatrix and Andres Cabrera will tell you that I have come with no such fears. I am at your mercy. There's nothing to stop you from locking me up in one of those jails in the tower of Hommage, where you once kept Afonso and me under lock and key."

Henry interrupted angrily: ". . . and tomorrow Ferdinand's soldiers would be under my battlements!"

He spun back to look at Isabella, his face a mask of torment, pallid lips twitching.

"What times we live in, Isabella! What misdeeds are we atoning for? The fruit is only just ripe when it falls from the branch and rots in the grass . . . then a storm kills the tree. And God doesn't listen to our prayers, doesn't redeem us from our sins. What must I do? To whom should I listen? What is the will of God? Let Him only show me the way, and I will follow Him as the sheep follows the shepherd's lantern at night. But my eyes are blind to that gleam, and absolutely no light penetrates them."

"I've seen this light." Isabella's voice was soothing. "You too can find it, if only you show that you really want to."

He looked at her in amazement, and then let out a grating laugh. "And you're going to ask me to follow you, am I right? Everyone who comes to me—the queen, Villena, Carillo, Borgia, Andres—all show me their own little light and say 'It's a sign from God.' How many labyrinths are there for me to get lost in? And now you, Isabella . . ."

The king turned to the wall, resting his brow on the cold stone, hands on his temple. Great shudders shook his back. When he turned back to Isabella, his eyes were streaming with tears, tears he didn't attempt to hide.

"I beg your pardon," he said. "When I pleaded with you to come and see me again, it wasn't with the idea of boring you with my complaints. I know now that the queen is a whore, her daughter a schemer, Villena a knave. You're the only one left to me."

"You can thank Andres for that: he it is who opened my eyes. He and I have fought each other recently, me to protect those I thought I loved, he to show me the emptiness of that love. We spent many a night quarreling. I heaped threats and insults on him, but when he wanted to stop arguing I would persuade him to continue. I needed this voice that could judge me and touch my deepest emotions, digging out the painful roots as with the blade of a dagger. Ah! What tortures Cabrera put me through—and how grateful I am to him!"

"All that's in the past. Now that I'm here, everything is simple."

The King's face lit up instantly, like a child who comes across an unexpected pleasure. He bowed formally, stepping back a few paces. Then he returned to Isabella, and put his hands on her shoulders.

"Isabella, do you trust me?"

"The fact that I'm here shows that I do."

"Then tell Ferdinand that I'm waiting for him. He performed great deeds at Perpignan, and I would be happy to hear him tell me about them."

Ferdinand arrived some days later. He left his army encamped on the banks of the Eresma, between the monastery of El Paral and the river itself, and together with a few of his captains he entered the town by the great gate of San Cibrian. Somewhat coldly, he saluted the Count of Benavente, whom the king had sent to meet him, and followed him in silence to the bishop's palace, where Isabella was staying.

"None of this makes me feel very confident," he said. "Your brother was very quick in making up his mind to receive me."

Pleased to see Ferdinand again and more or less satisfied by her conversation with her brother, King Henry, Isabella replied in a quiet voice, "We're at no risk here."

"Are we going to keep to ourselves?"

"Certainly not. Henry will soon come looking for us, to introduce us to his people."

The king arrived as expected, in the middle of a buzz of lively chatter. He hugged Ferdinand to his breast and called him "cousin." He seemed overexcited, rushing from Isabella to Ferdinand and talking in a voice so loud it rattled the window panes. He didn't seem to be aware of the young prince's shyness; the group of courtiers never once took their eyes off him.

Ferdinand went up to Cabrera. "The king's drunk, isn't he?"

Cabrera shook his head. The king was subject to such mood swings. In a few minutes' time, he would very probably groan and burst into tears.

When everyone had moved down into the palace courtyard, Henry invited Isabella and Ferdinand to mount the horses that had been prepared for them. Then he caught hold of the two mounts by their bridles, one in each hand, ordered the gates to be opened, and set out down the road on foot.

There was a moment of dismay among the crowds massed in front of the cathedral. Then gusts of laughter rang out, sounding like muffled explosions, and finally there followed rumbling cheers, which started from the arcades, swept over the crush of people, and burst around the king who—now very calm—walked on, still leading the horses by their bridles.

"Castile and Aragon!"

"Isabella and Ferdinand!

"Que viva el rey Enrico!"

"Long live King Henry!"

Small branches of boxwood were thrown in the path of the young couple. Paper flowers flew around them like so many butterflies; lace handkerchiefs fluttered down from windows and balconies. Dressed in rags, poor women from the seedy parts of Santa Cruz and Santa Lucia came to display their children, covered with scabs, which Isabella touched with the fingertip of her glove, following the old way of bestowing a blessing from royalty. Every so often the king turned to smile at his sister, or to throw her a kiss.

Near San Miguel, the stirring strains of a military band were soon heard mingling with the roar of the crowd, increasing in number as the royal group progressed. So great was the press that the Moorish guards had to intervene. Imperturbable, sabres unsheathed, dazzling in their white *burnous*, horses the color of soot, they cleared a narrow way through the throng.

The procession was passing by the boundaries of the Jewish quarter of town when Isabella's eye was caught by a group of schoolchildren. Looming over them was a strong profile, which she immediately recognized as David Ezra. Arms around the shoulders of his fellow Jews, he watched the parade with a severe expression.

⚜

His face, surmounted by a big straw hat, scarcely brightened when he spotted Isabella. He smiled and raised his arm in salute, without in any way taking part in the waves of rejoicing that lapped up to the white walls of the ghetto. Isabella returned his smile and his greeting.

"He follows you like a shadow. Whichever town we're in, he's there. Perhaps he multiplied, and now there's a David Ezra in every town of Spain," whispered Ferdinand. He went on: "Stop smiling at him, please. People might take it as an indication that we sympathize with these heretics." Then he added in a voice more bitter than before: "When will this farce end? Who is sincere amid all this?"

"The people are always sincere," said Isabella. "If we were indifferent or hostile to them, they would let us know right to our face."

"Sincere or otherwise, tell your brother that I'm anxious to get back to the palace."

"This evening," said Isabella, "Andres Cabrera will meet us there. Try to put on a good show, my Ferdinand. I didn't expect anything like this to be happening to us."

The princess's voice was lost in the sonorous thunder of the bells of San Martin.

⋆

During the meal, the king was a charming table companion; he even consented to sing, which he sometimes did on special occasions. But afterwards, Isabella was given the news that her brother had taken to his bed with a high fever and pain in his sides.

Salomon Ezra was with the sick man when Isabella came into the room. He took her to one side. "I thought," he said, "that the king was only pretending to be ill. We are used to that sort of play-acting, you know. But when I checked his urine, I saw that it had blood mixed with it."

"Poison?" Isabella whispered.

"I would like to believe not, but . . ."

"It's impossible! Who would have . . ."

"I am a doctor, your Highness, not a soothsayer."

"Is there a risk my brother might die?"

"It seems not—the dose was insufficient. Perhaps someone wanted to give him a warning. At the moment, he's resting. But I don't want to make a prognosis. It all depends on how well his body fights back—and the king is not in the best of health. Go to your room now, and come back early tomorrow morning."

⋆

Isabella bent over the sick king. His sunken, violet-hued cheeks rose and fell feebly in time with his breathing. His eyes were open, but he appeared to see nothing.

"Henry!" Isabella called his name softly.

He turned toward her, his face expressionless. "Somebody wanted to . . . somebody wanted to poison me, didn't they? Who?"

"Who would want you dead?"

He made no reply, and went back to staring at the fringe on the bed's canopy. Isabella repeated the question; the king shook his head.

"I trust no one any more, Isabella . . . no one." He closed his eyes as great tears welled up. When he opened them again, Isabella had gone.

❦

"He didn't say anything else?" asked Ferdinand.

"Nothing. But his last words hurt me deeply."

"You don't think they will suspect us?" exclaimed Ferdinand. "Our interest is in keeping him alive—at least until he has disowned la Beltranaja. She's the suspect—or rather, the queen is. They are the only ones who would reap any advantage from his death. Have you questioned the servants?"

"Yes, with no result."

Ferdinand walked back to the far end of the room and stood for a moment on tiptoe as he gazed at the Guadarrama snows sparkling in the deep blue of late winter. His curly hair seemed to be framed in a metallic luster.

"Listen, Isabella. We have to find out what's happening. What are the king's real intentions? We know nothing about them. He welcomes us with open arms, makes a great fuss over us, shows us to his people like a couple of performing animals—but refuses to reveal his plans. And if he dies—what then?"

"Ferdinand! "

"La Beltranaja is still his successor. All those barons who escorted us through the town are the same ones who are loyal to Jeanne. Tomorrow, if the king dies, they will all turn on us! There's nothing for us to do except to escape from there and take up where we left off, or to give up all claim to the throne and retire back to Aragon."

Ferdinand attempted to control his anguish. Sitting on an arm of Isabella's chair, he put his face close to hers. His features softened. He looked at her closely for a few seconds before going on: "You will keep going back to him, under the pretext of finding out how he's progressing. You will talk very gently to him for as long as he

can bear. You must get him to understand that only the queen would
wish him dead. There is plenty of evidence that that is the case."

"Next, you persuade him to name you as his heir. Make sure his
secretary, Juan d'Oviedo, doesn't leave the room during your
conversations—he must be there to record the king's words. You
mustn't be afraid to strongly influence his will, to push him in the
direction where his apathetic nature is loath to go."

"You're mad! First of all, I would never have the nerve to
dominate him so openly. Second, I'm sure he would go against all
my suggestions."

"So let's get started! As far as Henry is concerned, the last one
who talks to him is the one who is in the right. We must see to it
that we have the last word, that's all."

Ferdinand knelt on the ground before her; he took Isabella's
hands in his, kissed them, and touched them to his face. She let him
do this, sensing that she had lost the argument and would have to
follow her husband's lead.

"Never again do I want to see these dear hands chapped by the
coldness of a poor horse's bridle, do servants' work, cook and darn.
Never again do I want to see this shoddy jewelry, these gloves full
of holes because you've worn them too long."

"I'll go, my love," said Isabella. "I'll do what you want."

❧

"Still nothing?" asked Ferdinand.

"Still nothing," Isabella replied sadly.

But yes—the king seemed to be improving. He had asked for a
bowl of goat's milk, and had called for some of his friends.

"Are they the arrogant and conceited young cavaliers dressed
like wandering players of indeterminate sex, who we see coming
and going in the king's anteroom?"

Isabella nodded.

Ferdinand murmured softly, "To think that our future depends
on a man who even at death's door cannot obey the voice of his
conscience!"

"I can't go on any more, Ferdinand. The way his expression
goes blank when I come near him, the long silences, the feeling that

he's judging me . . . Just a little while ago, he pretended to fall asleep while I was talking to him. He suspects some hidden meaning in everything I say, and his disdainful smiles leave me helpless."

"That's enough for today," said Ferdinand. "Tomorrow, I'll go and talk with him. I know how it can be done."

"He won't listen to you."

"We'll see about that."

❧

The next morning, full of rage, Ferdinand walked to the room of King Henry. "Get out of here! Everybody—out!" shouted Ferdinand.

The male favorites exchanged glances of outrage, stuck out their chests and, whispering among themselves, left the room with great dignity.

Ferdinand slammed the door behind them. Almost immediately, the pointed hat and goatee of Salomon Ezra appeared at the half-open anteroom door.

"What's all the noise?" asked the doctor.

"I've thrown out all those gossips. Open the windows—I can't stand these girlish smells. I would like to see the king."

"I must point out to you that he is very tired, and that the slightest upset . . ."

"Don't worry about it."

Ferdinand entered the room. The king lifted his head from the pillow. "You!" he exclaimed.

"I would like to talk with you, and I would be much obliged if you would listen to me."

The prince couldn't suppress a feeling of pity. Henry's body looked skeletal under the counterpane. The taut skin of his face emphasized every high point of his bone structure, and the hollows were violet-shaded. Ferdinand softened his voice, but maintained its ring of assurance.

Ferdinand talked for a long time in a tone of authority that only dulled a little the impression he had that he was speaking with a dying man. Occasionally he asked, "Do you hear me, Henry?" The king would blink by way of response, and Ferdinand would continue.

When he had finished, the king replied: "There's no hurry, even though you might think otherwise. Those who tried to poison me missed their chance. But I still haven't made up my mind about the succession. I'll have to consult my ministers."

"Mendoza, Benavente, Villena, of course! As if you don't already know what their reply will be. Do you take me for a fool? I was right in thinking your friendliness was all a charade!"

No sooner had he spoken than Ferdinand regretted those last words. He saw the king knit his brow. In a voice charged with renewed nobility and self-assurance, he declared: "Threats, Ferdinand! You should be aware that if I have sometimes given way to hypocrisy, to cunning, to force, when my people's peace depended on it, but I have never given in to threats. You have been badly advised, cousin!"

"My words ran ahead of my thoughts. I spoke too quickly. Please forgive me."

"You may leave," said the king gently. Ferdinand left without a word.

⚜

An unusual commotion aroused Isabella from sleep. The bedroom was still in icy cold darkness. She slipped on a thick overcoat, looked for her fox-fur slippers, and ran to the anteroom, where she collided with dona Beatrix.

"Your Highness, the king . . ."

"Is he dead?"

"No—he's left the palace. Juan d'Oviedo is sure that he has decided to go to Madrid. It would seem your husband has provoked his wrath."

"I should have known this might happen. I must see him."

"He left at first light, about an hour ago."

Isabella knew that the queen and la Beltraneja were at Madrid. She clapped her hands to her face, muttering a few words Beatrix didn't catch. When she took her hands away again, she was so pale that dona Beatrix went to help her.

"Leave me alone."

She shuffled to Ferdinand's room and opened the door. He had dressed in great haste; the biting cold made him pull his head back into his shoulders.

"This is your work. My brother has just left for Madrid."

"That's insane! When I left him, he looked as though he had only a few hours to live."

"You pay too much attention to outward appearances, Ferdinand. Henry won't die until he's made up his mind to do so—death itself won't dictate the hour. Ten times I've seen him apparently ready to give up his soul, and then recover at the last moment without anyone knowing of his decision. While he yet has strength, he'll use it for the battle where he is still able to will!"

"Nonsense!" shouted Ferdinand. "I'm going to send a party out under Rocaberti's orders. We'll soon find out if he has enough strength to stand up against my men."

"That won't get you anywhere. Henry took his Moorish guard with him—two hundred men who would kill for him."

"Your brother must come back! If he reaches Madrid, all our plans will be ruined."

"Isabella is right," said dona Beatrix.

"Get out, you!" said Ferdinand.

Isabella stood with her back flat against the wood panels, arms outstretched. "Be careful! You made a big enough blunder yesterday. You must know you won't get anything from my brother by threats or by force. If you bring him back here, he will allow himself to die without making a decision—or after having already declared himself for la Beltraneja."

"It will be easy to make him talk, I promise you."

"You seem to forget that here you are nobody, Ferdinand. Poorer, more defenseless than when we were at Duenas, shivering from cold in your old mule-driver's clothes. Now we are only as rich and powerful as the trust people have in us. Any further thoughtless action could spoil everything. Let's be patient for a few days. We will go to Madrid to defend our cause. All is not lost."

"No! We can have real power, real riches today if we act boldly. Let me through!"

"If you go through this doorway, Ferdinand, the responsibility will be yours alone."

Ferdinand bowed his shoulders. Enraged, he ran his hands through his curly brown hair, and didn't say anything for a few minutes. Then: "Very well. Do as you wish. I'm going back to Aragon."

Henry opened his eyes. At first he was frightened by what he saw. He believed himself to be on the far side of death's dark divide, which he had been familiar with for a long time without making the decision to go across.

Villena. It could only be him—face craggy as the bark of a tree, small bloodshot eyes, smile revealing rotten teeth. It was only when he felt two cold lips on his hand that he realized he wasn't dead.

"It is I, Don Pacheco, Marquis de Villena."

"I recognized you, Marquis. What are you doing here? You want to see me one last time before I die, is that it?"

Villena shook his head. "You're not going to die yet, your Majesty. I was called to your bedside—that's why you see me here. I heard that Isabella wanted to make an attempt on your life so as to speed the moment when she might ascend the throne, and that your wife and daughter were threatened."

"Isabella? How could she . . ."

"As you reach the end of your reign, your Majesty, I'm sure you wouldn't want to show weakness by disregarding these schemes? Especially when your little Jeanne is about to become engaged to don Afonso, King of Portugal."

"What are you saying?"

"I wouldn't want to give you false grounds for optimism, but when I was in my retreat at Penafiel I learned of Afonso's plans."

"Can this be?" the king sighed.

"It's virtually certain."

"My good and dear friend—what relief you have given me! Where is Jeanne? I want to see her right away."

"There she is," Villena replied.

The king lifted himself up on his elbows. At the sunlit end of the great antique tapestry on the opposite side of the room, he made out the oval shape of a young face. Her color was heightened by emotion, head encircled with heavy black braids.

The queen stood behind her daughter: a pale face the king didn't like meeting, for to him it was an indictment of his neglect and cowardice.

"Who are all these people?" the king asked.

"Your secretary, your ministers. The Cardinal of Spain has come specially."

"Specially . . . for what?"

Villena toyed nervously with the insignia of the Grand Master of Santiago, which he wore on important occasions. He thought it best to smile with astonishment.

"Your Majesty! Don't you agree that the best way to stop Isabella and her barbaric Ferdinand is to confirm your recognition of Jeanne as your successor? After what happened in Segovia, this action would seem to be essential."

"Certainly," sighed the king.

Jeanne had come up to him; he put his hand on her head. Thirteen years old, she glowed with youth and beauty. That beauty she owed to don Beltran de Cueva when once he had been caught in the small hours of the morning, in a passageway near the queen's suite.

"Also, it would be as well, your Highness, if you cleared up any misunderstanding about the paternity of your daughter. It is your enemies key weapon."

"What misunderstanding?" the king cut in sharply. "Who would dare to question that?"

Villena bit his lip. "Nobody, your Highness. But your enemies wouldn't hesitate to lie."

"You're right, Marquis. Tell my secretary to come here."

The secretary arrived quietly. Searching for the words, Henry dictated a long text. ". . . and such is my desire," concluded Henry in a weak voice.

The quill pen scratched on the parchment. A star-shaped blot fell on the king's signature.

"Your Highness," said Villena, "you are the wisest prince in the Christian world."

The king silenced him with a wave of the hand. He dismissed everyone except the marquis; after Villena had kissed the royal hand, Henry caught him by his sleeve.

"Marquis, come nearer to me . . . nearer. May I confide in you one last secret wish—you who have seen more closely than anyone not only my wisdom, as you call it, but also my weakness? The desires of the flesh are still with me, no matter what I look like. Do you believe that the Almighty would forgive me if I gave this poor horse a free rein one last time before I appear in front of Him?"

Villena almost choked. "But, your Highness, the slightest overexertion could be fatal."

"Answer me: Do you believe that God would grant me His forgiveness?"

"If you are truly sorry . . ."

"I will be. Marquis, you must do me one last favor before you go back to your Penafiel mountains. This is what I want you to do . . ."

❦

It was far into the night. The room was filled to its high ceiling with the radiance of a thousand lights; it was as though it were broad daylight. The king had wanted it this way. He was afraid of the dark, which made him feel alone and vulnerable to the evil forces that menaced him. For him, darkness was full of blood-colored roses. As each petal fell, he felt as if life itself was ebbing from his veins.

Here, on the other hand, was a vivid display of light and of life. A platform had been erected at one end of the long banquet table; on it, the king's chair had been covered with a voluminous red cloth decorated with gold leaf. Two valets had carried the king there as music began playing at the other end of the room.

Henry wore a jacket of purple velvet tightly cinched in at the waist by a ruby-studded leather belt; a loop of gold chain decorated his chest. The sleeves, puffed out at the shoulders, made his face look even more emaciated, and the dark hues of his clothes, in spite of the colored powders that accented his lips, cheek bones, and eyes, suggested those of a corpse's shroud.

"Thank you, Villena," said the king, as the Grand Master came to take his leave. "You have done well. Will you be here tomorrow? If so, come back to me soon after daybreak. You won't be sorry to have spent a few more hours in Madrid."

It was a brilliant party.

Some fifty guests were seated around an enormous table that glittered with fine glassware, silver cutlery, Florentine water jugs, and Murano vases overflowing with beautiful hothouse flowers.

The marquis had gathered together all Madrid had to offer in the way of young and degenerate noblemen, sons of rich Jewish merchants, Moors and Christians, prostitutes, homosexuals. They were all jabbering away under the dazzling lights of silver and bronze chandeliers, even though the king, whose head was already aching, could scarcely hear the music—which in any case nobody was listening to. He nodded his head and smiled when the guests drank to his health and cheered him.

His last reserves of strength were gone. He had been as good as dead from the moment his valets had placed him on his pathetic "throne." He only stayed afloat on the sea of life by virtue of his senses, clinging to the fragile buoy of light and sound. Once the lights were extinguished and the noise hushed, he would no longer be able to withstand the black wave that he felt bearing down on him.

After the meal, the orchestra played fortissimo for dancing. Couples formed for a stately pavane, and it gave Henry great pleasure to see the elaborately choreographed figures come together and then slowly dissolve. He wanted to wave his hand to acknowledge a couple who bowed before him and placed a rose at his feet, but his hand would not obey his will.

This weakness soon became a sensation like being in a slow whirlwind, then like the rolling of a ship—one of the ships that cruised down Seville's Guadalquivir River in the spring. Then everything became very confused, and the king thought that his last moment had come.

A clash of cymbals roused him from his lethargy. He had the impression of rising to the surface of a dead sea, snared in a net of

colored seaweed. A gypsy dancer was pirouetting in the center of
the dance floor to the loud clacking of castanets. What a beautiful
girl! thought Henry, fighting against the leaden weight that pressed
down on the back of his neck.

After the gypsy, there came a beautiful young man, almost
naked, his head crowned with garland of carnations. The king
moaned with pleasure as he watched the lad leap from one end of
the room to the other. At the same time he pulled his head upright
as it started leaning toward one shoulder—he didn't want to miss
the rest of this fascinating performance. The beautiful young man
twirled in front of him, placed his crown of carnations on the king's
knees, and melted away into the crowd.

Next came the representation of a witches' Sabbath. Men's
laughter and girls' shrill cries echoed hollowly as though they were
in a crystal crater. Naked figures had been embroidered on the rich
trimmings of their doublets, jackets, and breeches. They looked like
human garlands, living vines moved by a wind of fire.

The King hiccuped. He opened his mouth and stiffened. Before
his eyes closed, he had time to see a large naked woman climb the
steps to his throne and offer him a goblet of wine.

Close to death, Henry was taken to his own room. A piercing
light made him open his eyes.

In a low whisper, he breathed, "Tell Cardinal Mendoza to come
. . . immediately."

⚜

Isabella's knees were giving her a lot of pain. Even so, she
completed the prayer she had begun. She had repeated it more than
a hundred times in three days, and each time she felt it renew her
strength.

"Lord, who knoweth the secrets of the heart, know thou that
fraud, injustice, and tyranny have played no part in my accession to
the throne of Castile . . ."

By the dancing light of the oil lamp's flame, the ivory figure of
Christ that Borgia, the papal legate, had brought her, seemed to be
alive. But what appeared to her to be moving at the statuette's base
was not the carnations and roses that had been placed there, but the

red tabards emblazoned with white crosses worn by the French soldiers besieging Perpignan. Perpignan, where her Ferdinand might even now be imprisoned, or perhaps dying as a soldier of united Spain.

". . . but that I attained it by refusing to surrender to foreign powers the sceptre that cost my ancestors so much blood . . ."

Why doesn't Ferdinand send any news? Isabella wondered. In a few hours' time she would be crowned queen, without having any assurance where her husband was, or even if he would ever come back.

Wherever she went, whatever she did, she would always be aware of the empty place by her side. His absence was particularly hard to bear at night; the cries of the nightwatchmen and of the *serenos*, the special concierges taking care of their buildings, would draw her out of a disturbed sleep in which she dreamed of many Ferdinands, disguised with hideous faces, come to torture her. The mournful litany of the *serenos* would then become solid reality, and Isabella would bury her head under the sheets so she would hear their cries no more, nor see the faces of the monsters giving voice.

"I therefore place in your hands, omnipotent God, ruler of kings and kingdoms, my claims and my cause. Thy will be done . . ."

A sudden draft blew the window open with a bang. A gust of north wind chilled her . . . she shivered, and warmed her hands around the wavering flame of her Jewish lamp. Hernando de Pulgar, a young court official, hurried to close the window. The noise of Segovia's bells, which had for a moment filled the room with muffled sound, ceased.

"Thank you, Hernando." Isabella's voice was low.

She continued, her voice quieter still: ". . . And if my claim is not legitimate, please know that my only sin is that of ignorance. But if it is valid, help me to uphold it by the strength of Your arms."

Isabella made swift signs of the cross on her forehead, her lips, and her breasts, before rising, legs heavy from so much kneeling.

"Let us go," she said.

She wore a gray velvet jacket banded with ermine, and a brocaded skirt, which dona Beatrix covered with a white silk robe. Isabella looked truly majestic, but no hint of joy illuminated her face. With the little energy left to her, she put on an expression that was severe, even indifferent. It was beyond her power to give any impression of exaltation.

The bells had been ringing ceaselessly for hours in the clear cold air, those same Segovia bells that had so joyfully run in her ears when the king had led the horses of Ferdinand and Isabella through the town.

The same bells had sounded the knell a few days before, when Henry's body, face uncovered, left Madrid to be laid to rest in the monastery of Guadaloupe. These bells—sometimes joyous, sometimes sad—she now wanted to silence with one wave of her hand.

Against all the odds, she was hoping Ferdinand would appear. The news of the king's death must have reached him; she would hear the noise of footsteps in the passage, a door would open. . . .

No, Ferdinand would not be there. Ferdinand was fighting the French in Roussillon. Isabella would reign as a widow. The crown she wore would be for her like a sad mourning headdress of black crepe.

She had known she loved Ferdinand more than ever since the time he had left her following their quarrel. Perhaps he would have come back before now if the war had not flared up again. Perhaps their love, a unique combination of emotion and reason, would have been able to break through all barriers.

Whenever she wanted to recall the face of her husband, Isabella would look at Isabel. But Isabel was playing in her room, listening to the noise of the bells carried on the morning wind.

As she turned around, Isabella was taken by surprise. Isabel was there in front of her. Dona Beatrix propelled her toward the princess, as though she had been reading her thoughts.

"Elisabeth, my daughter, my love."

The little girl tensed when Isabella took her in her arms. She didn't recognize her mother, and wanted to cry in the close embrace.

"Don't leave me!" Isabella whispered in her ear. "I want you beside me during the coronation. You will be given fine clothes and precious jewelry. You'd like that?"

The child made no reply. She would prefer to go back to her room, to her toys, her governess, her golden solitude.

"Prepare her," said Isabella. "She will stay by my side, where Ferdinand should be."

"But . . ." murmured Andres Cabrera.

"Do as I say."

Dona Beatrix bent down to whisper in the little girl's ear.

Cabrera persisted. "There's someone in the anteroom who wants to see you: David Ezra. Shall I show him in?"

"No." Isabella frowned. "I will see him alone."

Suddenly David walked into the room. He smiled, but his expression was grave.

"What are you doing here?" exclaimed Isabella. "You shouldn't have come today, David."

"I won't bother you any more after this. As soon as you are Queen of Castile, I will drop out of sight. You'll hear nothing more of me, I promise."

"That's not what I meant. This is not a good time for us to meet. Think of all those people who saw you come in . . ."

"I beg your forgiveness. I wanted simply to give you my very best wishes and to take my leave before departing. That is all. Good-bye, Isabella."

"No!" She spoke sharply. "Wait . . . I . . ."

"What is it, Isabella?"

She took her hand away from where she had placed it on David's wrist and sighed.

"Nothing, David. I thank you for coming. I won't forget you. You were the joy of my youth—without you, my early years would have been so gloomy that they would have scarred me forever. You know that I will always be ready to help you, David."

"I want nothing for myself. I simply wish for you and Ferdinand that your reign will be noted for its wisdom and kindness. Be lenient to the Jewish people, make them an ally and not an enemy—you won't regret it. That is my one desire. For myself, I ask nothing."

He added, in a quieter tone: "I will always love you, Isabella. Farewell."

Isabella stretched up on tiptoe to kiss David's cheek, close to his lips. He held her tightly, found her lips and kissed her passionately. She remained in his arms for an endless moment.

"Now go!"

Isabella waited for a few seconds, alone in the small room. Her lips moved as though her whole life had suddenly drained away. No Ferdinand, David gone, she experienced a sensation of emptiness. She felt her robe being tugged from behind.

"Isabel . . ."

The little princess was ready. She wore a robe of velvet brocade that covered her all the way to the tips of her shoes, shoes glittering with magnificent red garnets. Andres Cabrera came in after her.

"Your Highness, all is ready."

Cabrera was dressed in a padded red doublet that fitted close to his chest. A robe, attached to his shoulders by a fine gold chain, fell in broad pleats behind his back. On his right shoulder he bore, unsheathed, the heavy sword of the Trastamare family: the sword of Justice.

"We will follow you," said Isabella.

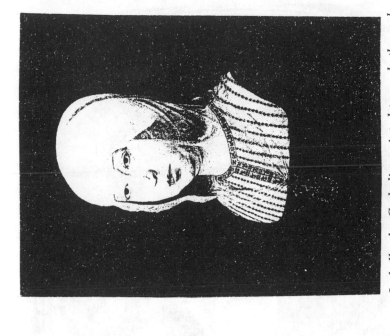

Isabella the Catholic, painted towards the end of her life, by Juan de Flandes (courtesy Patrimonio Nacional)

Isabella of Castile, artist unknown (courtesy Windsor Castle/copyright reserved to Her Majesty Queen Elizabeth II)

Ferdinand of Aragón, artist unknown (courtesy Windsor Castle/copyright reserved to Her Majesty Queen Elizabeth II)

4

The Ladies' War

Jeanne had to pretend not to smile when her elderly husband, King Afonso of Portugal, stood in front of her, struck a comic attitude, and launched into speech:

I, dona Jeanne, by the grace of God, Queen of Castile, of Leon, of Portugal, etc. To the Consuls, *Alcades*, *Alguazils*, *Regidors*, Cavaliers, Officers, Equerries, and Principals, greetings and blessings. You are doubtless aware, since this is a matter of public knowledge and well known throughout my kingdoms, that the king, don Henry, my lord and father of glorious memory, having married with the approval of the Church the queen, dona Jeanne, my dear and well-beloved lady and mother, and that, while they were living together as man and wife, I was born of them by the grace of God . . ."

Don Afonso's voice became less and less modulated as the endless parchment unrolled, and his deplorable Portuguese accent began intruding into the Castilian. The May heat was so intense in the Estremadura town of Trujillo that he paused to wipe his face with a black handkerchief, a face the color of old leather and framed with a close-cut crop of white hair.

My uncle, and my husband, Jeanne mused. How many kingdoms do I owe him? She counted on her fingers while resting them lightly on her knees, but stopped on the count of three when she realized that Prince Joao, Afonso's son, was staring at her. She blushed, then composed her features to show that she was again paying attention to the king's libelous tirade.

"This princess [he referred to Isabella] broke her pledge and left the court, and, knowing full well that the king of Sicily

["Ferdinand," muttered Jeanne] was a foreign king who, far from being associated with King Henry, was on the contrary obnoxious and unacceptable to him, she had him summon her secretly, against . . ."

"Hum!" Jeanne interrupted.

Afonso stopped short, as though he needed to sneeze.

"You would like to make a comment?" he asked.

The previous day, during the third reading, she had requested that this last passage be dropped: It didn't seem truthful to her. It wasn't Isabella who had Ferdinand summon her; he was urged by his father, King John. Jeanne had no love for Isabella, but there was no need to systematically pervert the truth.

A powerful voice rang out behind her:

"The truth," said the Archbishop of Toledo, rising from his wicker chair, "the truth is that Isabella wanted don Ferdinand with all her heart. The end result is the same . . ."

Jeanne lifted a weary hand, and don Afonso continued.

Joao's stare . . . The thin face that leaned toward Jeanne, and which he fanned with his gloves . . . why wasn't it he she'd been made to marry, instead of this old man, her uncle, who brought nothing for her except his wealth and his past history as a hero of the African wars and great lover? Great lover!—Afonso? In the weeks since they had been married, he hadn't touched her: "We must wait for Rome's dispensation, senorita," he would say, stroking her hair.

"It is common knowledge that my father, the king, to lay to rest the false rumors being put about concerning the legitimacy of my birth, declared on oath that he recognized me as being truly his own daughter."

Through the window opening on to the Altamirano palace out-buildings, la Beltranaja's attention was caught by the golden dome of Maria la Mayor, where flocks of pigeons swirled around. The reddish-brown roofs of Trujillo stood out against the blue distance of Estremadura, toward the west, toward Portugal.

The previous day, Joao had talked to her about Lisbon, while they were riding to Santa Cruz de la Sierra, an old Arab town. So oppressive was the heat that they had made a halt in the shade of some olive trees. Joao began talking of Portugal, a land about which she knew little, and where she would now be called upon to live. Joao was fairly persuasive, but Jeanne knew that it would be difficult to tear herself away from Castile, that she would prefer to go on living there, in spite of Isabella.

She had stood up, cheeks aflame, when Joao had tried to kiss her. He made her sit down again, and soon afterwards took her hand and pressed it to his lips.

Jeanne continued talking silently to herself while Afonso droned on. After swallowing a pitcher of barley beer, the king continued, even though most of Spain and Portugal's great and good attending the council were thinking of other things.

"With all my heart, I would like to prevent the evils that will be inevitable if this difference of opinion is put into the hands of the law . . . if Ferdinand and Isabella do not accept, I hereby declare that the murders, arson, banditry and all the other barbarities that this war brought about will again fall only on them, and not on my wife and me."

The war . . . on the horizon of Estramadura the little queen saw the banners of Portugal being raised, the richly caparisoned cavalry advancing, the regiments of lancers, the infantry swarming over the hills like the clouds of locusts that sometimes swept through the south. The statement to which she was being forced to put her name appealed to justice; but she knew too well that the only justice would be that of military might, and not that of God.

Fighting was already going on throughout Castile. At the same time, as the Marquis of Villena's son in Madrid was trying to pull together a great alliance, Ferdinand and Isabella were raising their standard on the highest church steeples and castle keeps. The coming summer would be one of battles, and that distressed the little queen even more than the prospect of spending her whole life either in a Lisbon jail or in the house of this old man called don Afonso.

"Given under our hand at Placentia, May 30, 1475."

"Why Placentia?" Jeanne asked absentmindedly. "We are in Trujillo."

Carillo's voice again trumpeted behind her. "Yes, but Placentia is a much more important town."

Jeanne turned round sharply, and stared coldly at the fat archbishop. She wanted to slap his face, all glistening with sweat, to shout out loud that all this was false and that it would lead to disaster. Had she drafted this proclamation? Not a single line! It was Carillo's inspiration; he dictated and corrected it after taking advice from the dry little fellow who trotted around after him like his shadow: the astrologer, Ferdinand of Alarcon.

Jeanne was the victim of this crank, of this aggressive man of God, of this senile King. They used her; the first two to satisfy their need to dominate, the third to expand his kingdom.

She felt an enormous fatigue overwhelming her, and dreamed that Joao was rising up and brandishing a sword of fire, throwing out all these beasts, and carrying her away at full speed to the ocean.

"Let's get it over with," said the King of Portugal. "This heat is exhausting." He spat drily between his feet.

The storm created little whirlwinds of carnation-scented dust along the track. The band led by Isabella to find Ferdinand at Tordesilla was only two leagues from the city; but the plain seemed to stretch to infinity under the harsh yellow light and the ovenlike heat.

Isabella's plump filly was usually a placid-tempered animal, but now it balked with skittish nervousness at the wind squalls. Captain Gonzales de Cordoba rode alongside the queen. He kept raising his head to watch her from under the peak of his cap; he thought he had several times seen her look rather unsteady, very pale, her eyes closed. The wind tore at her light woolen cape, giving a glimpse of her protuberant belly.

She's not going to make it to Tordesilla, thought the young captain. He moved closer to the queen, and shouted to make himself heard: "Let us stop under this elm tree. It's not sensible to press on."

The queen's reply was lost in a strong gust of wind. She shook her head, and continued on her way. Gonzales didn't take his eyes off her. They had gotten as far as where the river Duero was bordered with poplars when he saw Isabella pitch forward. He only just had time to leap to the ground and catch her in his arms.

The saddle-cloth was stained with blood, and a red blotch soiled the queen's robe where it wrapped round her thighs.

"Dismount, everyone!" he shouted. "Give me some help!"

When Isabella opened her eyes, she saw silhouetted against the burning sky above her the brown, clean-cut features of Gonzales, and a circle of hairy heads, of dusty beards, of eyes reddened by the shimmering white light. She had been carried to the shelter of a clump of gorse, but its shade hardly covered her face. No one had yet dared to touch her.

"Go away," she ordered in a weak voice. "You, Gonzales, stay. You must find some water, even if it means emptying the flasks."

"Are you in much pain, Madame?"

Isabella gritted her teeth. "No, Gonzales, I'm not hurting. At least, my physical suffering is nothing compared with my feeling of regret. I held on to this baby—I was taking it to Ferdinand as a gift, as a promise of peace and prosperity for our people. Will he forgive me?"

Gonzales went away, and came back with a helmet full of water. "I have sent a rider to Tordesilla to forewarn the king. While you are waiting, don't move, don't even lift a finger. I can give you the proper attention. Can you accept that?"

"What, you, Gonzales?"

The young captain smiled. His forehead reddened with embarrassment. "I planned to be a doctor, but fate decreed otherwise."

Isabella turned her head away while the captain operated. She felt confident in the touch of his supple hands, and could sense through her closed eyelids that sometimes his shoulders shielded her from the fiery sky.

Otherwise, she felt almost nothing. A calming smell of fennel filled her nostrils between the gusts of wind. She heard Gonzales tell her that she had lost a lot of blood. Then she fell asleep, or perhaps just lost consciousness—she would never know.

༺❀༻

"Gonzales . . ."

He was no longer there; Ferdinand appeared in his place. His expression was stem and mixed.

"Do you blame me very much?" asked Isabella.

He nodded his head to show that he did.

The coat of mail he wore under a low-necked sleeveless silk jacket emphasized the roughness of his appearance. He was still wearing his sword and his red leather boots. They could hear the stamping of soldiers and a distant bugle call.

"Yes," said Ferdinand, "I do blame you. Didn't I tell you many times to wait for me in Valladolid, and not to stir from there? Instead of which, you gallop from one town to the next. And so this is what happens."

"Please look where I am—in what condition! But look how I have helped you—in only one week I have recruited 2,000 lancers."

"And we have lost a son and heir!"

"How do you know it was a boy?"

Ferdinand spun round on his heels without answering. Isabella knew that he must have consulted a sorcerer to have his horoscope read.

"We mustn't go on arguing—it's really not a good time," said Isabella.

The time hadn't been any better when, soon after Henry's death and Isabella's solitary coronation, Ferdinand, boiling with rage, had burst into the Alcazar at Segovia with a group of Aragonese. Had he forgotten that he was Isabella's husband, and King of Castile?

Isabella had let the storm blow over without taking a really hard line, but she had remained firm nevertheless. It wasn't until the time that she had seen the upheavals caused by Ferdinand and his clique—dismissing government ministers, replacing them with men they thought more reliable—that she had made up her mind to act.

"In Aragon," retorted Ferdinand, "men do the governing. Women are content to look after the children."

"It's not that way in Castile," Isabella had thrown back at him. "And you forget that we are in Castile."

The palace was in revolution. Castilians and Aragonese looked at each other with scorn, and settled their arguments with the sword, on the banks of the Eresma by the light of early morning.

All this time, the son of the Marquis of Villena (the father having died shortly before) was scheming and plotting in Madrid, while Jeanne and old King Afonso were raising armies in Portugal.

Isabella and Ferdinand agreed to place their own disagreement in the hands of the Cardinal of Spain, who made his rulings with great authority and even-handedness. The coinage of the realm would bear both their likenesses; Isabella kept the right to appoint castle governors; for a long time they thought about a design for their heraldic device, and the cardinal suggested as a theme:

"Each as powerful as the other, Isabella the same as Ferdinand."

"Tanto manta."

On the evening of Ferdinand's coronation, they once more slept in the same bed.

"No," said Ferdinand. "We won't quarrel. Forget all the criticisms I've made of you."

He leaned toward his wife and lightly kissed her brow. Isabella breathed in an odor of carnations that reminded her of the storm sweeping over the town as evening drew near.

"I was waiting for you, for the blessing of the royal standards," he said. "We will postpone the ceremony until tomorrow, if, of course, you are able to get out of bed."

"What does our military strength add up to?"

"Twelve thousand cavalry, thirty thousand infantry. Afonso has no advantage over us. What's more, we have taken the important town of Badajoz."

"What I can't fully understand is why the king of Portugal hesitates to attack. He seems to be afraid to go far beyond his frontiers, afraid of falling into some trap. Isn't he sure of his Castilian allies?"

"He isn't sure of anything. The letters he sends me are just meaningless boasting, the messengers in clerical dress spout nothing but ambiguous phrases."

Los comentarios de Gayo Julio Cefar.

The royal shield of Isabella and Ferdinand. The shield incorporates the royal insignias of Castile and Leon (the castles and lions) and the bars and eagles of Aragon. At the base of the shield are the words "Tanto Monta," meaning "One Is Equal to the Other." At the bottom, center, is a pomegranate, the symbol for Isabella and Ferdinand's conquest of Granada. Beneath the shield to the right is Isabella's personal symbol for her marriage to Ferdinand, flechas (arrows) to symbolize F. Beneath the shield to the left is Ferdinand's personal symbol for Isabella, the yugo (yoke) to symbolize Y (I). The final element is the Gordian knot, to symbolize indissoluble union. (Courtesy of The Hispanic Society of New York)

The Seal of "Isabel la Catól-
ica" (courtesy Archivo His-
torico Nacional)

A fifty excelente gold coin from
the reign of Ferdinand and Isabella
(courtesy The American Numis-
matic Society)

Isabella lifted herself onto her elbows. "I would like to get up."

"You think it's all right?"

He folded down the sheets, then put his cheek and lips on her bruised belly.

"Gonzales says that there will be no marks," said Isabella.

Ferdinand frowned, and quickly pulled the sheet back over her.

⚜

Ferdinand was talking to the town. He took a mouthful of the sweet-smelling *estofago de toro* and leaned back, chewing. "There is an opening on the north side, patched up with lime and sand. It could easily be broken through."

"Only if you have artillery. And you have none."

"That's true," sighed Ferdinand.

This braised *toro* was a true delicacy. Every herb on the mountainside had been used to prepare the smooth, creamy sauce. Ferdinand smiled when he thought that the town he was besieging was aptly named Toro. He turned to Isabella to make a sign of mutual understanding; she was sitting on a camp bed, engrossed in an old Bible dating back to the beginning of the Reconquest.

She did not stir. She knew that Ferdinand was in the habit of holding these one-sided dialogues with fortresses he intended to storm—it was a ritual he seldom missed.

He had a servant spread the awning of his tent and place a camp table beneath it, then ate alone, eyes riveted on the town's battlements.

Ferdinand was waiting for the return of the knight Gomez Manrique, to whom he had given the responsibility of delivering a formal challenge to Afonso and Joao. The summer season was progressing, the end of July was in sight, and one way or the other it was evident that decisive action would have to be taken before the winter months. If not, he would have to dismiss the troops and start operations again the following spring.

Gomez Manrique put on his glittering ambassador's full dress to present Ferdinand's proposals to King Afonso, who was in an execrable temper because of his gout.

Manrique started by saying: "Leave the town. We can dispose our respective armies between the Duero and the castle battlements."

"I'm not ready," groaned the king of Portugal. "Besides, the chivalric code imposes a thirty-day delay for consideration."

"Would single combat be acceptable to you?"

Afonso felt like throwing his bowl of herb tea in the ambassador's face. "I'm sure that you can see I'm in no fit state to mount a donkey!" he bellowed.

"Your son is fit."

Afonso grumbled. Joao . . . He was a poor duelist; there were too many fancy trimmings on the sheath of his sword.

Afonso concluded by saying, "I'll consider it. In any event, there is no great hurry."

The King of Portugal was playing for time. Gonzales Manrique came back to the attack several times in the ensuing weeks, always with no more success. Afonso counterproposed that his own wife, la Beltranaja, and Queen Isabella be exchanged as hostages.

"This old fox is playing with us!" exclaimed Ferdinand. "Let him go to the devil! We will come back next year."

"Now calm down," Isabella told him.

She rested her hands on her husband's chest and drew his lips close to hers. They stayed for a moment clasped in each other's arms, in view of the red-brown fortified walls of Toro.

"When this war is over," said Isabella, "when we reign in peace, I'll give you children—lots of children."

"Isabella," whispered Ferdinand, "Isabella—what would I do without you?"

They paused at the entrance of the tent. Naked grooms were leading the horses two by two down to the river. A mile away, on a vast plain, cavalrymen were practicing their maneuvers in a pearly cloud of dust, lances at the slope. Dusk was gathering. The warm light of this September evening gilded the stones of the Arab battlements. Ferdinand kicked over the table where he had taken his meal, and, swaying his shoulders, worried about giving the order to break camp.

That winter saw feverish activity, with much coming and going of troops and messengers. Almost every day wagons arrived at Valladolid, where Isabella and Ferdinand were living. They were guarded by armed and touchy monks: they brought for the Castilian monarchs vases of gold and silver "borrowed" from the churches, which were transformed into silver reaux coins and gold doubloons to pay the troops who would be launched against Toro and Zamoro in the early spring.

Things were going well for the young sovercigns of Castile. One by one, the Castilian lords, pockets still full of Portuguese gold, relinquished their loyalty to the king of Portugal and Queen Jeanne. The Duke of Arevalo led the movement; others followed.

The young Marquis of Villena abandoned the Portuguese cause to pursue his own affairs. Carillo kept repeating: "I put the scepter in Isabella's hands; I turned it into a distaff."

To fill the cup of unhappiness, the old Queen Joan, widow of Henry of Castile, was found one morning dead in her bed, one hand on her heart, her fat white lips open as though seeking a last kiss, eyes open to the ceiling where pink Cupids frolicked. A page's belt was found hanging over the back of a chair.

Afonso looked at his young wife, and it was the old queen he saw—her death mask frozen in an expression of pleasure. He had never really wanted to possess la Beltranaja, and it mattered little to him whether the papal dispensation came or not.

His inner eye focused on Africa, and he dreamed while those early spring showers fell on the rich earth: he dreamed of the shores of Mauretania and Goa, where he had spent the best years of his pugnacious youth. This coming fight, he sensed vaguely, would be his last.

It had only needed Ferdinand to appear at Zamora for the town to throw open its gates. As soon as one of his guns had damaged a watchtower on the castle, the white flag was hoisted.

That first evening after Zamora's surrender, Isabella and Ferdinand climbed to the top of the castle, which towered above the old town and the cathedral. They could see the Duero flowing around its midstream islands, its waters green and yellow in the fading evening light. And they knew that they had reached the last stage on their road to the throne.

The long struggle had not been in vain. A moment like this was worth all the hunger, the cold, the deprivation; it repaid the uncertainties each had brought, the intolerable burden of exile, and the shame they had felt. They held tightly to each other, their capes flapping about them in the icy wind that whipped around the fortress's high walls.

They slowly looked over the land that was beginning to grow dark in the cold spring night, a land of rocks and water, a plain exposed to the four winds.

"From this point on," said Ferdinand, "we won't be parted from each other again."

"Never again," Isabella echoed.

There was one more battle to be fought, but it was as good as already won. Isabella didn't know if the distant rumbling noise was the sound of the river washing against its isles, or the king of Portugal's powerful cavalry. Either way, it meant little to her, and after a while she heard it no more.

The Portuguese artillery barrage made an appalling racket. When the smoke cleared away, the tower of Zamora bridge had lost some of its parapet and a number of its defenders. Captain Valdes retaliated sharply, and the base of a Portuguese field-gun was blown to pieces, leaving its horses milling around chaotically.

In a few minutes, the Cabanales area of town was cleared of its last inhabitants. There was some sporadic fire, but at noon there was a lull. In the fortress, Ferdinand was waiting for messengers from Afonso, who was besieging the town; after each attack, the old king put forward peace proposals, which Ferdinand rejected.

On several occasions they had agreed to meet at night on one of the islands in the middle of the river, but each time the current had proved too strong, and they never made it. Carillo pressed don Afonso to attack, but the king of Portugal stuck his head out of his tent and withdrew, shivering. It was far too cold to think of attacking.

One night, however, Afonso came to a decision. While his envoys were haggling over arrangements for single combat, he ordered his army to strike camp. Shortly before dawn, tents folded, his rearguard took off in the direction of Toro.

When the darkness of the night gave way to the dawn, Valdes saw that the Cabanales plain was deserted. He rubbed his eyes, believing that he was being tricked by some illusion. Then he rushed to the fortress, where Ferdinand was still sleeping, and woke him to urgently call his staff together.

"You, don Alvaro de Mendoza, take five-hundred light horse and harass their rear unceasingly. They must be prevented at all costs from closing the gates of Toro, or we will be besieging that town until Whitsun."

Massed drums started beating at first light. In the Candelaria quarter, where the bulk of the Castilian army was massed, confusion reigned. The cavalrymen looked gloomy, but they managed to eat hunks of bread as they sat in their saddles, waiting for a command.

Ferdinand moved around, checking the flexibility of his armor. His steel gauntlets were supple, the joints working smoothly.

"Let me come with you," Isabella begged. "I don't want to stay in Zamora and miss the battle."

Ferdinand protested that it was no place for a woman, but at last granted her request.

"Hurry up and get ready. You can join me later."

"I'm ready now."

Isabella half opened her red topcoat, revealing battledress: a chain-mail coat covered by a sleeveless silk jacket, buckskin breeches, and decorated leather boots. Ferdinand couldn't help smiling. He took her in his arms.

"Let's go," he said.

A few leagues outside Toro, the valley narrowed down to a gorge, so that at the foot of the hills there was only room for the river and a very constricted passage. Ferdinand was extremely disappointed to find that the valley was deserted. He was already late, the morning well advanced, and neither Alvaro de Mendoza nor the Portuguese rearguard were in sight.

Ferdinand looked around at the crests of rosemary-covered hills where herds of sheep and black goats were grazing. He had ordered the Cardinal of Spain to dispatch a reconnaissance unit to this high point, from which the wide plain in front of Toro could be observed. He told his leading company, which had joined him, to keep silence. Nothing could be heard, other than the goatherds' whistles and their calls—"*Prrt . . . tsch . . . tsch . . .*" and the clattering of thrown pebbles as they rolled down the stony hillside.

"I don't hear anything," said Isabella, "so why is the cardinal waving his arms and shouting?"

They saw him pull his horse around sharply, and head back down straight across the dangerous stony scree. He stopped in front of Ferdinand, bubbling with excitement.

"They are in battle formation. Alvaro has placed his troops on each side of the gorge so no one can get in."

Ferdinand sent a dispatch rider to inform the main body, led by Gonzales de Cordoba.

"It's rather unwise to attack in this situation," said the cardinal.

It was true that circumstances did not seem very favorable. Unlike the Portuguese, the Castilians had nowhere they could fall back. They had fewer cavalry. What was more, they had the sun in their eyes. Ferdinand shrugged.

"In battle, conviction and courage are more important than the conditions," he said pompously.

"I agree with you," Isabella rejoined.

She turned around to watch the main body moving up, headed by Galician cavalry. Gonzales was alone at the head of this mass of men and horses, of lances and banners that glittered with brilliant color in the March sun. Gonzales smiled: Isabella smiled in return, with a little wave of her hand.

The silence of the Portuguese army was unnerving. It was disposed in two wings, solid and unmoving as stone. The fluttering of banners was the only sign of life in the lines of men and horses drawn up like a barrier across the expanse of the plain. In the distance the red walls of Toro could be seen.

Ferdinand bit his lip. He suddenly feared having fallen into a trap, and quickly glanced around to be sure that don Afonso hadn't left other troops to surprise him; but the hillsides were deserted. He stopped short, hypnotized by this motionless host; his own army, equally unmoving behind him, kept silent.

At that moment a knight rode up. It was Loys de Tovar, and he said, without looking at the prince, "Don't wait, your Majesty! The least hesitation could cost you dearly. You must fight—or give up your kingdom."

These words had a galvanizing effect on Ferdinand. He called his captains together in a wood of pistachio trees; all agreed that they should adopt the same combat formation as the Portuguese. With some five hundred men each, the two opposing forces were evenly matched.

Don Afonso harangued his troops, and Ferdinand did the same. Then the drums again began beating. Shortly afterwards, there were signs of movement in the Portuguese left wing. It advanced slowly, lances lowered, toward the Castilian right wing under the command of Gonzales de Cordoba. The Castilians immediately began advancing as well.

Just as the two opposing wings were about to meet, Ferdinand was rooted to the spot by a dramatic turn of events. The Portuguese lancers altered their formation into small groups, and about fifty *arquebusiers* slipped through the gaps with their light field pieces. Small flames flickered over the guns, and before Gonzales' men could fall back there were fifty simultaneous flashes and fifty detonations.

The panic-stricken Castilian horses spun convulsively and, with blood spouting from their wounds, dragged their riders behind them, armor shattered, helmets torn off, shields broken. The whistling and hoarse shouts of the captains trying to regain control further added to the confusion and chaos.

One piece of Gonzales' leg armor was severely damaged. He was losing a lot of blood, but continued to battle the leading lancers, and only lost ground one step at a time. But soon he was put right out of action; a Portuguese soldier slipped under his horse and disemboweled it. The poor animal managed to carry its rider for a few more minutes before collapsing with a whinny. After that, the battle became a rout.

Even through the din of the fusillade, Ferdinand's ears still rang with the words: "Fight or give up . . ." Then the second volley of the arquebus threw him from his horse. Should he counter-attack, or fall back on Zamora? He glanced around for Isabella, and saw that she had taken a group of lancers from Leon to join up with Gonzales' men. Her lone presence was enough to put new fire into them.

While Gonzales and Isabella were holding on in their salient, he barked out some orders. The fifty small flames flickered again as the Duke of Alba led his left wing forward into hell, against the Portuguese right, commanded by the Count of Faro and Archbishop Carillo.

A little later, it was the turn of the infantry squares that constituted the core of both armies to move forward. The fray became widespread.

Isabella was no longer aware of her body. Wielding sword and shield, first leaping to the attack and then breaking away from an attacker in the swaying mass of humanity, she felt herself driven by the desperate strength of an overwhelming passion. But when she pulled back from the center of the battle to catch her breath, when she dismounted to rest under the protection of an equerry, she burst into tears.

How long could she keep going? She looked at the sun, about to disappear behind layers of red clouds. She swallowed a mouthful of beer, and with great difficulty remounted to rejoin Gonzales. His leg bandaged, the young captain had immediately gotten back into the fight, and succeeded in forcing back Prince Joao's Portuguese lancers. The *arquebusiers*, faced with the unbelievable fracas that resulted from their tactic, were forced to abandon their weapons.

Suddenly Isabella tensed. Standing up in the stirrups, she could see a woman coming on to the field, accompanied by ten cavalrymen. Jeanne? That was her first thought, but Loys de Tovar, who had followed the queen's gaze, corrected her: It was dona

Beatrice Pacheco, the young Marquis of Villena's sister, lady-in-waiting to la Beltraneja.

Her calm bearing and the elegance of her attire, which she could see under the coat blown open by the evening wind, fascinated Isabella. She spurred her filly, and with several horsemen following her, swooped down on the young woman. The name of Villena rang in her ears, that hated name that left the bitter taste of poison in her mouth.

The terror-stricken damsel turned her horse around and made off while the armed horsemen confronted each other. Isabella pursued her and caught up with her.

"Who are you?" asked Beatrice.

"The Queen of Castile."

Beatrice's expression hardened. "That's not true. The Queen of Castile is a long way from here, and she doesn't look like a camp-follower."

"Beautiful and bold, in spite of appearances," Isabella murmured.

"What's that you're saying?"

"I'm saying that there is only one Queen of Castile, and that I am the wife of King Ferdinand. Are you armed?"

Beatrice's face again looked like that of a startled doe. She showed her belt; suspended from it was a pathetic little dagger.

"So—we'll duel with daggers," said Isabella.

"You will certainly kill me—I'm not trained in the use of a dagger. Anyway, what's the point of dueling? By tonight, we will know who are the true rulers of Castile."

Isabella smiled scornfully and shrugged. "Your reasoning is sound. But don't bank on don Afonso's victory—you could be disappointed. Look what's going on over there!"

Isabella pointed to the thick of the battle. The Portuguese flag was being passed rapidly from hand to hand among a Castilian company. Carillo's men started to pull back toward the Duero across a wheatfield, raising a cloud of yellow dust as they went. In the rays of the dying sun, the dust looked like the reflection of a great fire.

"The battle will be over," said Isabella, "and you will have been beaten. Henceforth the unity of Spain is assured, and neither Afonso nor Joao can do anything about it. The road has been hard and long, but from the very beginning I have been sure of victory. All the misery, all the problems that we've had to overcome have been caused by your father. But at this stage I'm inclined to be forgiving. Don't look so remorseful! I don't desire your death. Forgive me for having stormed down on you a little while ago."

Isabella jumped from her horse, and Beatrice followed suit. She was a vivacious blonde, with golden eyebrows, but now looked weak and deathly pale. Isabella observed her closely, with no feeling of hatred. Nothing about her called to mind the terrible marquis.

All around them was a mad stampede. The Portuguese horses were galloping from the battlefield, the Castilian cavalry in hot pursuit. Isabella recognized Gonzales and waved to him. Gonzales reined back his horse from its headlong charge, and leapt to the ground. His face was ashen, his lips trembling, and he staggered as he came forward.

"You have done enough," said Isabella. "Lie down. The battle will be won even without more help from you."

"Prince Joao," he said in a toneless voice. "I had him within my grasp . . . he escaped . . . with the others. . . ."

"Don't worry about it," said Isabella. "Senorita Beatrice will take care of you."

Beatrice nodded her agreement. Isabella climbed back in the saddle and went to join Ferdinand. He was watching the rout of the Portuguese, who were swimming across the Duero, under attack from Galician and Aragonese archers. It was nearly night.

"Don Afonso fled first," he said. "Joao tried to make a last stand, but we threw him back into the river. It's a great victory, Isabella. And what plunder! Look what I've just found."

It was a dagger decorated with inlay work, its sheath gilded with fine Lisbon craftsmanship. It bore the arms of the count.

"I would like you to have it," said Ferdinand. "You fought better than any of our men."

A detail from the fresco Batalla de la Higueruela in the Library of El Escorial. The fresco illustrates a fifteenth-century battle between the Spaniards and the Moors, including the use of the cavalry, lances, and crossbows. (Courtesy Patrimonio Nacional)

A detail from the fresco Batalla de la Higueruela *in the Library of El Escorial. The fresco illustrates a fifteenth-century battle between the Spaniards and the Moors, including the use of the cavalry, lances, and crossbows. (Courtesy Patrimonio Nacional)*

5

David: Shield of Israel

Isabella slid quietly from her wide, low bed, threw a light silk robe over her shoulders to conceal her nakedness, and moved toward the window.

Through the tiles she could feel the strength of the afternoon sun. Inside, the walls were warm to the touch. The heat clung like a flow of lava to the front of the Alcazar and seemed to have crushed all the life out of Toledo. The Tagus was no more than a thread of reddish mud.

Isabella ran her tongue round the inside of her dry mouth to find a little moisture and tasted again the flavor of the overspiced paella she had eaten for lunch. What was the cause of these sudden feelings of unease, these spells of tiredness that came upon her without warning? The birth of her son, Juan, and of her second daughter, Juana, had weakened her, and only with great difficulty had she regained a fragile stability. And then these endless horseback excursions from one end of Spain to the other all the time.

The war against Portugal, ended nearly five years before, had left its aftermath all over Castile. Isabella and Ferdinand believed that they had destroyed their enemies, but they sprang back up like a hundred-headed hydra that would not die.

Isabella heard a low moan. She turned back to the bed, and saw a naked body bathed in sweat, sit up and immediately fall back again. Ferdinand's lips made a wet noise, and with a groan he went back to sleep.

Let him sleep, thought Isabella. Ferdinand needed to restore his strength for the journey he was going to make to the south. The

King of Granada, Moulay Hassan, had broken a three-year truce with Castile, unleashing on Zahara thirty thousand foot soldiers and three thousand cavalry. Hassan hadn't wanted to wait until the Castilian monarchs had paid all their enemies before again pursuing his grand vision of Islamic expansion.

Isabella pulled her feet free of the warm, sticky wax on the wooden floor, and returned to the bed.

Ferdinand was sleeping, mouth open, arms flung out, one knee slightly bent, in the position of a javelin thrower. He occupied the whole width of the bed, and Isabella could only sit on the edge. Selfish even when he's asleep, she thought. I must give in to his slightest wish, only go where he sees fit, say nothing of which he doesn't approve. A light sweat moistened his powerful body, marked in two or three places by the scars of war.

He hasn't forgiven me for wanting our wishes to be in step, for wanting the coats of arms of Castile and of Aragon to be displayed side by side on our standards, for wanting to sign together the royal proclamations: "I, the Queen, I, the King." He is quite surprised to see me alive each morning, to hear me give orders, to see me smile and talk. Yet what would he be without me? King of Sicily, King of Aragon after his father's death. Spain would have been but a soulless body. torn between France and Islam, If that's what you want, Ferdinand . . .

Certainly, we are the Catholic Monarchs, and we are perceived as being the most united royal family in the west. But what storms beneath the calm!! When I come back from an expedition, tired, features drawn, you frown and scold me. But I don't want sleep—that would be to give up. I want my share of fatigue and worry—and the greater share. I want Spain to be grateful to me as well as to you for its unity and its happiness. I will carry on until I'm exhausted.

Give me more children: I will go on bearing them endlessly, without stopping the horseback tours from one town to the next, to give them a feeling for the castles, the farms hidden in the mountains, the shepherds' cabins. I will scatter along the route princes who will make Spain and the world of tomorrow. Ferdinand, whatever you wish . . .

Ferdinand sighed. His head came so close to Isabella that his brown curls brushed her naked thigh.

From the love they had made a little while before, there remained with Isabella a sort of light-headedness and a quickened heartbeat. In these embraces, she sensed an annihilation of her body and of her soul; there was nothing except flesh against burning flesh, the hair where his hand wandered, the breath of fire that burned her shoulder. He was the only man she had ever loved. For a few months, Gonzales de Cordoba had stiffened her spirit just a little, but this had been mere burning straw, which left only a warm memory.

She could not deny her feelings for David Ezra, the confidante of an ambitious and fiery princess, an emotion that was more than friendship, but not quite love. David Ezra was a Jew; at the palace, where Ferdinand's own anti-Semitism was popular, the spirit of challenge in David's gaze and in his attitude meant that his presence was not welcome.

David still came down occasionally from his little castle hidden in the Guadarrama highlands, where he lived among his peasants and his goats, to pay his respects to Isabella, when the court was away in far distant towns. His openness pleased the queen; she would have made him one of the greatest individuals at court if he had agreed to be baptized, and if he had shown more flexibility in his relationships with the powerful barons.

"I love you," said Gonzales. "I love you," said David. But it was Ferdinand's voice that Isabella heard.

How many women had heard Ferdinand utter the same words? Isabella knew of a few, but paid little attention. Her heart recoiled from such unfaithfulness, but her intellect forgave it.

An exceptional person, Ferdinand had exceptional needs. From this constant battle that went on in the secret depths of her soul was born a strengthening but unconfessed passion, which ultimately became as clear and as unchanging as a diamond.

The palace was sleepy in the summer sun. In its silence Isabella listened to Ferdinand's heartbeat and the sound of his breathing.

What inspired her undying love for him? It was the long, long time they had to wait before their marriage, the sense of despair that came afterwards, the tears and the blood they had spilled together. But just as important was the profound popularity they had with their people, an unspoken surge of national feeling that upheld them, just as it had upheld Spain's leaders against the barbarian hordes in times past.

The royal couple were God's gift to the country, at a time when Spain needed to assert its nationhood. Their sense of mission was too strongly rooted in history for them to have any doubts or to hold anything back in their devotion to it. Their lovemaking was an act of faith. The birth of each child—Elisabeth, Juan, and then Juana—was a rekindling of the flame of Spain's destiny.

Isabella could hardly bring herself to look on the face of her sleeping husband, with its expression of peace, self-confidence, and strength. His selfishness, unfaithfulness, cruelty to his enemies were beyond her power to imagine. But he was Ferdinand, and she loved him.

With his defeat at Toro, King Afonso of Portugal had lost everything. He had abdicated, and sought refuge first in Rome; then, disguised as a pilgrim, in the French court. He had forfeited his young bride, Jeanne-la-Beltraneja, who had withdrawn into the religious life in Coimbra.

After his son, Prince Joao, has ascended to the vacant throne, there was nothing more for Afonso but death. He was found one morning, body blackened by plague, in Sintra castle, where he had retired among his beautiful gardens between the ocean and the Tagus estuary.

The death of King John of Aragon caused more of a sensation than that of Afonso. One winter's night, wind howling around the roofs of Saragossa palace, a horseman rode hell for leather past the black cathedral walls in the direction of Castile. The old king had gone to bed after a light meal. Two hours later, a loud cry woke the chamberlain. The king had died a sinner, before the archbishop and his chaplain could administer the Eucharist for the dying. His furniture had to be sold to pay for the funeral, and for the coffin where his wasted body was laid like that of a child.

When Ferdinand reached Saragossa, exhausted after his long journey through the snow-covered *meseta*, he found nothing but empty rooms where his footsteps echoed strangely. Even the tapestries and hangings had been torn down, dark patches showing where they had been. In the throne room, where old Rocaberti sat shivering on a stool, someone had left a portrait of the king. The foxy face peered sharply from under a broadbrimmed hat, smiling sardonically.

Ferdinand greeted the old captain and stood motionless for a few moments in front of the painting. The king's features seemed to come to life, and Ferdinand believed he could clearly hear a quavering voice:

"I leave a kingdom to this rascal, but an incomplete kingdom. What will he make of it?"

"He really said that, Rocaberti?"

"Yes, Sire."

"He didn't like me very much, did he?"

"No, Sire. He didn't trust you. But to tell you the truth, he really didn't like anybody—and he trusted only himself."

"Did he say anything else?"

"He became delirious, and called for his mistresses."

"What do you think of me, Rocaberti?"

"Disguised as a goat-herd, I took you to Castile, left you and an equally poor young princess to the mercy of those savages, the great Castilian lords. What can I believe, other than that God must have truly called you to this high office?"

The old Catalan captain coughed, spat between his down-at-heel slippers, and went on:

"Take care, Ferdinand, not to fall short of God's expectations for you. He has chosen you to be powerful but not a tyrant, brave but not cruel, adaptable but not deceitful."

"What do you find fault with in me?"

"Nothing, Sire . . . yet. Nothing of any importance. However . . ."

"You can speak freely, Rocaberti. You have nothing to fear from me."

"Resist the temptations of power, and continue to be magnanimous now that Spain is yours and now that you have shown your courage to be beyond question. When a man at last possesses a weapon that he has desired for many years, he may be impatient to see it stained with blood.

"Explain yourself," said Ferdinand, his voice changed.

"You intend to wage a long war against the kingdom of Granada. People say also that you plan to exterminate the Moors, or at least chase them back to Africa."

"That's true. I want to rid Spain of these infidels. There is no longer a place for them in my Kingdom. What else do they say?"

"That your justice, Sire, is rather arbitrary."

"If an abscess is ready, it must be lanced. The slightest delay could be fatal. Is that all?"

Ferdinand's voice had grown angry. He marched back and forth in front of the captain, his cloak touching him as he passed.

Rocaberti continued in the same even tone:

"They criticize you for wanting to bring back the Inquisition's court system. Be careful. As soon as the first convert is tortured, you will unleash the people's fury against them and against the Jews. Your action will be interpreted by the public as permission to trample on them. Blood will run in all the ghettoes of the kingdom, in every town. That blood—added to the blood of all the wars and revolutions we have been through—will weigh heavily on the future of Spain."

"The blood of Moors and Jews doesn't weight heavily on the future of my country," Ferdinand countered, rage in his voice. "Take off your mask, Rocaberti! You stand up for the Jews—I hate them. You respect the Moors—I loathe them."

"At Valladolid, the palace was full of Jews. They sniveled and swarmed round Isabella and me, and I was afraid when I went to sleep at night that they were under the bed and in the closets. They reckoned that luck would be on their side. They paid for Isabella's bridal dress, our wedding breakfast, the musicians, the candles. Then they waited to see what fate had in store for them. When things didn't move fast enough for them, they pestered us with complaints, those Judases, those goateed moneylenders!"

Ferdinand turned and mounted the throne. "That's their game. They take everything they can, and have no respect for the crown. I'm sure that don John, my father, would agree if he could hear me."

He looked questioningly at the king's portrait. It seemed to him that the smile had become a thin-lipped grin.

"Ferdinand," said Rocaberti, "I'm afraid that this anger that drives you is not really caused by your resentment of Jews and Moors. The truth is that you need gold, a great deal of gold, to undertake the conquest of Granada—and your coffers are empty. You know where to find gold; the Jews have plenty."

"The Inquisition is a convenient method. You throw the Jews into prison and gold will rain down from their tortured bodies. That outpouring of blood will be successful in causing you to be seen as a dispenser of justice. But future centuries will judge you differently."

"Future centuries will judge me for the achievements of my reign. I will be remembered as the one who gave birth to a united Spain. The world is going to see some amazing things, Rocaberti. Our race will put down roots so far afield that the people of this earth will shake in their shoes. You and I won't be alive to see these marvels, but they will take place, and they will be well worth the sacrifice of a few thousand Moors and Jews."

Rocaberti noticed that Ferdinand had not once mentioned Isabella's name. He had forgotten how much he owed her, even forgotten to ask her advice on his plans. In spite of his efforts, and those of Philippe de Barberis, Inquisitor of Sicily, and of Alfonso de Hojeda, Dominican Prior of Seville, Isabella had not permitted the Holy Office to be re-established in Castile. The Papal Nuncio, Nicolas Franco, had received nothing but a promise. 'Patience," Ferdinand had said to him. "I will soon convince her to yield."

"Men may forgive you this sacrifice, Ferdinand, but God will hold you responsible. You can't cheat God."

"I will build monasteries. I will cover Spain's cathedrals with gold."

"You cannot bargain with God, either."

Ferdinand shrugged, then caught the old man by the neck in his iron grip and shook him. "What are you trying to do, Rocaberti? Destroy everything my father and I have worked for—you, who have served us all your life? Answer, you driveling old fool! Answer, or by God you'll pay for your silence!"

Rocaberti stayed quite calm. "At last—genuine anger, Ferdinand! Your voice was shaking a little while ago, but your eyes

were cold. This is your real face. All is not lost, because you cannot
hide your feelings."

He spun round as the blow burst open his lip, and sat down,
groaning, on the steps to the throne. Blood trickled into his beard.

"You will be a great king, Ferdinand, a very great king."

Ferdinand shrugged again. He walked up the few steps between
him and the throne and sat there absorbed in thought, sword across
his thighs, fingers drumming on the armrests.

It was then that he became aware of a group of men watching
him from the darkness at the far end of the room.

❧

The disheveled little girl came up to David Ezra and tugged at
his leather jacket. David turned around, smiled, and picked her up
in his strong arms.

"You are Senor Ezra?"

"Yes I am. What is it you want?"

"The constables want to take my father and brother to the
palace. They haven't done anything, senor."

"Who are your parents?"

"My father is Joachim Daud. He is a clothes dealer, and his
store is over there. He knows you well. Can you come and see him
right away, please?"

David looked where the child was pointing. A wide gash
scarred her forearm, and the drying blood looked like a number of
small bracelets.

"But you are hurt!"

"Oh, that is nothing. But unless you come quickly, they will
harm my parents."

"Let's go!"

They hurried along alleyways cool as water buckets coming up
from a well. People turned as they went past, greeting David Ezra.
Many of them hadn't seen him in Toledo's Jewish quarter for
months or even years, but they hadn't forgotten the broad-
shouldered giant with the long, muscular legs and a way of walking
rather like a cat. Once having seen him, he was unforgettable: Pull-
necked, face bronzed by the mountain sun, and framed by blond

curly hair, wiry as heather, tumbling over the back of his neck. His sleeveless leather jacket, wide open at the chest, revealed a thick growth of tow-colored hair, where a large medallion glittered. David walked with long strides, carrying the little Jewish girl.

At last they came into the Street of the Virgin, where Joachim Daud lived. The street had been invaded by a crowd of yelling Christians and by a mob of thugs from the *barrios* of Martin and San Juan. The constables were pointing their gaudily plumed lances straight at them, in front of the Daud house, where the crowd was at its thickest and most menacing.

David used his shoulders to barge through the mob, and managed to get behind the constables in time to see something that for a moment stopped him in his tracks. A policeman was dragging along the cobblestones a large, completely naked woman by her hair, her face covered with blood.

The child tore herself away from David's arms and ran between the legs of the men-at-arms, crying "Mama!" This brought some coarse laughter. A hand holding a mace rose above the girl, but before it could come crashing down on her, David jumped into the circle of constables and caught hold of the fist, twisting it violently. There was a brief moment of astonishment.

"Where is the sergeant?" asked David.

A man with a short brown beard came and stood before, him. "That's me. Just let us do our job. Take yourself off."

David heard the crowd muttering angrily. He put his back to the wall to be ready for any surprise attack. "Not until you have cleared this street. What have you done with Joachim Daud?"

Someone in the crowd replied: "He's been baptized, he and his family, and yet they go on living by the Mosaic law!"

From another: "They've been caught singing Psalms!"

"Joachim had his last son circumcised!"

"He cuts his nails and burns the clippings!"

"Judas! Judas!"

The circle, charged with hatred, slowly closed in on David. He caught hold of his sword as a young man-at-arms tried to tear it away from him.

"Where are Joachim and his family?"

"In the passageway," replied the sergeant. "We had to use force—they were thrashing around like monkeys. The little girl managed to get away. Are you David Ezra, the friend of the queen?"

"I am," said David. "And once more I suggest that you leave."

The sergeant took two steps back, and shouted an order. The constables formed up and left. Voices from the crowd went on shouting:

"They conjure up demons!"

"The wife is a witch! She has marks in her left eye!"

"Get back!" roared David. "I will run through with my blade the first one to come near me."

He drew his sword and flashed it in the sunlight that beat down on the flimsy roof of reeds over the alleyway. The people melted away, muttering. Soon there was nobody left other than quiet passers-by. With some trepidation, neighbors began to open up their window shutters.

"Come and help me!" shouted David. "There's no danger now."

A fat woman came down first, and bent over the bruised and battered form of Joachim's wife.

"They've killed her," she said.

The little girl continued to cry. "Mama! Mama!"

David went into the store's passageway. All the rest of the family were sitting on the steps leading down into the shop. Clothes had been half pulled off the shelves; a store mannequin covered in brocade seemed to be dancing.

"Where is Joachim?" asked David.

A large, sad-faced young man, with a deep gash on his cheek, pointed to a body stretched out on a counter, the head beaten in. David pinched at his lower lip.

"Get me a wagon, right away. Bring it behind the store."

Other than the little girl and the lad who was leaving to find a wagon, David counted three children. That would make five orphans. The housekeeper was holding a newborn baby in her arms, her lips trembling.

David had been present at several pogroms, and on some occasions had risked his life, but he had never been able to hold back the emotion they aroused in him. The sight of such suffering and misery made him do things that under normal circumstances he would never have dreamed of doing.

He was not very clear about what he was going to do now, but he couldn't accept the idea that today's dead should lie unnoticed in the shadow of their store, that the Jewish quarter—and, indeed, the whole town—should forget them, that they would simply be two more deaths among all the rest. The blood on their faces was a sign that they would not be lost in the anonymity of death.

Wooden wheels rumbled over the cobbles: the wagon David had called for. Helped by the big son, he place the two bodies in it, took the donkey by its bridle and the little girl by the hand, and signaled the others to follow.

The procession caused a sensation. David's powerful presence started the group moving. Many Jews joined and followed in silence. Some wore the yellow cross; others were dressed in the *sanbenito*, that oversized yellow coat that brought down upon them the opprobrium of Christians.

Soon, the group became a crowd. Several rabbis accompanied their flocks and sang Psalms, which were taken up by the rest, first timidly and then more boldly, until all were singing with one voice. David Ezra set a fine example: his beautiful bass voice resounded between the dazzling walls of the ghetto.

He walked at a leisurely pace, making a path through the crowd as Moses did through the waters of the Red Sea. He waved to the Rachels and the Esthers who were smiling graciously from their windows at the blond giant, throwing him geraniums and pomegranate flowers.

David felt himself guided by a tranquil force within him. He had allowed the two dead bodies to remain in view so that the Jewish people of the barrios could take heart. They were the ones now urging him onward, and he felt in his heart the force that made him keep moving.

Where would this funeral march end? By the time the procession arrived at the limits of the Jewish section, he still didn't know. It was dangerous to venture outside. If they fell in with the constables or the guards, they would be attacked, and Jewish blood would flow again. David, however, knew that he was not in charge of events. Shouts rose behind him:

"To the Archbishop's palace!"

"To the Alcazar!"

"Let's show the Christians what their justice looks like!"

Strong shoves now shook the wagon, and the donkey moved forward, pulling David with it. In the streets they were passing through there was no one except those trying to get away. Children stopped their playing to hide in the passageways. Storefronts and windows were barricaded. Two constables who encountered them took off in the opposite direction, blowing their whistles, piercing calls that were quickly taken up by others.

David Ezra drew his sword and turned toward the procession. A long round of applause greeted him, and he felt himself wrapped in a warm cocoon of support. He was the general of the Jews, their champion. The few words of Hebrew that remained in his memory seemed to counsel calm and dignity. With his big hands, he picked up the little girl, who was playing with the flowers thrown from the windows, and lifted her above his head like a banner. He trembled when he heard the strains of an ancient Israeli battle song.

"Let's go!" he said.

At the end of the deserted street a patrol of constables was waiting for them—a wall of men bristling with lances. He maintained his steady pace; the constables retreated.

As they came into the cathedral square, David felt a lump in his throat. Isabella must be at the Archbishop's palace with Ferdinand, back from the borders of Granada; the Moorish guards were stationed in front of the palace walls.

As well as the fifty mounted Moorish guards, a company of constables were in front of him, lined up as though for battle.

He went forward.

"What is all that singing and shouting?" asked Ferdinand. "Are our good people celebrating the news of my successes at Alhama?"

Cardinal Mendoza, Bishop of Toledo, smiled and leaned his head to one side.

"There is no doubt about it. Haven't you yourself said that your popularity will increase remarkably over the next few weeks? No exploit would be as pleasing to Spain as the conquest of Granada, which God has called upon you to undertake."

He turned toward Isabella: "And this reputation will reflect on our good queen."

The din grew louder. The firing of an *arquebus* made the queen leap out of her chair. She rushed into the corridor, followed by Ferdinand and the Cardinal, and collided with an out-of-breath courier, who had come to tell them what was happening. Hurrying out opposite the cathedral square, the first person she saw was David Ezra.

She shouted, "Stop! The Queen orders it!"

She was just in time. Hit by the shot from the arquebus, one hand on his bloody shoulder, the other holding his sword, David would certainly have been killed by the second shot, which was about to be fired when the queen shouted.

"It is a riot fomented by the Jews," a sergeant of the guard told them. "The whole Jewish population of Toledo is here in this square. What shall we do, Sire?"

Ferdinand swore heavily, pushed the constables aside, and went out into the open space between David and the men-at-arms. He muttered angrily.

"What do you want, David Ezra? I thought I told you never to show your face again in Toledo—or in any other town!"

David indicated with his head that Ferdinand should look behind him. Ferdinand shoved past him roughly, saw the bodies, and gave a start. Isabella, following him, let out a weak cry.

"Your work, King Ferdinand," said David. "I hope you're satisfied. Joachim Daud's wealth is now yours."

"I don't understand. Why do you accuse me of this murder? What has happened here?"

"Explain yourself," echoed Isabella.

David related the day's events. Behind him, the Jews were hushed, listening. The point of a pike sparkled in the sunlight.

Ferdinand protested, "All the same, you are surely not going to hold me responsible for a crime carried out by a few officers? I swear that I knew nothing of this murderous attack."

"That's a lie!" shouted David. "If the order didn't come from the king, it came from his ministers. This is not the first atrocity to be perpetrated against the people of the ghetto, and neither will it be the last."

"Be silent!" cried Isabella. "You are drunk, David!"

Ferdinand took three steps back, and barked out: "Arrest this man!"

A captain of the police came forward with five men. David raised his sword to the *en garde* position, and spat out at Ferdinand: "Don't have your policemen killed uselessly, King Ferdinand. This *arquebus* is more effective."

The captain had already drawn his sword when Isabella came between them. "You have done what you came to do," she said to David. "Now, go away and tell your followers to leave as well."

"It's not that simple!" David shouted.

He turned around, and lifted the little Jewess off the donkey where she had been perched. She moaned when David's great hand gripped her wrist.

"What about her, Isabella? And the other four sons and daughters of Joachim Daud, and all those who have lost one or both parents in your dungeons, who will look after them? Isabella, you are an accomplice in these crimes, and that grieves me more than anything."

Isabella looked bewildered. She closed her eyes, pulled a cambric handkerchief from the small purse attached to her belt, and wiped the end of her nose. She was on the point of replying when Ferdinand's voice rang out behind her.

"You have just two minutes, you and your rioters, to clear this square. If you don't, instead of two bodies there will be a hundred!"

"Who cares about a hundred dead Jews, King Ferdinand?"

The King signaled to the artilleryman, who adjusted the weapon on its trunnions.

"All right," growled David. "We will go. But think carefully of how the future will judge you."

"And you, Ezra—think carefully of your life."

"You sent for me, your Majesty?"

Isabella spun around. Cardinal Mendoza, Primate of All Spain, stood behind her, motionless, a little stooped, hands tucked into wide sleeves, a cape of rough material like those worn by sentries, thrown over his shoulders. It was almost nightfall, and the shapes of the small Visigothic columns around the cloisters of Santa Cruz de Toledo could hardly be discerned.

The king and queen had taken their evening meal there.

Mendoza seemed astonished as he looked around him. "You are alone?"

"The king stayed with the prior. I needed a few moments of solitude to let some understanding come into my soul. I thought that you could be a great help to me. Are you not a confessor?"

"I have that honor, your Majesty."

Isabella smiled at him. From the stone bench on which she sat, she could easily see the cardinal's too-pale face, his features rather heavy but full of distinction and nobility.

"Would you like to sit next to me, your Eminence?"

"Would you object if instead we were to walk a few steps?"

Isabella had forgotten that the Primate of Spain did not like what he called "conversations between statues." She stood and walked toward him.

"What a beautiful evening, your Eminence. While waiting for you, I was breathing in the scent of the orange trees and the myrtles, listening to the rippling of the water and the nightingale's song. I watched the sky over the cypresses darken, and I have to admit that I felt peace descend on me—but a spurious, unsatisfying peace. I am too worried about the events of this afternoon for a fragrance, a song, a beautiful sky to give me peace for long."

"Do you want to talk about these Jews who started the riot?"

"Yes." Isabella's voice was dull.

The cardinal felt Isabella put her hand on his arm. She went on in a hesitant voice: "Your Eminence, would you vouch that I am sincere in my relations with God?"

"You are the most pious princess that Spain has ever known."

"Are you quite certain? I go through the motions that our religion requires, I attend church services as often as I can, I confess my sins and misdeeds, but only those sins and misdeeds that are respectable . . ."

The Primate turned away to hide a faint smile.

"So you have unrespectable sins? I am sorry that you are afraid to place total trust in me. Your confessors should hear everything;

you must tell them everything." He continued in a lower voice, as they reached the gallery: "What I find difficult to understand is the connection between this Jewish riot and the sins that you mention."

"Do you mind if we stay in the garden? I need this time of dusk to help me with my confusion. You were present at the scene in the cathedral square. The young Jew who led the rioters did not go unnoticed by you."

"Indeed. In fact, I really only paid attention to him and to the two bodies."

"He is called David Ezra. He is the son of my brother Henry's doctor. David lived with his father at court for years, and he and I saw each other often. He taught me how to ride a horse. One day, at a time when Henry was keeping me locked up in the Tower of Hommage, in Segovia, David came at night to release me. I had sent him a hastily scribbled note, telling him of my thirst for freedom. David risked his life for me. We left, just the two of us, across the *meseta*, without knowing where we were headed. It was a miserable October night. There was a suggestion of snow in the air. David wanted to take me to his castle, in the Guadarrama, mountains, but we had to stop at San Ildefonso when the snow started to fall heavily. We took shelter in the bakery of the Posada, not far from the monastery. We slept quite innocently in each other's arms, and next morning the monks of San Ildefonso woke us up. They recognized me, and we had to follow them back to Segovia. As luck would have it, my brother didn't find out about my escapade, and so David Ezra was able to stay close to me. From that time on, I knew that our destinies were linked."

The Primate lifted his white hand. "Childhood loves are the most difficult to forget."

The changed voice of the queen brought a chill to his heart. "I fear that I shall never be able to forget this love."

"What are you saying?"

"I'm saying that I love David Ezra."

"A Jew!"

"Would you have granted me absolution if he had been Christian?"

The Cardinal side-stepped the question, which Isabella had thrown at him in an assertive tone. "I can only absolve you if you sincerely regret these guilty feelings and if you promise to renounce them."

"I regret nothing, and I promise nothing."

"So what can I do for you?"

"You won't help me?"

"I cannot give sight to the blind and hearing to the deaf. If I were to counsel you, you would not listen to me. Have you at least the desire to redeem yourself."

"Yes, I have such a desire; I feel that it comes from somewhere deeper than myself. But then David comes back into my life, and everything is again thrown into question. It was like that this afternoon. I hadn't seen David for months, and I was beginning to believe that he was fading from my memory, that I would see him no more, that I was free of him at last. But when I saw him standing in the square, his leather jacket covered with blood, his shoulder pierced by a shot from an *arquebus*, I could sense that the fragile wall of security that had been building round me for so many weeks could crumble. So there you are—you once again have a sinner in front of you. Tomorrow David will come knocking at my door, and I will not be able to refuse him."

The cardinal's face was set. "May I ask a favor of you?"

"To promise something that I don't think I can do?"

"Try, your Majesty, I beseech you. You and Ferdinand are the two most united rulers that history has ever known . . . you are a couple chosen by God to make Spain great. The slightest stain would undermine your mission, make you unworthy of the faith God has placed in you."

"I will try to be worthy of this divine confidence, and to be worthy of it for the two of us."

She turned to the Primate and fixed her blue eyes on him. "I mean it when I say 'for the two of us,' your Eminence, for you are not unaware of Ferdinand's notorious misconduct. 'The most united rulers,' you say? No doubt that's the way history will see us. But what heartbreak is hidden in that union! I love Ferdinand, you know that, and if I were sure that he would be faithful to me I would no more see David, I would calmly accept his disappearance or even his death."

In the darkness, Isabella could imagine the Primate of Spain's sad smile. "God will be able to weigh the merits of each of you."

Isabella didn't hide the irritation that this reply caused her. She knew that, when David came back to her, her door would be open. They would spend long hours together, looking at each other and finding out more about each other. The very thought made her so giddy that she closed her eyes.

With nightfall, the orange trees' fragrance became very strong, almost palpable, and Isabella imagined it clinging to her dress, her skin, her hair. David will stay with me, but will not touch me. I have forgotten the taste of his lips, the texture of his skin under my hand. I have forgotten the excitement that such contact aroused in me, long ago, in Medina and in Segovia . . .

"I haven't told you everything yet, your Eminence, but the rest need not take long. The methods of the Inquisition disgust me. I wouldn't go so far as to praise my brother, don Henry, but in his time the authorities contented themselves with apprehending overzealous Jews, putting a crucifix under their noses, and making them sniff the fires of our hell. Many were converted, either by fear or by rational argument. The ones who were not went back in complete freedom to their synagogue. Today, they are hunted down, flayed alive, burned after having been submitted to interrogation."

Again, the cardinal was taken by surprise. He threw out his arms like the black wings under the military badge.

He's going to mention God again, thought Isabella.

"God . . ." began the Primate.

Isabella interrupted sharply. "Your Eminence, you know that my conduct is that of a good Christian, but—just for once—stop making God responsible for our actions. It's not God who gave us the idea of reviving an unforgivable Inquisition, but St. Peter. And how persuasive he was! Ferdinand went along with it, for two good reasons: He needs the Jews' gold to fight the Moors in Granada; and he needs the support of Rome for his policies in general. You couldn't imagine that he would refuse . . ."

"Might I remind your Majesty that God is the inspiration for St. Peter's decisions?"

"It is the Popes who God refuses to support, and to whom he denies authority."

The cardinal coughed to hide his embarrassment.

"I want you to clearly understand me," continued the queen. "My greatest concern is to see my country free of the aftermath of lawlessness, and to create a Christian land. But not by lying and murder. Those dead Jewish bodies deeply distress me."

The Cardinal steadied his voice. "You are allowing yourself to be blinded by sentimentality, your Majesty! What are two dead bodies compared to the price of the blood spilt by our Lord because of the Jews? Spain will only be truly great and worthy of its destiny when all the falsely converted Jews who infest our towns, monopolize the important posts, hide under soldiers' greatcoats, priests' soutanes, and judges' robes, have been driven out or died. That, or when they have resolved unreservedly to make common cause with Christianity. The fact that Ferdinand uses their gold against other enemies of Spain offends me not at all. He is only returning to Spain the gold the Jews squeezed out of it."

"If it were only those two bodies . . . but there are thousands who in just a few months have had their throats cut or been burnt at the stake. When will the carnage cease?"

"I would remind you that you signed the bill to reinstitute the Holy Office in Seville."

"You well know that I couldn't refuse without forfeiting the support of Pope Sixtus and losing Ferdinand. Now I would like the hand that signed the document to wither away and fall off. My slumber is full of the cries of children, the light of the fires round the stake, the dreadful smoke. I pay dearly for that moment of weakness."

The cardinal assumed a fatherly air. "My child," he said, "I can see into you clearly, more clearly than you can see into yourself. Although you appear to be defending the Jews, it's really your wretched passion for this David Ezra that you are protecting. His are the cries you hear in your sleep. It is he whom you see burning at the stake. And to save him, you would go so far as to break your word, or to turn the spear in Christ's side."

By now it was almost completely dark, and the queen and the cardinal could see each other only as faceless figures. The night seemed to concentrate the fragrances of the land and its flowers between them. Through that odor, their words lost all their power. The queen heard only the nightingale's song. A cloud edged with streaks of fire hung in the sky like a sword.

"We are not speaking the same language," said Isabella.

⚜

David punctiliously completed his evening prayers, and readied himself to leave before the curfew.

He had arranged a meeting with Rabbi ben Samuel, Rabbi of the Toledo Jews. The rabbi had been so distressed by the news of the riot that he had taken to his bed. Before setting off, David looked out of the window of the little house where he lived, not far from the bridge of San Martin, overlooking both the ghetto area and the gorge of the Tagus.

The temperature had fallen. A great sword of fire seemed to be suspended in the sky above the surprisingly quiet alleyway.

David decided to go unarmed. Knowing David's fiery temperament, the rabbi didn't like to see him carrying a weapon, and his bushy eyebrows would knit in a frown whenever he saw a sword by his side.

A police patrol came down the street, passing a line of mules whose hoofs clattered on the cobbles. One of the men carried an *arquebus*, and David instinctively placed his hand on his wounded shoulder. He had used some ointment compounded by his father to prepare healing plasters. They made his shoulder swell and hindered his movements, but the pain was nearly gone. In any case, the ball had only caused a flesh wound, tearing some leather from his jacket.

David breathed in the orange trees' fragrance that hovered over the baking-hot roofs, and thought, tomorrow, I will go to see Isabella.

He had more than an hour before the bells would sound the curfew. David started to walk his slow, quiet, big cat's walk. As he passed by windows open in the warmth of dusk, he saw families gathered around the little lamps for their evening prayers to their

Jewish God. He saw a hand raised in salute, and a woman following him with her eyes.

Soon after stepping out of his door, David passed a small group of constables going in the opposite direction. They stared at him and slackened their pace. David continued on his way, but a warning bell sounded in his head. He could sense danger whenever it threatened, and he was seldom mistaken. This time, his instinct was reinforced by an obvious fact: after the afternoon's episode, some might find it advantageous to have him disappear.

David broke into a cold sweat. The houses in the alley seemed to close in on him. Behind him, the constables must have stopped, for he no longer heard their footsteps.

He kept going, every sense on the alert. Odd snatches of his evening prayers ran through his mind, but he could not focus on them; it was as though they were outside him. A hand waving would seem to him like a flash of light inside a house and make him jump.

At the end of the street he encountered what he had half anticipated: another police patrol advancing, lances leveled at him. He spun around, and saw that the patrol he had passed earlier had changed direction, and were now heading his way.

David had no choice. A very dark, narrow alley was close at hand to his right. He dived into it, and realized almost at once that he had fallen into a trap. He banged on the first door he came to, but there was no reply. He had no better luck at the next one, which was closed and double-locked. Then he caught sight of a passageway, which he cautiously entered. He sniffed a comforting smell of cabbage boiling, then a strong fragrance of spices, and guessed that he must be at Jace Crequel's house. He pushed open a door and found himself in an empty hallway. At its end, a glimmer of light showed under another door. He called out:

"Jace! Jace Cresquel!"

A scraping of bolts, and two huge frog's eyes appeared, magnified by the pince-nez lenses in front of them.

"Jace! It's me, David Ezra."

"It's you! What do you want, my son?"

"I'm being hunted, Jace. You must hide me."

Jace bit his fat wet lips, and closed the partly open door even farther.

"You must understand that I cannot do that, David. Not after what happened this afternoon. They would destroy everything here, and kill me and my family."

"Then show me some other way out, besides this one."

"Go on up the stairs. You'll come to an attic. The right-hand window opens on to a flat roof. From there you can jump across to the opposite roof, and make your way to the synagogue orchard. Good luck, David Ezra."

"Thank you."

He followed the route Jace had given him. When he came to the flat roof where Jews' shirts were hanging out to dry, he heard muffled voices in the alley below. He carefully leaned over, and saw the constables talking and pointing in all directions.

"You can jump across to the opposite roof," Jace had said, crediting him with superhuman agility. The synagogue was not far. David could make out its domes, and a little light twinkling in a window. The orchards' feathery trees were blurred in dark green shadow. If I can make it there, thought David, I am saved.

He climbed onto a gently sloping roof with infinite caution, so as not to crack the tiles. As he leaned over to check on the police, he spotted a wide-open window from which came a regular noise, like the chiming of a convent bell. He smiled, recognizing an old Jewish coppersmith who was beating a copper bowl with his mallet by the dim light of a candle. The smith lifted his head and saw a great shadow outlined against a fiery cloud that filled the sky. In sudden agitation, he let fall his work to go to the window.

"Is that you, David?" he shouted.

Down in the alleyway, those words were the signal for a wild stampede. David steadied himself, leapt onto the roofs, breaking tiles with his heavy tread. He stumbled on a skylight, crossed some flat roofs, then some sloping ones, and suddenly, just as he reached a point opposite the synagogue's orchard, he saw the barrel of a culverin pointed straight at him. A little flame fluttered over the gun's fuse. David counted to three, then threw himself down flat as the shot roared over him like a thunderclap. He leapt forward and seized hold of the weapon by its barrel, ignoring the intense pain of the burning heat. With one blow of the butt, he knocked the constable senseless, and saw him spin round before falling down into the alleyway.

Not a moment too soon. The constables' footsteps were growing louder. In a few seconds, they would burst onto the roof, and then it would be too late to escape them. The block of houses ended a few yards farther on.

David quickly estimated the distance between his position and the wall that surrounded the synagogue orchard. With a short run, he had a chance of landing in the branches of a great fig tree just behind that wall.

With a brief prayer to Jehovah, he leapt into space.

⁕

Princess Isabel stepped forward timidly into the circle of ladies, curtsied, and stood looking at the tips of her pointed shoes, which protruded from under the hem of her richly embroidered dress. She was tall for a ten-year-old, but sickly-looking, with features too sharp, complexion too pale.

"Let's start, Isabel," said the queen. "We are expected at dona Inez de Castro's poetry recital."

The little girl remained silent, so the queen whispered in her ear: "When I was in Tordesillas . . ."

"She is overawed," said dona Beatrix Cabrera.

"Give her a moment to remember the words!" added dark-haired dona Leonor de Soto.

"Let's begin!" said Isabella.

The princess let out a sigh, placed her long pale hands flat on the crimson velvet of her dress, and recited without raising her head:

"When I was in Tordesillas—for my pleasure and relaxation . . ."

Surreptitiously, she threw distraught glances at her brother Juan, her sister Juana, and at her mother. The queen tapped her fan on her knee in time with the cadences of the old poem.

When she had finished, the ladies gave voice to their pleasure and clapped their hands. Dona Mencia de la Torre called for another recitation, and the child, with great lack of enthusiasm, was about to comply when the queen's chamberlain came in quietly, his face ashen. He bowed, and whispered a few words in the queen's ear. She gave a start.

"What's this you're telling me? He's here, and wants to see me?"

After some hesitation, she went on, "Let him wait for me in the red room."

In the same monotonous voice, Isabel began reciting "The Little Princess": "The knight is going hunting—hunting, as is his custom . . ."

Isabella waited until the end before rising and excusing herself. She appeared deeply troubled.

David was waiting for her in the small room, examining two Flemish paintings by Van Eyck, which don Henry had bought long ago. When he turned around, Isabella let out a cry. David's face was like a mask of Christ lacerated by thorns. He was scarred with numerous wounds, and his right arm was bound up to the elbow with a thick bandage.

"Have you been fighting?"

"Yes. With a tree. Looking at these landscapes of Van Eyck, I doubt if the painter ever fell into a tree. If he had, he wouldn't have painted them with such softness and flexibility. What can be nastier than a tree?"

David told her how he had been the target of an attempt on his life. He gesticulated while talking, and Isabella had the impression of being at the foot of a great oak tree shaking in the wind. After recovering consciousness, he did not know how he found the strength to drag himself to Rabbi Samuel's house and to hide in a cellar, so as not to disturb the old man's sleep nor to involve him in the affair.

"To tell the truth, I was expecting to pay with my life after the Dauds were murdered. But not so quickly."

"Who would be interested that you disappear from my surroundings forever!"

Isabella realized at once how naive her question was. Ferdinand had left that afternoon, and before setting off for Mocejon, where he planned to spend the night, he had had a discussion with the short-bearded police captain. Isabella had seen them when she looked out of the window.

"I will talk to the king this very evening."

"That will do no good at all. Sooner or later, Ferdinand will achieve his goals. He detests me because he knows what bonds unite us. As a Christian, he would have exiled me. As a Jew, he will kill me. But I'm not scared of that, Isabella. I can look after myself—not so much to save my own life as to continue fighting and to keep the trust of my people. For they live in terrible times, don't they?"

"Yes," Isabella said, somberly. "Terrible times."

David bowed his head, and with his hand wiped away a bead of blood that had formed on a scar on his face. She pulled from her red leather purse a small cambric handkerchief, and moved closer to David.

"Don't move," she said.

She moistened a corner of the handkerchief in her mouth, and dabbed it on the wound. "Are you in a lot of pain?"

His voice was hard when he replied. "I don't have time to feel sorry about my own injuries. Joachim Duad and his wife suffered much more cruelly than I. Others are agonizing in the cellars of the Inquisition, tortured by pincers and the garrotte. So these little scratches . . ."

His cut lip started bleeding again. Isabella stretched up on tiptoe, one hand on the back of the giant's neck. Her lips met David's, and her mouth was full of the taste of blood. David pulled himself away from her.

"I must leave," he said.

"Where are you going?"

"I'll go back to my old castle in the mountains, to my goats, to my sheep. I am tired of this world where men are more savage than the Guadarrama wolves."

"You should not have come to Toledo. I should not have agreed to see you once more. And in any case, you promised not to seek me out again. Every time you're close to me I start having doubts about everything—my mission as queen, the future of Spain, my faith! I am poorer and more defenseless than the miserable turkey-keepers of Toledo. Your broad shoulders hide the world from me. One look from you and all my problems disappear. When it's your voice that I hear, the words of my confessors seem as devoid of sense as the bleating of the goat."

"Isabella."

She turned and looked at him, her gaze direct. She saw only his tortured face, his large frost-blue eyes, and the tears welling up.

"I would with serenity give up seeing you again, I would erect a cross over your name, whatever the cost. I would never again leave my mountain if I had your assurance that you would hold back the Inquisitors' zeal. My people . . ."

"Your people . . . that's the only thing I hear you say! And what can I do for 'your' people?"

"You could do much, if you wanted to. You share power equally with Ferdinand—what he can do, so can you. The Spanish people love and respect you. The army commanders swear by you. The Church looks on you almost as a saint. Isabella, I beg of you. Do you know how much Spain owes to the Jews and to the *conversos*? Long ago, they made the country rich. They came to Spain ages before Christ died, and the name 'Judas' was then unknown. Your doctors are Jews, Isabella! And your bankers, your advisers, even some of your prelates. Is it their gold that the king needs? Remember that they themselves suggested that they should finance the conquest of Granada. Ferdinand himself has Jewish blood in his veins."

Isabella's face hardened. She said in a tone of indifference, as if replying to a beggar, "I will consider your request."

"Joachim Daud's children left Toledo at dawn this morning. I gave them all the money I had with me. Do you know where they are heading? To Granada. To the Moors. Yes, Isabella, that's where liberty and tolerance have fled to."

David bowed his head and made a gesture of impotence.

"I can tell that what I am saying is not touching you. Good-bye, Isabella. We have nothing more to say to each other. You will never see me again. That will be best for both of us."

Just as he put his hand out to open the door, Isabella cried out in a quite different tone of voice, "Don't go!"

"I must."

"Then come back soon. I can't go on without you. I love you, David."

"I love you, too. But even so, it must be farewell, Isabella."

She stayed for a few moments in the little red room, looking at a painting by the Flemish artist. Through her tears, she could see angels swirling over blue-green trees.

⚜

Ferdinand came back from Mocejon in the cool of the early evening. Still wearing his boots, eyelashes white with dust, he entered the queen's rooms where Juan and Juana were playing with a Valencia mastiff dog. The queen was leafing through a printed Bible that Cabrera had sent her from Madrid.

Ferdinand kissed his wife, then sat beside her and said, "I've good news and bad news. Which would you like to hear first?"

"The good," she replied, with an air of indifference.

"Pope Sixtus has just awarded us the title of Catholic Monarchs."

"Really?"

Ferdinand frowned. "That doesn't interest you?"

"I am delighted," she replied coldly. "Now the bad news."

"It only concerns you. Last night your friend David Ezra met with an accident. He was walking in the Jewish ghetto, after the curfew. When challenged by police, he ran away. A bullet killed him. You must understand that I had nothing to do with this. Ezra was a hothead, the most dangerous of all the Jews in Spain, but I respected him for his courage. If he had shown himself as being more diplomatic in his opposition to the Holy Office, I could have appointed him to command a cavalry company . . . but you're not listening, Isabella. Aren't you upset that David . . ."

Isabella lifted her eyes from the Bible, which still smelled of fresh glue, and closed it with a bang.

"David Ezra has just left me," she said.

Granada

6

The Little King of Granada

War was again flaring up on the border with Granada. One morning, a tall white-bearded old man, who was known as one of the most celebrated Moorish astrologers in the royal city, came coatless down the alleys of the Albaicin. He was crying out that the end of Granada was near, that he has seen in a dream the great walls of Zahara falling on the people of Allah.

The astrologer was taken before the aged King Moulay Hassan, who nodded his head as he listened to him.

The old man foretold in a wheezing voice: "Yes, I have seen the walls split in two like a knife through butter, and two kings, each carrying a royal banner."

"Two kings?" asked Moulay Hassan.

He let the old fool run on until his story came to an end, smiled with amusement when he had finished, and ordered his head to be cut off. Then he called for Soraya, his favorite, whose name meant 'Morning Star,' and asked her to sing as she played her *guzla*. The beautiful voice of the Christian girl, who had only recently been converted to Islam, pronounced the Arabic syllables in a strange fashion; but this pleased the king. He interrupted her:

"Do you believe what the astrologer foretold?"

"What did he foretell, great King?"

"That Granada would be conquered by the infidel dogs, and that we would perish in a deluge of stones."

Soraya's thoughtful gaze wandered to the curving red battlements of the heights of the Albaicin.

"This prediction will come true if you continue to let yourself be controlled by a shrewish wife and tyrannical children." Looking tenderly at him, Soraya added, "*Li sahhad el aafya, jakhod roumiya.*"

Startled, the king said, "What are you saying?"

"Must I teach you the sayings of your own country, great King? 'He who loves tranquillity, let him take a Christian wife.'"

The great king stoked his beard and gently rubbed his rheumy and myopic eyes. He thought that Soraya had a lot of good sense and would make a most acceptable wife. But there was the queen, and, of course, the six children.

"Sing," he sighed. "Sing some more, Soraya."

჻჻჻

Isabella was working night and day. At daybreak, the boatmen who came down the Guadalquivir on their way to Seville could see a little light shining on the floor that the queen occupied in the bishop's palace in Cordova, and they thought, we are much blessed that God has given us a queen such as Isabella.

She left her work table, overloaded with state papers and thick ledgers, and leaned out of the window overlooking the Arab mills and the Roman bridge. The cool crisp air was pleasant to her uncomfortably perspiring brow. She watched the boatmen, and thought, good people of Spain, people of the *pueblos* and the cities, goatherds, boatmen, the bourgeoisie—I work for all of you.

She shook the shoulder of the scribe, who was falling asleep over his inkwell, chaffed at a yawning Gonzales, and finally sent them stumbling sleepily away.

She sat down, blew out the dying candle, and plunged back into her accounts.

"To the medical service of the tenth company of Ponce de Leon, stationed at Loja: 10,000 *maravedis* . . .

She repeated to herself, "Loja . . . 10,000 *maravedis* . . ." and suddenly her mind became confused, her expression clouded over, and she could no longer feel the paper on which she was writing.

She only had just enough strength to stand up and walk over to kneel in front of Borgia's ivory crucifix. The words "Loja" and "*maravedis*" mingled with her prayers until she collapsed on the rug, overcome with sleep.

"You are working too hard," Ferdinand would tell her. "You can only keep going at this rate for a few months."

But Isabella felt that she could go on for years. She had managed to wrest from Ferdinand the responsibility for supplies and medical care for troops in the field. She was acutely aware of what would happen if Ferdinand alone were to win the victory over the kingdom of Granada. He would take all the glory, as he did on the battlefield. The name of Isabella would disappear from the bottom of the royal proclamations, to the greater glory of the name of Ferdinand.

For all the love and trust she had vowed for her husband, she had always to remain vigilant. Ferdinand would never easily accept the power sharing she had brought about.

This selfishness did not quite deaden in Ferdinand the love he had vowed—and still vowed—for his wife. None of his mistresses, Aragonese or Castilian, Moorish or Jewish, gave him the pleasures he enjoyed with his wife. Isabella knew how to be a woman even while remaining queen. She never gave herself to Ferdinand. He had to win her by gentleness and by paying her a lot of attention, sincere or otherwise. Each of their embraces held a taste of conquest, which for him was far superior to the easy but self-seeking submissiveness he found with other women.

For Isabella, this taste for conquest assumed another form. Her fight was primarily against herself, and she was careful to give to Ferdinand only that part of her from which David was excluded. This was not always easy; what Ferdinand sometimes took for tiredness was usually the result of her internal conflict about the young Jew.

She would not allow herself to visualize his narrow face with its strong features, his colossal shoulders, his childlike skin nourished but not harmed by the sun, his strength, his gentleness. David was most often defeated in these mental battles, but sometimes it might be Ferdinand who lost. On such occasions, Isabella was left with a feeling of dissatisfaction and bitterness that would not leave the young queen.

Ferdinand did not grow tired of this demanding love. Isabella was blooming. Her eyes were still like those of a young girl, set in a face that reflected pride and intelligence. At thirty, time had not robbed her body of youth and beauty. Spain had never had so beautiful a queen; Ferdinand had never loved so perfect a woman.

Her struggle against David Ezra not only made itself felt in these problems in her relationship with the king. It would strike her like lightning even at the calmest of times, wherever she was or whatever she was doing. At those times, weary of this internal war, the only thing for her to do was to pray. David may have left her, but it seemed to Isabella that his smile meant he would return.

She had not seen him again at the bishop's palace in Cordova since their meeting in the red room. She avoided spending any time there. When she had to go through it, she did so with her eyes lowered; even so, she could not prevent herself from seeing the outline of David gliding over Van Eyck's trees.

Since the events that had so shaken Toledo's ghetto, the Jewish community was enjoying a period of relative peace. The tribunal of the Inquisition continued to function under the skillful direction of Tomas de Torquemada, a little-known Dominican priest whose zeal, exemplified by the scourgings to which he was devoted, had called him to the position.

Conversions were in full flower, obtained sometimes by threats, sometimes by conviction; but they were almost always spurious, and the *conversos* would secretly return to the synagogue.

Torquemeda was tireless in his preaching, his threatening, his condemnations. Jews were put to the question; they were decked out in the *sanbenito*, the infamous gown marked with a great yellow cross. Those who were swallowed up into the cellars of the Holy Office only came out in secret, drained of blood, mutilated, fit only for the grave.

Isabella was not unaware of these activities. But what could she do? Her counsels of moderation came up against Ferdinand's implacable will, for he needed the Jews' gold for the war in Granada; against Torquemada, for whom Jewish blood was a precondition for his accession to the right hand of God; and against Pope Sixtus, for whom the gold and the blood meant both wealth and redemption.

The queen felt alone in this maelstrom of squalid desires and ferocious idealism. She could not recall without terror the dreadful words addressed to her by the Cardinal of Spain, Monsignor Mendoza:

"You must fight against the memory of David Ezra, humiliate it, wound it, destroy it. If you live with this memory in you, your ability to fulfill your mission as queen will gradually be eroded. You do not have the right to accept failure. You must be worthy of the trust that God has placed in you. You struggle, you tell me. But you struggle feebly, against a ghost. David is on the side of the Jews and the *conversos*, this rabble of unbelievers, of traitors, of usurers, of money-grabbers. By fighting against them, you will fight against him. By crushing him, you will demonstrate your greatness. You will oblige me if you sign with a steady hand the bills that the Holy Office will present to you. Be a queen, Isabella."

One day in June, on her way back to Segovia, the queen had passed within a few miles of the black highlands where David lived. She hesitated before taking the mountain road that led to his estate, but after hours of indecision she resolved to do so in spite of the delay such a detour would cause in her program. She made her way on foot to the cliff on which his castle was perched. But then she lacked the courage to go farther, and with the darkness of death in her soul she retraced her steps.

Just the previous week, her shaking hand had signed the arrest warrant for three Jewish merchants from Toledo, accused by Grand Inquisitor Torquemada of having eaten unleavened bread at Easter time.

Soraya was as smooth and as fragrant as a rose petal. Silent when she needed to be, talkative when it pleased Moulay Hassan. Always ready to obey the whim of her master. When he tired of the grumbling of his wife, the old Queen Aicha with a face lined like the trunk of an olive tree, and went off to find his favorite, it seemed to him that as he crossed the threshold of the suite in the Generalife where he had installed her he left behind him thirty years of emptiness and worry.

She would sit on his knee and, with her sharp tongue, play with him until the stumps of his teeth shook in their gums. Her provocative games delighted Moulay Hassan. They made him feel at least twenty years younger.

One morning, the king found his favorite deeply distressed. Very early, while the king was still asleep, Aicha had burst into the Generalife, dagger in hand. Had it not been for the quick action of the devoted *rakkas*, the huge Sudanese blacks charged with the monarch's personal security, Soraya would have been stabbed to death.

"She swore that she would come back again, great King. So I have decided to leave your Kingdom."

Moulay Hassan felt as though his heart would burst. "My Morning Star! If you leave me, I will die."

Soraya climbed up on his knee. She had moistened her ear lobes with essence of cloves, like an Albaicin prostitute, for she knew that although she detested it herself, this perfume gave the king pleasure. He guessed that she was about to ask a favor of him, a favor he would be unable to refuse.

"You must choose, great King, between the Morning Star and the Ugly Moon."

She put out her pink tongue, threw back her thin veil, and lightly licked the king's face from his ear to the quivering royal nostril. What was she going to ask of him? Already a black eunuch she suspected of spying had been flayed alive on his orders. That had been a great loss; the slave had cost nearly three hundred mithkals, the price of four horses. Surely Soraya would not ask that Aicha should die? That would trigger a revolution in Granada.

She said, "I will stay, but only on one condition: that you put the queen under guard."

Moulay Hassan breathed again.

Some days later, he found his favorite packing her bags, even though he had thrown the queen into a dungeon. Soraya explained that the princes had stormed into the Generalife in the middle of the night—six demons in black capes, armed with *alfanges*.

"They killed ten guards. To escape from them, I had to hide in a clump of myrtles and stay there until daybreak. I thought that I would die of fear and cold."

"I will have all six of them thrown in jail."

Soraya sighed, sitting on a leather chest with a cover of golden Arab designs. From inside the chest hung the sleeve of a mauve silk seroual.

"No prison would be strong enough to stop them escaping and venting the hatred they feel for me. No, great King! I am going back to my family in Salamanca, and you will see me no more. Then peace will return to your home."

"I will have them whipped until they bleed!" bellowed the king.

"That wouldn't do any good," said Soraya. A tear, blue with khol, ran down her cheek. She turned away with the poise of great nobility. The movement dispersed a fragrance of sandalwood. The king closed his burning eyes and felt completely shattered.

"I will do whatever you want, Soraya. I will give up my religion, my ancestors, my home and family, my country. Everything! We will go to Mauritania. With my personal wealth, we will have the means to live in luxury for years."

Soraya burst into tears and collapsed on the floor, her head on the gilded chest cover. Her rumpled hair fell in a dark wave down her back. Her golden skin showed through the white zihara.

"Yes, Soraya, anything you want!"

"Anything, great King? Truly anything?"

She slowly rose to her feet and came toward him.

"My eternity for you, Soraya!"

She half closed her eyes. Her voice took on a hard tone. "I don't ask for that much. Just understand this: As long as your sons are alive, you will see me no more."

Moulay Hassan reeled away. With a shaky hand, he adjusted his turban, which had slipped over his left ear, and stepped back with a panic-stricken look. Then he disappeared without a word.

Singing, Soraya took the decorated cover off the chest, and a slave helped her to put her clothes back in the wardrobe.

※

Ferdinand arrived in Cordova with a wildly excited expression on his face. He ran to the queen in such haste that his spur made a hole in an expensive wooden table, and he became tangled up in the carpet. The queen frowned. Was it not unusual that his victory at Tajera should have left Ferdinand in this state?

Ferdinand placed himself in front of her, both hands on her worktable.

"Granada is ours," he said.

"What do you mean?"

"I tell you that it cannot be long before Granada surrenders. It is a certainty—Gonzales interrogated the Moors we captured at Tajera. They told us astonishing things. Revolution has just broken out in the kingdom. There are going to be two kings, father and son—Moulay Hassan and Boabdil. I hurried to you the moment I heard the news."

How good of Ferdinand! He seemed to scorn his wife's advice, but didn't hesitate to travel many miles at breakneck speed to bring her the latest news from the war in Granada. He fell into a chair, his arms dangling over the sides, and caught his breath.

It appeared that to please his favorite, a certain Soraya, the Moorish King had not stopped at condemning his sons to be beheaded. The old Queen Aisha, hearing the horrifying news, bribed one of her guards, had him take her to the chamber in the Alhambra where the executions were to take place, and reached there in time to save two of her sons, of whom Boabdil was one. She had fled with him to Gadix.

One day, while Moulay Hassan was engaged in combat in Loja, under siege by Ferdinand, Boabdil and Aicha covertly made their way back into Granada. There, they had the council depose the murderous king and appoint Boabdil to the throne in his place.

When Moulay Hassan returned to Granada, he found the gates closed against him. Boabdil sent him a message that from hence forward he was to be considered dethroned. Together with his favorite, and with his brother, Zagal, Moulay Hassan went away with his head bowed low.

"What did he do? Where did he go?" asked Isabella.

"His first concern was to secure the other great cities of the kingdom—Malaga, Almeria, Baza. From now on, Isabella, Granada is at war with itself."

Isabella didn't completely share Ferdinand's optimism.

"They will become more united in the face of danger. They won't worry about things that divide them when it's a question of defending their kingdom. Islam will become as one when threatened by our armies. You seem to forget that they put their faith and their patriotism above all their quarrels.

"War against Granada is inevitable, Ferdinand, and it will be long and terrible. The Moors will hold on the mountains, to which they have given Arabic names, to the plains they have made fertile, to the steppes where they raise their horses. They will oppose us every step of the way, and at each of those steps Spain will shed a little more of its blood. How many men did you lose at Loja, Ferdinand?"

Ferdinand clenched his teeth and made no reply. Isabella hadn't expected an answer to her rhetorical question. In the hells of Loja, the *infiernos*, as they called them in the country, he had seen hundreds of men perish. That fortress held a fascination for him; if he managed to take it, the *vega* of Granada would be open to him, and he would make camp under the walls of the Alhambra. But Loja was strongly defended.

Los infiernos. A country of stone and fire. Ferdinand had launched an attack only on the Alcazaba; it had been so murderous that he had not followed through. The memory of Loja was lodged within him like a bolt from a crossbow. But he had not given up. One day he would come back to this town with a great army. On that day, all Islam would be shaken.

Ferdinand left for a new campaign in the southern territories, and Isabella returned to her state papers.

Her only real joy was being with her children—Elisabeth, Juan, and Juana. She did not see them very often, and even then not for as long as she would have liked. But on each occasion she marveled to see how they were growing, how the flame of youth was burning ever brighter in them, and it seemed as though she had left them for months.

At times she told herself that she was not a real mother to them. Once, she went into the room where a maidservant was washing the

dust off them, after they had ridden far along the banks of the
Guadalquivir. Isabella was startled; she didn't recognize her own
children. How long had it been since she last saw them in their
naked innocence? She couldn't recall the little brown mark on
Juana's hip; she had forgotten the scar where Juan had hurt his
knee; and surprise mingled with guilt when she noticed that
Elisabeth was becoming a woman.

From that time on, her heart was not quite so fully in her work.
She would suddenly leave her work room, seized by a desire to see
her children again, to hold them in her arms. Such unplanned
displays of maternal feelings first surprised and then amused them,
and Isabella was herself amused.

"Mother," said Isabel, "when you come to spend some time
with us, you seem to become ten years younger. Please come and
see us often. Don't just rely on what the servant tells you about us.
You are the best mother there could possibly be, but you do not
spend enough time with us."

"My child . . ." Isabella whispered.

She caressed the princess's chestnut hair, and took the two
younger ones in her arms. Then she sat on the floor to join in Juan's
games, helping him set up his wooden soldiers, ready for their next
battle. But gradually the sight of the toy warriors faded, and it was
other soldiers, other armies, that she could see on the move.

She rose reluctantly, kissed the princesses and the prince, and
promised to come to see them in their room more often.

Once she happened to go into their room while it was still dark,
just before dawn. She leaned over their beds, but sleep separated
them from her like a veil, and she felt herself to be a stranger in
their lives.

Let this war come to an end, the queen prayed to herself. Let me
become the mother they don't have. the mother they have never
had.

Let this war come to an end . . . she felt that Ferdinand was
drawing away from her as well. She could read her failure in the
faces of his mistresses when she came across them in corridors or
at court gatherings. She knew that for the king they were an
essential part of a day's riding or a day's fighting.

Am I going to throw away my whole life in the attempt to make my reign successful? Isabella asked the question of herself. Let this war come to an end. . . .

❧

Zagal, brother and ally of the old King Moulay Hassan, scored a victory over the Christians, who were attacking Malaga. This news not only caused consternation in the Spanish Court; it also aroused the young rebel King Boabdil's jealousy.

The Little King, *el Rey Chico*, called together his Council of Elders. In front of this assembly of white beards and jeweled turbans, he declared that he, too, wanted a victory over Isabella and Ferdinand.

The sound of Boabdil's war drums reached Lucena's lookouts like noisy heralds of an impending cataclysm. It was as if the whole mountain was talking. It started quietly, as the gentle noise of a fast-running river. Then louder, and the valley of Lucena soon resounded to a muffled mumbling. Finally it was a deafening thunder that echoed and re-echoed endlessly.

When the first white *jellabas* appeared below Granada's green banners, there was real panic in the fortress. The Governor, Fernandez de Cordova, was a man of strong will: He was capable of inspiring the very stones with courage and fighting spirit. A courier had already left for Cabra, a small fort a few miles away in the mountains, where a substantial Castilian force lay in reserve. They had been equipped with artillery, purposely to terrify Boabdil's men.

While awaiting the reinforcements from Cabra, Fernandez couldn't overcome his desire to meet the *Rey Chico*. He asked for and received permission for such a meeting, and went unarmed into the Moorish camp, early in a morning busy with the comings and goings of men and horses.

The King's *mazall*, the lavish royal tent, was surrounded by athletic-looking Sudanese dressed in immaculate *jellaba* that emphasized the darkness of their skin. They opened their great ash-wood *harbas*, ornamented with many colored ribbons, to let the governor through.

In the *mazall* the heat was stifling. The fragrance of sandalwood rose from a small silver perfume-burner mounted on a tripod. The sides of the tent were festooned with helmets and their attachments of chain mail, with bucklers, with darakas, great round shields of damascene leather bearing a prominent boss, with *alfanges*, with scimitars in costly scabbards, with bows fashioned from antlers, and with wide, gold-studded belts.

The *mazall* was vast, and Boabdil was at the far end, sitting on an enormous sofa. Fernandez hardly noticed the eunuchs, the chiefs, the wives, who all bowed as he passed them. His feet trod on precious carpets the color of clay and old wine.

"Health be with you," said Boabdil, bowing. "May your day be happy."

Fernandez performed creditably during the preliminary rituals, which gave him the time to observe Boabdil. He had thought to find in his opponent a man of small stature, and he smiled when he realized that the name "Little King" referred not to Boabdil's height, but to his age. He appeared to be about fifteen years old, and still had a child's face, on which authority had not yet set its stamp.

"You will find here my family and my household," the Little King went on, formally.

"I need nothing more than your company," Fernandez replied, with the same formality.

These Abencerages were a race of great beauty. Noble, powerful, cat-like. Boabdil's wide green eyes, lids lightly powdered, rested briefly on Fernandez, but the governor guessed that he was concentrating on reading his intentions under his mask of politeness. For his part, Fernandez's gaze never left the young king's face. He read in it an oriental fatalism, a well hidden distrustfulness, tempered by a strong will. Other than his stature— Boabdil's height was above average—the young king was as Fernandez had imagined him to be. He would have liked to have seen him smile; Boabdil had the sort of personality that could be completely transformed by a smile. But during the conversation, Boabdil maintained a serious expression.

Fernandez suggested that it would be well for the king to think hard before attacking a fortress such as Lucena, which was stronger

than it appeared. Moreover, the Catholic Monarchs were less
worried about losing it than they were concerned with destroying
Moulay Hassan and Zagal. Boabdil's eyes narrowed at the sound of
those hated names. It was even possible that peace proposals from
the two rulers might soon reach the king of Granada. Their
Highnesses were preparing a brutal revenge against the two
conspirators of Malaga.

Boabdil listened to him without interruption, and promised to
examine most carefully the matter he had brought up. Fernandez
felt a burden of anxiety lifted from his shoulders—Cabra would be
with him in two days . . .

They drank mint tea served by a very black, very fat matron.
Under his goatskin jacket, sweat was pouring from Fernandez. He
was amazed to observe that, beneath his white *jellaba* with gold
facings, Boabdil's skin was clean and dry.

The Count of Cabra arrived even earlier than the governor had
expected. The Moorish lookouts perched on a ruined atalaya gave
loud cries to warn of the arrival of the Castilians.

Fernandez looked around for the Little King. He saw him
coming toward the battlements on a small Spanish horse to observe
the citadel, hand shading his eyes. He stayed motionless for a
moment, deaf to the threats shouted by the foot-soldiers assembled
on the covered way, oblivious of the arrows flying around him.
When trumpets announced the rallying of the Granadan army, he
reluctantly turned his horse and galloped away to take his position
behind the vanguard of his troops.

Not a moment too soon. A troop of Cabra's cavalry was pouring
out from the town walls.

"We cannot pursue them," said Cabra, mopping his brow. "In
the mountains, they always hold the initiative."

Fernandez pointed to the river, now in full spate following a
storm that had swept over the mountaintops that morning.

"You're not taking these floods into account," said the
governor. "At this stage, they have to get their infantry across. As
soon as they reach the other bank, we will attack. Don Alfonso
d'Aguila's cavalry will swoop down on them like an avalanche,

Cabra! During this time, we will press the Moorish cavalry against the torrent."

The small Castilian army left Lucena at a feverish pace, and arrived in sight of Boabdil's troops just as nearly all the Moorish infantry had crossed to the far right. They attacked at once.

Fernandez did not let Boabdil out of his sight. He saw him jump on his spirited Andalusian horse, *alfange* in hand, trying to restore some order to the appalling panic that had seized his fragmented army. Fernandez vowed to himself to take the king of Granada alive. His delicate skin, his air of pride fascinated him. It seemed to him like having a beautiful wild animal with a fabulous coat in the line of sight of his crossbow. He would offer that coat to the king and queen.

Once he saw him surrounded with a circle of Castilian lances, then a cloud of dust hid him from view. When a gust of wind cleared away the dust, Boabdil had disappeared, and Fernandez felt so disappointed that he started swearing like a heretic. He spurred his horse, and positioned himself on a rocky outcrop. He knew that Boabdil had not been killed. If the Little King had taken flight, he wouldn't hesitate to go after him, as far as Loja if need be.

The battle came to an end when the peak of a mountain hid the sun. A few Moorish cavalry and infantry were scattered over the mountain—the Governor did not try to follow them. Groups of black guards were still fighting; they would go on to the last man.

Fernandez came down from his vantage point, and questioned the Moorish prisoners. Nobody knew where the king might be. The interrogation completed, he sat down on the ground, head between his bent knees, when he heard calls. Quickly he jumped back on his feet and caught sight of a group of Cabra's cavalry holding a Moorish soldier at bay, whose white *jellaba* could be seen through his horse's legs.

He leapt to the scene, pushed his way through the cavalry, and recognized Boabdil. The Little King was leaning back against a hole surrounded by bushes where he had been hiding, still defending himself, weapon in hand. Fernandez whispered, "God be praised!"

"Boabdil," called the governor, "it is useless to resist. Surrender. We will treat you as a friend."

"Liar! Son of a liar! Coward! Son of a coward!" yelled the Little King. "One day, I'm going to have your teeth ripped out!"

Fernandez had the Little King locked up in Lucena Castle, which from then on became known as The Castle of Courage. Occasionally he would open the judas hole, and for minutes at a time, watch him dream, eat, sleep. One day he even saw him cry, and the old warrior felt rather remorseful.

He kept him locked up for a few days more, waiting for King Ferdinand's reply. When he saw the Little King saddled on a mule, hands tied behind his back, he felt the sadness of a hunter from whom has been taken away a quarry pursued since childhood.

The decision to free Boabdil came like a bolt from the blue.

It was Isabella's idea. At first it took Ferdinand by surprise, but he came around to the view that the proposal, taking everything into account, was more than reasonable: It was inspired.

"Let the Little King of Granada go free," said Isabella, "and the war between his supporters and those of Moulay Hassan and his ally, Zagal, will grow much fiercer. I agree that we will be giving the Moors of Granada a wonderful present . . . but it is a present that will be fatal for them. Then, to avoid a subsequent alliance between those two opposing factions, all we need do is to get the *Rey Chico* to sign a peace treaty. He is a man of his word, and will honor it."

"As far as the treaty is concerned," said Ferdinand, "it is I who will lay down the conditions. They will be tough."

"Be careful! Boabdil is proud and arrogant . . ."

To the great surprise of the king and queen, Boabdil read the terms of the treaty without batting an eyelid, signed it with a steady hand, and bowed to those whom he had come to regard more as hosts than jailers. Ferdinand slowly rolled up the parchment scroll and handed it to his private secretary, Juan de Soria, who took it away. The king could not hide his amazement any longer.

"To be quite frank," he said, "I thought you would have reviewed each article, point by point. Particularly the one about the meeting of the General Staffs."

"To be equally frank," Boabdil replied, "I would have accepted even if the conditions had been stricter."

Ferdinand bit his lip. Was Boabdil as disarmingly naive as he appeared, or was he just pretending to be, the better to outwit his opponent? Ferdinand needed to find out.

"I imagine," he said, "that as soon as you get back to Granada you will once more take up the sword against your father and your uncle?"

Lines of cruelty creased the Little King's small dark face. His left hand gripped the handle of the gold-encrusted dagger, which was slipped into the wide green belt holding in the waist of his flowing *jellaba*.

"All my life, I had never encountered hatred." His voice was heavy. "Then it hit me so brutally that it is branded on my heart. A whole eternity of kindness could not remove those marks."

One day, after much hesitation, he told Isabella the story of the terrible night that made him revolt against his father. He had seen his brothers beheaded, one by one, in a little room in the Alhambra. The muscular black executioner exuded great drops of sweat, as much from fear as from the heat. The severed heads rolled into a bowl, and the blood flowed down channels between the flagstones to the feet of the stone lions on guard around a little pool.

While this was taking place, festive music could be heard coming from the Generalife. The hill was aglow with a myriad lamps. The last two of Moulay Hassan's sons, Boabdil·and his younger brother, were about to be executed, when a group of rebels led by the queen burst into the Courtyard of the Lions. Boabdil followed his mother out to where horses were waiting for them. They took the road to Gadix at full gallop.

"We will help you," said Ferdinand.

Boabdil slowly lifted his head, and stared intently at the King of Spain. "You will help me, you say? You will help me fight my enemies?"

"Would you agree to let us?"

"What reason would I have to refuse? Do I have any choice?"

Ferdinand hid a smile with his hand. Beyond any doubt, Boabdil's naiveté was extreme. He stole a glance at Isabella, who averted her eyes. Deep inside, she wanted to cry out, "Wretched Boabdil! Can you not see the traps being set for you? With Moulay Hassan and Zagal crushed, what chance would you have against our armies?"

She experienced strangely mixed feelings of pity and wicked pleasure. Ferdinand was right when he announced that Granada could be thought of as vanquished from the moment the revolution broke out. Isabella imagined herself again at the top of the brick keep at Medina del Campo, facing the chalky expanse of the *meseta*, while her brother wallowed in a feigned deathbed scene. At that moment she had felt that there was no better reason for living than to conquer the kingdom of Granada. The tales of her old *duenna*, dona Albonza, had given her a taste for its warm fruits . . . and for blood.

Hardly had she regained her composure when an astonishing thing happened. Casting all reserve to the wind, the *Rey Chico* put one knee on the ground, kissed the hem first of her robe and then of Ferdinand's, and stood up again, his face beaming and overwhelmed with gratitude.

"Thank you! Thank you!" he stammered. He stepped back a few paces, and bowed. "If you will excuse me," he said, "I must withdraw. It is time for prayer."

Isabella watched him closely as he left. Every day at the same hour, accompanied only by two guards, he went to the middle of the ruins of Medina-Az-Zahara. Here, in great deserted rooms inhabited only by reptiles and wild birds, among thousands of pink Tunisian marble columns, he chose a spot where he would lay out his prayer mat.

Ferdinand patted her thigh and burst out laughing.

"What did I tell you? You could strip the *jellaba* from his back, and he would still say 'thank you.'"

"While we're on the subject," said Isabella, moving closer to her husband, "Fernandez came back this morning."

"The Governor of Lucena? What does he want now?" grumbled Ferdinand.

"He asked to see Boabdil, as usual."

"And you agreed?"

"I told him that this would be the last time, that it would be pointless for him to come back again. Boabdil is not a phenomenon. Fernandez looked very unhappy. He begged me to include him in the escort that will take the Little King to the gates of Granada. I agreed."

Isabella could not get out of her mind the expression on the face of the old soldier as they went from the upper level of the cloister, where he had observed Boabdil for several minutes. A face of leather. An old wound on his cheek, standing out in sharp contrast to the weather-beaten skin, seemed ready to start bleeding again.

⚜

The *Rey Chico* had misjudged his people's welcome. The cheering that greeted his entry into Granada deteriorated into cries of rebellion after he revealed to his council and to the old queen the conditions of the Catholic Monarchs' peace treaty.

He did his utmost to convince the council and the people of the good and increasingly effective intentions of Isabella and Ferdinand. But Zagal chose this moment to attack, and the impact of that blow turned against the king even those who had still believed in him. Zagal had not been a traitor, they said. Zagal alone had fought against the infidel. Zagal carried aloft the green banner of the Prophet. And Boabdil waited.

At last he had to flee from Granada and seek refuge in Almeria. From the top of the castle's red walls, he turned his gaze seaward. Through the mists, he thought he could see the African coast.

Instead of Boabdil, it was Zagal who was now in power in Granada. Every evening, he would surround himself with his favorites and treat himself to the spectacle of a few beheadings. There was no longer any mention of Moulay Hassan. The old king, more enamored than ever of Soraya, the beautiful Christian girl,

A relief of Boabdil's surrender at Granada Royal Chapel. The fall of Granada, combined with Ferdinand and Isabella's marriage in 1469, made Spain a unified kingdom.

Granada's Muslims sally forth in an attempt to break the siege of their castle, in a typical action in the last century of the Reconquista. *By astutely exploiting internecine strife among the Granada nobility, King Ferdinand of Castile gradually eroded Muslim power.*

Returning to the Alhambra after his capitulation, Boabdil broods over his fateful decision, which would have grave consequences for Spain's Muslim and Jewish populations.

prayed to Allah to be allowed to die in peace, basking in the light of his Morning Star.

"Everybody has abandoned me," Boabdil mused. "My subjects, my friends. Ferdinand and Isabella are mocking me. Where are the troops they promised? One day I will leave this ungrateful land behind me, and set off for Africa."

The old queen was always yapping at his heels.

"A child! You're nothing but a child! Act, instead of just dreaming! If Zagal were to suddenly appear, you wouldn't know how to defend yourself. That man is a snake. Poison runs from his nose."

Boabdil shrugged and looked at his misty Africa.

"Zagal will bite off much more than he can chew." This was his only hope. In Granada, they were beginning to grow restive about Zagal's cruelty, and against Moulay Hassan's senility.

Ferdinand finally arrived after Boabdil had given up waiting for him. He descended on Malaga with a powerful army. The dust of June was raised in clouds by the wheels of his cannon as they rolled along.

All summer long, Ferdinand fought on the frontiers of Granada. Towns fell, garrisons capitulated. A few artillery rounds would knock down the brick castle keeps, tear apart the defensive earthworks, and then *arquebus* volleys would throw the fortresses into a state of panic. The dust of powdery clay raised by the guns was a torture for the Christian king. Every evening when he got back into his tent, exhausted by the heat and by the noise of gunfire, he found clay dust even in his ears and armpits.

Using these tactics, he took many towns, and imagined them as a bouquet he would present to his queen at the end of the summer.

"And Boabdil?" asked the queen.

"I didn't see him. He's probably still in Almeria with his mother. It's possible, however, that I took some towns from him without his being aware of it . . . In the spring, I will take Malaga."

"In the spring, " said Boabdil, " I will retake Malaga."

"And how do you think you are going to do that?" yelped old Queen Aicha. "You can't even depend on your own guard of Sudanese *rakkas*."

"I will retake Granada without an army."

"You must have learned how to get drunk when you were with the Christians."

"I am not drunk, Mother, I'm in full possession of my senses."

"And you are going back to Granada next spring! Good! Good! But try to make up your mind before King Ferdinand makes a move. It is said that he intends to besiege Almeria with fifty thousand men. Maximilian, Duke of Austria, would dispatch a fleet to blockade the town from the sea."

"The sea . . ." Boabdil dreamily repeated.

"Are you paying attention to what I'm telling you? What are you always looking at in the distance?"

"Africa . . ."

The Little King disguised himself and a few supporters as merchants, and without too much difficulty managed to enter Granada.

They hid themselves in the densely populated maze of the Albaicin, in the home of one of his loyal followers. After prayers each morning, he would turn his gaze to the square tower of the Alhambra, where his uncle was living. Then he would take up the bridle of his small donkey and go around all the streets of the Albaicin to recruit supporters from among the town notables, officers, and simple men in the street.

He risked his life ten times a day, but at the end of a few weeks, he had succeeded: The whole of the Albaicin acknowledged him and rallied to his cause.

Zagal could not take this without retaliating; he attacked. The Albaicin endured a terrible time. Ferdinand's intervention added to the confusion. He had cleverly calculated the scale of the reinforcements he sent to Boabdil—not too many, not too few. Too many, and it would hasten the end of a civil war that was helping to further his own plans; too few, and there would not be enough to stop Zagal triumphing over his rival.

After forty days of street fighting, news came through that caused consternation in Granada: the Catholic Monarchs were marching on Malaga with fifty thousand men and powerful artillery support. Velez, a town near Malaga, was already under fire from their guns.

On the evening of that same day, Boabdil received envoys sent by his uncle. Zagal proposed a truce, on the basis that it would be advisable for all Islamic forces to make common cause against the Christian danger.

"A truce!" exploded Boabdil. "Agree to a truce that this cruel traitor would break at the first opportunity? Never. There will only be one truce between us—and it will be signed either with his blood or with mine."

So Zagal left the city without Boabdil and headed for Malaga. He took up position in the mountains that led to the port, and waited for the Christian army. He had foreseen a rushing stream, but what came along was a mighty river. He was forced to break off the engagement, and pull back his troops to Granada.

When they arrived at the gates of the city, they found themselves locked out.

Dusk brought its own perspective to the mountains surrounding Malaga. It seemed to bring them into sharper relief, outlining each ridge in blue. A whole multitude of mountains seemed to be reborn each evening, created on the vast empty sierra facing the sea.

Ferdinand and Isabella loved this peaceful hour, which coincided with the Spanish evening meal and the Muslims' prayers. The *muezzins'* flute-like voices echoed from one minaret to another, and thousands of men bowed to the east.

Ferdinand had said, "In the spring, I will take Malaga." Malaga was still holding out. Once, a group of defenders loyal to Boabdil came to give him some *atalaya* and a few acres of the mountainous land surrounding them. On another occasion, the Catholic

Monarchs saw groups of Moors coming toward them, making signs of peace and proclaiming the name of Boabdil.

"Treat them as allies, as if they were true Castilian subjects," the Little King had requested. Isabella and Ferdinand let them keep their riches, exacted no tribute from them, made them suffer no humiliation. They simply gave them into the clever, slim hands of the Dominican friar Ximenes Cisneros, who taught them to worship one God only: that of the Christians.

Ferdinand and Isabella enjoyed these times when Malaga gave the appearance of surrendering to them.

Ferdinand finished his solitary dinner, and was standing at the entrance to his tent, his back to the red sky. Isabella came to join him, and before retiring for the night they rode around the line of battlements and the banks of the Guadalmedina, where naked children were swimming. As soon as they noticed them, the children scrambled out of the muddy, stinking water, black and shiny as fish, and shouted in broken Castilian, "Money! One *maravedis*, kind sir, kind madam!"

Isabella and Ferdinand always carried their leather *barjoletas*, full of small change, which they scattered in the dust for these urchins.

Riding at anchor a few cables offshore, the Duke of Austria's *caravels* moved gently with the swell. More were cruising a few miles from the port, so far out to sea that it was hard to discern their billowing sails. Had this fleet not arrived at the very moment it was most needed, the monarchs would have despaired of ever bringing the Malaga siege to a successful conclusion.

It was the most important and richest town in the whole of Granada. All the merchants of Africa and the Orient had warehouses there. From its gates set out the mule trains that carried supplies to the wealthiest towns and the humblest villages in the kingdom. Once Malaga was taken, Granada would wither away like a flower deprived of water.

They loved this time of the evening because they were able to be free from the elaborately dressed courtiers who were close on their heels throughout the day. They were able, too, to use words other than those they spoke all day long in conversing, he with his officers, she with her stewards; rough-and-ready words, like that coarse-milled flour handcarried from the mills to bake bread in camp, bread of which they quickly grew tired. Now they had other things to talk about, in another tone of voice, with other words.

"I worry about Juana's health," said Isabella. "Eight years old, but she looks like six. All food repels her. I have to threaten to get her to swallow some white chicken meat, and if she's punished she has a fainting fit."

"This will pass," Ferdinand answered. "She should breathe less incense, and more fresh air. When I think that she has never mounted the foal that I gave her for her seventh birthday . . ."

By the grace of God, Isabel, the oldest, who was nearly seventeen, was in better health—it was never necessary to chastise her for not eating. She was a tall girl, slim and intelligent. People though that she might marry the prince of Portugal.

Little Juan, one year older than Juana, was, like his younger sister, also in delicate health. He rode a horse most gracefully, but was reluctant to take part in military activities. He was more often to be found in the forest, roaming endlessly and listening to the blackbirds, than practicing cavalry maneuvers. Ferdinand was not very fond of him, thinking him effeminate. There again, the young prince liked nothing more than the company of the ladies of the court, and he was always to be found with Beatrix de Bobadilla or Leonor de Soto.

How could the king's children possibly be of robust constitution? During her pregnancies, the queen did not call a halt to her travels on horseback between Castile and Aragon, and gave birth wherever she happened to find herself. Isabella was aware of the error of her ways, and promised herself that she would correct them.

But was it perhaps too late? Now thirty-six years old, she had virtually given up the idea of giving more children to Spain. The monarchs' hopes were centered on Juan, but he did not show great promise of being able to carry the future royal burden.

Riding in the warm air of twilight, they went on to less gloomy subjects.

It was a frequent occurrence for foreign military officers to come into the Malaga camp. For Isabella and Ferdinand, they were a wonderful source of interesting and often light-hearted conversation.

These men, attracted by the crusading spirit that was the main feature of the Granadan war, were the successors of French, English, and German lords who had rushed off to the Orient centuries before. Like their forebears, what they wanted out of this adventure was not so much a place in Paradise as earthly rewards, and also to quench their insatiable thirst for action.

"Did you notice," said Isabella, "the look on the face of the Count of Cabra when he saw Lord Scales come into the camp with his five horses, his equerries, and his whole retinue?"

"If what I hear is correct," replied Ferdinand, "Lord Scales—in spite of his small hats, his effeminate clothes, his ceremonial shield—is a remarkable warrior."

There was one individual in particular who always put them in a good mood. In 1485, two years earlier, he had come to visit them in Cordova. He was an unusual man, enigmatic and fascinating. He spoke Castilian with a Portuguese accent, and said that he came originally from Genoa, where his father was a textile merchant. His name was Christopher Columbus.

This man was not dreaming of a crusade against Granada. He wanted *caravels* and money, convinced that he could reach the Indies by the westerly route. King Joao of Portugal had dismissed him from his court, so Columbus had taken refuge in La Rabida, a Franciscan monastery situated in the Palos mountains, in the far south of Spain.

This little man—tenacious, voluble, enterprising beyond belief—would not countenance the failure of his mission. He had succeeded in convincing the Duke of Medina-Sidonia, who swore by him and helped him financially. Columbus had begged the duke to present him to the Catholic Monarchs, and the duke had complied.

"This man is crazy," said Ferdinand. "Reach the Indies by heading west? Who would dare to risk himself and a fleet in such a venture?"

"I can't deny that," the queen acknowledged. "But how assured he sounds when he talks about the Island of the Seven Cities, and of those West Indies that are crammed with gold, and where the men go around naked."

"How does he know about it?"

Columbus didn't try hard to prove—or at least, he pretended not to—the existence of these fabled islands on the route to the Indies. He always arrived with a chest from which he took charts drawn up by his brother, whom he had left in Portugal.

"I ask that your Majesties listen to me carefully," he would begin.

Ferdinand would listen for a few minutes, and then send the inveterate beggar away. Isabella, on the other hand, never tired of hearing him. Once, she rather thoughtlessly said to him:

"Columbus, you are Spain's greatest poet."

Columbus had folded up his charts and sketches in silence, jaws clamped shut.

"I beg your Majesty's pardon. If she heard a poet speaking with my voice, I would rather remain silent."

"Stay, I beg you, and pardon me if I have offended you. You were saying that at sixty degrees west . . ."

Columbus went on with his explanations, quite tireless. On those evenings, Isabella would dream of great forests where parrots flitted about. The Island of the Seven Cities . . . the West Indies . . .

One day in July, Isabella and Ferdinand stopped their evening rides around Malaga. The Duke of Medina-Sidonia had just arrived with substantial reinforcements. The siege was about to enter a decisive phase.

Also, Boabdil had written to Ferdinand: "Capture the three main towns of my uncle Zagal—Baza, Gadix, and Ameria. Save me from this monster. Thirty days after the last of these three towns has fallen, I will hand over Granada to you. On the one condition that you will let me peacefully spend the rest of my days in a town of my choice."

Then one morning all the Spanish cannons roared simultaneously. The Governor of Malaga, Ahmed-Zeli, realized that these would be the final days of his town under the green flag.

Malaga resisted with flagging energy as they were demolished by Spanish cannonballs, and finally surrendered.

"Be lenient with my fellow Muslims," Boabdil had asked. Ferdinand was ferocious. He had lost many men and his money-chests were empty. He ordered a great massacre of Jews and Muslims, confiscated their wealth, and sold the rest of the population as slaves.

"The war in Granada is over," said Ferdinand. But Zagal's three towns had still to be taken.

7

Castle in the Mountains

Isabella's small group stopped at a simple *venta* between Madrid and Segovia.

There were only a few pilgrims gathered around the fire, which had been lit as the evening shadows darkened. The queen took the best room; she had her chests brought in, and hung Borgia's crucifix and the little Jewish lamp at the bedhead. As soon as she was alone, she knelt on the bare floor and began to pray, both hands on her face.

It was nearly evening by the time she had finished. She used her sleeve to wipe some dust from the window pane—and her heart beat faster. In the gray October twilight, slanting rain and snow swept across the high forests of Guadarrama.

After telling Beatrix de Baladilla in confidence that she would be away from her room, she made her way stealthily to the courtyard. Certain that no one in her retinue had seen her, she went into the stable and asked a groom to prepare once more the mare he had only just unsaddled. She greased his palm with silver to keep his lips sealed, and departed through the deserted orchard that farther on led to the Madrid main road.

On the main road, she galloped steadily. But when she got onto the narrow track that wound through great rock outcrops, the mare had to be more careful. She knew the way. One spring day a few months earlier she had taken it, and found herself close to David Ezra's haven. She had turned back her horse.

This time, she would go the whole way. She had to see David. A force more powerful that herself impelled her to do so. Waking or sleeping, she could always see his face, as through a mist.

When signing a warrant condemning a convert to prison or to the stake, she could see David's face full of suffering. Her hand would tremble, but she could not find the courage to stop the quill pen as it hovered over the parchment. Torquemada, de Ximenes, Cardinal Mendoza, Ferdinand . . . with their gazes fixed unwaveringly on her, the slightest hesitation would have been a betrayal.

Mendoza knew. It was Mendoza who had said to her one day, "You must fight the memory of David Ezra. Crush the very thought of him."

Isabella had thought that she could obliterate his memory by joining in the battle against what the cardinal called the 'Jewish heresy.' But she couldn't hate David. However, the cardinal believed she had the intention of destroying him, an intention that in truth she could never possess.

By now, Isabella was in the middle of the forest. The first screened out the last of the daylight. The mare was jumpy; she balked sharply at movements in the bushes, at the patches of mist wreathed around the trees.

When she saw the high walls of the castillo glowing faintly against the jet black sky, Isabella breathed more easily. The first snowflakes fell as she crossed the threshold.

An old manservant met the queen and guided her to the main room. David had just returned from wolf hunting. He seemed to be asleep in a high-backed armchair, legs outstretched toward the flames crackling in the hearth.

While the servant whispered in David's ear, Isabella stopped in the doorway, awed by the austerity of the place. Firelight pierced the shadows enough for her to make out bare walls rising to merge awkwardly with the vaulted ceiling. Here and there she saw bundles of softly gleaming barbarian lances, squat, gloomy furniture, ill-laid flagstones.

She shivered when David rose to come to her. Isabella didn't see his face, but sensed his agitation, for his voice shook when he said,

"You here? At this hour? And alone? You're very brave. My servants don't dare to venture into the forest after sunset."

He pushed back Isabella's headdress and kissed her on both cheeks, just as he had those times long ago when they came together again after many weeks of separation.

"We stopped at the *venta*," she said. "As your estate isn't very far, I felt that I could visit you without arousing suspicion. Are you glad?"

"More than you could possibly imagine." He added, his voice lower. "All the more because we won't be seeing each other for a long time. Perhaps never . . ."

"Never?" she echoed.

David took Isabella in his arms, led her close to the fire and, taking off his coat, sat her down by the hearth. He sat on the bare flagstones, legs bent beneath him. Even so, he was so tall that his head was level with her bosom.

She repeated, "Never?"

He put his big, dry hand on Isabella's and gazed at the fire in silence for a few moments. Then he said,

"I'll be leaving Guadarrama when spring comes, maybe never coming back. My brother will see to the running of the estate."

"Are you going to be married, David?"

He smiled weakly. "Yes, Isabella, I'm to be married. Married to misery, to suffering, to war. I know that the day is coming when the Holy Office will send its henchmen to arrest me, torture me, throw me in prison or burn me at the stake. So—I'd sooner leave. Many Jews have taken refuge with the Moors, and for the time being they don't need any sympathy. Others are hiding in the mountains and on the plains, determined to fight to defend themselves. These are the ones I'm going to help. My belongings, my life are theirs."

"Things could be easier for you if you wanted."

"I know. It would be enough to renounce my religion, ask to be baptized. But I can't pay that price. Cowardice is a widespread sickness, and many of my fellow Jews have the disease. Not I."

"You are Spanish more than Jewish, David."

He drew his hand away. "Are the two irreconcilable?"

"They are. Your destiny is to be Catholic . . ."

"'. . . and we will kill all heresies with iron and fire.'
Torquemada said that, or something very similar. You are a good
student, Isabella, and a great queen. Future centuries will pay
tribute to your memory. To plant Christ's banner in the belly of the
Jews—what a victory!" He lowered his head to his knees. "Why
did you come, Isabella?"

"To see you again. Because I love you, David."

"You're betraying Ferdinand, your religion, Spain itself."

"Do you think I don't know that? Do you think I don't suffer?
This love is my joy . . . and my shame. Don't destroy it, David.
Without it, what would be left of me?"

"You'd have your king, your country, your religion. And the
glory of being the great Catholic Queen."

"What would you do if you were me?"

"We are actors in the same drama, in different ways. We each
stand up for our people and our religion. But if I had been you,
Isabella, I would never have walked through that door!"

Isabella stood up quickly, and threw her cape around her
shoulders. "Good-bye then, David. Forgive me for having been so
greatly mistaken."

He forced the cape off, made her sit down again.

"We'll have dinner," he said. "Afterwards, I'll take you back
home."

They ate in silence, seated opposite each other, by the light of
rough tallow candles that gave off a pungent odor.

It was a frugal meal; water was the only drink. David got up
first and went to close the heavy wooden shutters. "It's snowing,"
he said.

Isabella closed her eyes. The small raised brazier that David
had positioned behind her warmed the nape of her neck.

"I must go," she said.

"Go whenever you wish. But if you'd like to stay the night . . ."

Isabella shook her head. She didn't want to run the risk of
anyone other than dona Beatrix discovering that she was away from
the *venta*. There was a risk, even though she had given instructions
that she was not be disturbed for any reason.

David seemed tense. He poked the fire briskly, sat down, then got up again to ask the maid to serve. When they were alone once more, the silence was unbearable.

Isabella hadn't yet made up her mind to leave; neither was she ready to accept that the old question brought up by their exchange of words must remain unanswered.

There were signals of expression she could send, gestures that she had practiced in her mind's eye as she had climbed the misty mountain trail. There were words she had silently rehearsed, but neither word nor gesture came forth. They remained dormant within her.

Stillness, silence. She was as still and silent as a statue. She let the minutes slip by as the snow fell.

"David, do you remember teaching me how to mount a horse— an unruly mare? Once she used every trick she knew to throw me, because a wasp had stung her ear. I let go the reins, you caught me in your arms, and we rolled down the bank. We stayed there for a moment, pressed together, not moving. The *meseta* smelled of flowers, of fire. . . ."

"Come and sit beside me," said David.

Isabella got up and slowly walked around the long olive-wood table. Passing a doorway half concealed by a thick yellow wool curtain, she glanced inside.

"My bedroom," he said. "You see how humble my abode is! No reception room, no drawing room. You want to go in?"

Before she had time to reply, he picked up a candlestick and led the way with its light. An iciness permeated the room. Great gusts of cold air blowing through the open window reminded them of the snow falling outside.

"Tomas isn't doing his job properly. He should have closed the window. So many things like that . . . he forgets. But I can't bring myself to dismiss him. He's old and sick—he wouldn't understand."

Together they leaned on the windowsill, one on each side of the slender stone mullion, and looked out on the night where the snow was beginning to settle on the thatched roofs of the out-buildings. A warm smell floated up from the sheepfold. The dogs barked at the wolves they imagined to be hiding in the fringes of the forest. The mountain sky was like a black triangle set against the ashen sky.

"Close the windows," said Isabella.

David's bedroom was even more austere than the dining room. Old furniture, old fabrics. The only decoration was a tapestry. It dated back to the early Trasatamares, and was lined with dark streaks.

Everything in this place spoke of austerity, even of poverty. David had sold the expensive houses he'd owned in the Jewish sections of Madrid, Segovia, and Toledo to help Jewish families plundered by the Inquisition. All he had left was this old *castillo*. Eventually, it would be his brother's. He would give to the Jews his only remaining possession: his life.

David had closed the window. He came back to Isabella, who was sitting under the bed's patched canopy. He knelt, rested his head on his lover's knees. He felt the warmth through the material of her dress.

"How simple everything seems now that we're alone," he said. "No problems. Why am I Jewish? Why are you Christian? Why am I on the side of the suffering, you on the side of the torturers? All these questions go away when we are alone together, when we want to think of nothing but ourselves. It's good to spend a few minutes on oneself, Isabella. My only moments of true peace are thanks to you. You are my rest, my sleep, the spice of my life. But soon I will have you no longer. I won't even have the certainty of seeing you ever again."

When he lifted his head, Isabella was crying. He shook himself like a big dog and started to laugh, as if everything he'd been saying was just a joke.

"Come on," he said. "You must get back to the inn now. It's possible that someone has realized you're not there—they could be looking for you everywhere. I'll ride with you. Come along . . ."

She pulled him to her, unlaced the top of the heavy silken bodice, and guided his lips over her firm warm flesh. His hands caressed her breasts, slid down to her loins, smooth and rounded as a marble column.

"What does it matter?" she breathed, uncaring of whether he heard. "What does it matter. David? I want to be with you tonight. Let me stay. Afterwards we will forget each other, but let me . . ."

He pushed her away roughly.

"No, Isabella! Do you really think that I could forget you after that? Do you think that I could bear being away from you? Tomorrow, I might have to fight against your soldiers—I wouldn't want my rage to be mingled with anger against your husband. . . ."

He hadn't finished speaking when Isabella ran from him. He caught up with her in the main room, already dressed in her coat.

"Good-bye!" She flung the word at him.

Just as she was about to lift the heavy tapestry hanging over the doorway, David's powerful hands grabbed her by the ankles. She lost her balance, and collapsed into his arms like a rag doll.

He carried her gently to the bed. She was aware of nothing except her overwhelming passion for David. As though she had lost her senses, possessed by an incredible power, she wrapped her whole body around his, grasping for him, giving herself totally and furiously to him. It was as if she was determined to merge her body with his.

David responded by unleashing all the passion that had been building in him for so many years. For a long, long while they clung together, two beings fused into one.

The first light of a dawn all white with snow crept in to caress their naked, exhausted, empty bodies. The fire had gone out. David was lying heavily on Isabella. She rubbed her eyes carefully, their lids heavy with sleep. Then David opened his eyes. She stopped him from saying anything by kissing him for one last time.

Indicating with one hand that he was not to move, she reluctantly began to dress . . . but without taking her eyes from him, as though he were a being from another world. David dared not move.

Stepping back from him, her gaze fixed on her lover, she moved toward the heavy door.

The door slammed behind her. He heard the click-clack of hurrying wooden heels. As he drew near her again in the courtyard, she was leaping into the saddle. Before slapping the reins on her horse's neck, she turned to him.

"You've hurt me deeply, humiliated me, David, and I'll never forgive you. But in one thing you've been right: for both of us it had to end, once and for all. That's all there is to be said."

"You can't go alone—that's absurd. Wait for me!"

He ran to the stables, quickly threw a saddle on his horse, secured it with swift, practiced movements, and leapt up. Isabella had gone.

"Isabella! Isabella!"

Isabella spurred her mount. She envisaged the trail as a narrow cutting through the forest. When she heard David's voice from afar, she wanted to reply, to wait for him. Instead, she urged the mare to an ever faster pace, though the animal was reluctant to go forward.

"Isabella! Isabella!"

It seemed to her that the whole mountain was calling her name, that a thousand voices were breathing it, that hands were reaching out across the trail to stop her. With bitter pleasure, she realized that David's voice was growing fainter, that it was weakening into a cry too feeble to raise the faintest echo.

It had stopped snowing. A fresh breeze blew off the slopes.

Lying in the straw, the groom was waiting for Isabella.

"Did anyone notice my absence?" she asked.

The groom shook his head. Isabella went back along the path through the orchard, found the stairs leading to her room, and collapsed on her bed. She fell asleep without undressing.

The crowd grew hourly around the acre of fenced marshy land on the banks of the Guadalquivir, just a few yards from the Triana bridge. A platform for the condemned had been set up, together with a grandstand covered with an enormous red canvas awning for members of the court and other notables. Four stakes had been erected on the river bank.

In 1480 the Inquisition was established. Executions were carried out in dramatic public gathering known as autosdafe—like the one in this picture.

It was apparent that by two in the afternoon all Seville would be here. The only people to be found at home would be old folk confined to their beds, women in labor, and tiny children.

A murmur of satisfaction arose from the crowd when the cathedral's great bell began to swing in the oppressive August heat. The procession had just started to move after the sermon of the Inquisitor General, Father Tomas Torquemada. He had arrived that morning, paler, thinner, more sickly than ever.

With him were the entourage of the Inquisition, and a personal bodyguard to protect him against attempts on his life. Such attacks were not infrequent; they were a reaction to his rigid, merciless morality and to the savagery of punishments meted out to heretics.

He had eaten his midday meal—a few lettuce leaves and a mouthful of water—with the queen. She had noticed that he would occasionally slide his hand into an inner pocket of his cassock where he kept a charm, supposedly a unicorn horn, as a safeguard against poison. So shocked had she been to see this lack of confidence on his part that she had been quite unable to carry on a conversation with him.

The disquiet that Isabella had felt during the Inquisitor General's sermon deepened into nervousness as the procession drew closer to the *quemadero*, the pyre where soon the Holy Inquisition would offer the heretics' mortal husks to the purifying flames.

Torquemada, with fire seeming to leap from his eyes, had earlier announced from his pulpit the names of the condemned. Isabella could remember only two: those of Samuel and David Ezra. Only the bones of the former, dead these many years, would be burned. As for David—still alive, she strongly believed—he would be burned only in effigy. This punishment in absentia had been ordered for the heretic, Jewish trouble-maker that he was, for openly taking up arms against the soldiers of Christ.

In the baking heat, walking in the slow, formal procession was becoming painful. Tomas de Torquemada's robe swept a path through the dust, a path that Isabella followed. The Archbishop of Seville, Monsignor Borgia, walked to her left, his heavy-set face bent forward, shiny with sweat. To her right, Mendoza, Cardinal of

Spain; he kept a surreptitious eye on the queen, taking note of her growing nervousness.

Mendoza was aware that she had signed the order against David Ezra in his absence, with the usual endorsement "as it appears," but he was less certain how sincere she had been.

"You will not know true peace," he had told the queen, "until you have extinguished the flame of remembrance of this man who has brought such turmoil to your reign. If you don't, serenity and freedom of spirit will not be yours."

Isabella would have found it even more difficult if Ferdinand had been present. She wanted to be alone for the task of expunging David's memory, of "killing him in herself," as the Primate put it.

Ferdinand had remained in Malaga. That very morning, the diarist Hernando de Pulgar had reported to Isabella that he was busily involved with Jews and Moors who had come to submit to him. These people were too wealthy, so the king had decided to eliminate the richest: he had them subjected to the torture of the "pointed reeds," assuring them a slow and awful death. His soldiers choreographed the spectacle he wanted.

Isabella was horrified, finding it difficult to believe the scribe's story. David in Malaga's main square. David pierced with reeds, bleeding on the cross from ten wounds, drop by gory drop. David despairingly holding death at bay with wild spasms.

"It's too dreadful, Pulgar. If I were there, the king would not have done such a thing. He would have acted in a truly royal manner. The Jews' gold is important to him, but so is the respect of his men."

Torquemada's robe now left no marks. Grass replaced dust as they entered the enclosure.

The Grand Inquisitor took his place, and gestured to his two assessors, Jean Guttierez de Chabes and Tristan de Medina, to sit beside him. The queen, Archbishop Borgia, and Cardinal Mendoza took the remaining seats.

This day, Torquemada was king. The queen could see nothing of him but his shriveled hand with its iron ring, resting on the arm of his chair. That dry hand rose, and the reading of the sentences began.

The Clerk of the Court first brought forward those who had been held in the "prison of mercy," charged with pardonable sins. They stood bareheaded on the platform and listened to the public reading of extracts from their trial proceedings. Each was dressed in a *mantela* of brown cloth, to which was fastened a big yellow sash, standing out in vivid contrast. On this sash was written the name of the accused and a list of his sins . . . the casting of spells, superstitious practices, refusal to be an informer, calling forth demons. Sentences read, they were given the cross and the Gospels to kiss before being dismissed.

The *auto-da-fe* continued its measured pace.

After the convicts from the mercy prisons came those from the jails of moderate severity. These establishments housed those violent and impulsive creatures who truly repented of their sins. The Clerk of the Court ended each sentence with "As it appears: I, the queen, I, the king."

One of them, a *zahori*, accused of magically divining hidden underground objects, had been the victim of an epileptic fit during his trial, interpreted by the Inquisition as a case of demonic possession. The trial had been halted for review. The court condemned him to a secret prison—no, not a prison, a torture chamber—until such time as he vomited up the bile of his sin on the wheel or the garrotte.

Isabella could scarcely support the sight of these ghosts who shuffled forward in line, unsteady, disoriented, blinking in the bright sun. The *mantela* seemed to crush them, and the grotesque miter with which they had been decked out kept falling over their eyes. They came from hell itself.

Shortly afterwards, they were publicly undressed. They were a grievous sight: bodies covered with bleeding wounds, limbs broken on the wheel, chests burned with red-hot pincers.

"How many are to be burned?" asked Archbishop Borgia, leaning on an assessor's shoulder.

"About two thousand—but two of them in their absence," replied the monk.

But two of them in their absence. David and his father. Isabella looked round to see David Ezra's effigy.

It was last in the line of condemned men, a ridiculous tattered dummy in no way resembling the young Jew's muscled and athletic body. The nightmarish mask was nothing like David's calm, fine, sensitive features.

Isabella was disgusted. Inwardly she struggled to eject from her brain the remembrance of David as she had last seen him. She fiercely fought against her own obsession with his final appealing cries . . . she heard them still echoing through the forest of Guadarrama that snowy dawn when they had parted.

She had hated him, had never forgiven him for the humiliation of being rejected when she had come to him full of love, ready to give that love to him for the first time—and almost certainly for the last.

Now she persuaded herself that hatred was still alive; but the persuasion was more of her head than her heart. Even if she could have been sure of the truth at the rational level, at the emotional level she would still have been troubled. She went deathly pale when she felt the cardinal's hand on hers.

"Courage, my child. God will help you through this trial. Wipe from your heart the real David. Let this mask be for you his eternal memory."

Isabella stiffened. All the lies she'd been guilty of recently were a dead weight on her soul. To obliterate David's memory, to erase the marks of the passion she had felt for him, she had sent these poor devils, guilty only of being Jewish and rich, to an awful death.

She knew that if she had refused to sign their death warrants it would not have saved them. But this, in her own eyes, did not absolve her of responsibility. Had she wanted these crimes? No. But she had approved of them. Her reluctance to sign, and her remorse after doing so, changed nothing.

"Do you recant?" cried the Clerk of the Court. Most of the condemned men renounced their Jewish heresy, which allowed them the single favor of being garroted before being consigned to the flames. Those who refused were tied to the stake, standing in the pile of sticks and logs.

The crowd had broken through the barriers and pressed close to the execution spot, silent and watchful. Firelighters busied themselves stroking the braziers. Children gathered around the Inquisition banner, caressing its heavy folds. The queen's distress grew.

A murmur could be heard from the throng as the royal guard forced them back to the barriers. At the same moment, the firelighters ignited the pyre. The victims still alive screamed hoarsely as the first flames licked their legs. Then nothing could be seen but smoke shot through with faint lights. And there was the smell—the disgusting smell that, although she held her breath, still forced its way into the queen's throat and nose. And the ceremony went on for hours and hours. At the end of this interminable day, Torquemada looked a little tired, but happy. Two thousand babies, children, women, men, of all ages, had been burned alive, "purified." As they said at the end, late in the evening, like an apotheose.

The figure representing David was carried like a battle flag to the last pyre, where it burned quickly with a clear bright flame. Samuel Ezra's bones were thrown into another fire, amid the prayers of monks carrying crosses and Gospels.

In the press of people, crying children and hemmed-in women, unable to move, some fainted, as the wind blew a cloud of smoke and smells over them.

"Are you finished?" asked the queen.

"Yes," replied Cardinal Mendoza.

She became aware that the prelate had not removed his hand from hers. A chill ran down her spine.

"Your Majesty, are you sure he's now dead? That he's nothing but cinders, with no power to live on in your thoughts? Are you sure? Are you sure? An answer please, Your Majesty."

"Let us leave," said the queen.

A large black cloud of smoke was floating over the town. It was very difficult to breathe. To purify the town of "this Jewish atmosphere," masses were celebrated for one day, nonstop, in all the churches.

⚜

She knew David was still alive. More than ever he was the champion of the hunted and tortured Jews. He was their only hope. He was a father to orphans, a son to those whose children had been snatched from them. He rode through wild nights from one mountain range to the next, slept on straw in the cowsheds of the miserable highland pueblos where Moors and Jews sought safety.

His only companions were the men to whom he had dedicated his life. That life was precious to him now that he had left remote Guadarrama to offer life itself as a gift to his people.

His greatest enemies were not Ferdinand's troops seeking his capture, but the fear and cowardice he could read in the faces of the merchants of Toledo, of Seville, of Cordova. In losing their gold they had lost their all. David despised gold. The yellow metal smuggled past the customs men burned his hands; he was not happy until it had been distributed among all his fellow Jews.

"You are the ones who are lost, not your gold," he told rich merchants. "Gold won't do you any good."

The Jews had to hand over to him all their money, down to the last penny hidden in the lining of their doublets. In return, he supplied them with weapons and a horse.

One day a Toledo rabbi asked him,

"The cause you stand for, my son, is a desperate one. Where do you find such courage?"

"In the very fact that it is desperate," replied David. "I fear nothing so much as hopes that slowly crumble away. They lead to renunciation of the cause, to desertion from it. We are at the bottom of a well. Our night can grow no darker. We are the living, fighting dead. We may have nothing to gain—but Ferdinand has everything to lose."

Even as he spoke, he was laughing in the face of death. He would imagine himself caught and thrown into a torture chamber, where his blood would spatter the inquisitors' documents like a red rain. Or ambushed and stabbed to death. Or killed by a traitor.

In truth, he didn't much care one way or the other what his end would be. The whole matter of his life and death was of little importance to him.

One morning, he handed his sword and belt to his friends for safekeeping and disguised himself as an *arrieros*. He loaded up a mule with bags of olives and onions, and headed for Seville. He had grown a beard, and in the ragged clothes of a mule-driver, he ran no risk of being recognized by the *alguazils*.

Once in the city, he mingled with the crowd and made for the *quemadero*, where an *auto-da-fe* was in progress. From his vantage point he could make out the inquisitors, the nobility, the high, and the mighty. The queen was seated behind the Inquisitor General, Tomas de Torquemada, whose tall figure partly hid her from view.

Teeth clenched, David Ezra witnessed his own sentencing and the enactment of his own execution. He almost gave himself away when his father's bones were thrown in handfuls on the fire. He swore to himself that never again would he be present at one of these ceremonies.

The sight of Isabella was shattering to him. He wondered if she would have signed his death warrant with so firm a hand if he had been not a free man, but behind the bars of an Inquisition jail. That aweful question would not leave him, and even woke him from sleep. But he vowed to keep a stout heart. Sooner or later they would meet again, he and the queen. When they did, he knew that he would be risking his life.

Sooner or later . . .

8

The Green River

Baza. Gadix. Almeria . . . Ferdinand reflected.

I have only to conquer these three towns held by Zagal and Granada will be ours. For seven months his troops had made no progress toward breaking into the first of them, and he was tired of trying to remain optimistic.

But one day in December 1489 envoys arrived from Zagal. The old lion had got wind of Boabdil's promise to surrender Granada when the Catholic Monarchs had taken his rivals' three strongholds. He had decided to play games with his nephew. Their quarrel had reached the limit, and he wanted now to have the last word.

His message to the monarchs was:

"I will hand over these three towns. In return, I ask little: recognition of my title of King after Boabdil has laid down his arms, and a pension of ten thousand ducats."

The King of Spain accepted his proposal. And so it was that one morning the old Muslim lord came in through the gates of the town and bowed before him.

"Sire," began Zagal. "I am keeping my promise. Here is my army. They will obey if I tell them that tomorrow they must fight against their comrades in arms, since they refuse to leave Boabdil's service."

In company with the Catholic Monarchs, Zagal set off for Granada. His banners mingled with those of Spain. It was a strange army. The main body of the Spanish troops were flanked by corps of *adjnah*, formidable light cavalry whose attacks had inflicted so many losses on the besiegers of Baza.

For a league behind them, in the mud and the dust, trailed an endless line of leathercovered wagons containing Zagal's treasures, his chattels, his clothes chests, and his slaves with their guards mounted on mules. There were litters with red and green velvet canopies sheltering wives and favorites guarded by gaudily dressed eunuchs, thoroughbred horses, and small high-spirited Andalusian steeds with Moorish saddles and gilded pommels.

In spite of the splendor he displayed at every opportunity, and in spite of the fiery spirit with which he attacked the fortresses, Zagal seemed to be worried. Isabella, who had brought Juan and Juana with her to join the king, noticed this, and ascribed it to delayed feelings of remorse.

She would sometimes see the Moor leave the camp and climb to the top of a hill along a dried-up steam bed. There, motionless on his jet-black Barbary horse, he would sit for a long time, gazing at the horizon. One day soon, Zagal would leave Ferdinand. This war was no longer his war. He had taken his revenge on Boabdil by loading the military dice in favor of the Catholic Monarchs. His task was done.

Isabella tried in vain to drag some of these secrets out of him, but she learned nothing to satisfy her curiosity. As for Ferdinand, he was sure Zagal would rouse himself from his torpor when they reached Granada. He was mistaken.

At last the Moor asked Ferdinand's permission to withdraw from the operation. There was nothing more for him to do in Spain. He owed some debts to the Sultan of Fez, and could not disregard his authority.

Ferdinand did not try to hold him back. On the whole he would prefer to be on his own when confronting Boabdil, so that his own army would receive all the credit for victory in Granada.

For the Little King had just refused to hand over the town.

Ferdinand launched a military expedition into the *vega* of
Granada, sacked some mountain villages, captured some
strongholds over which he raised the three flags: the banner of the
cross, the flag of St. James, and the national standard of Spain.
Then he had maps drawn up, and returned to spend the year 1490
in Seville, with the queen.

It was there that the echoes of their fame reached their ears.

Italy, whose coasts were being plundered by Sultan Bajazet's
Barbary fleet, could not speak highly enough of the Catholic
Monarchs. In the streets of Naples, peddlers were selling songs
glorifying the conquerors of Islam. Pope Sixtus decreed services of
thanks to St. Peter, and the lighting of thousands of candles for a
rapid end to the war. Parents who believed their children were
destined for greatness christened them Isabella or Ferdinand.

France was astonished, Germany delighted. The Duchy of
Austria, threatened by Islamic hordes, asked Ferdinand to assign
them some of his officers.

Isabella and Ferdinand settled into Seville as undisputed rulers.
In their eyes, Granada was nothing more than the last piece to
complete the jigsaw of their glory. A fresh revolution had broken
out there. Boabdil, surrounded by the elders in his beloved
Albaicin, strove to promote unity and to remove the name of his
uncle Zagal from where it was inscribed in stone.

Zagal had returned from Africa. He was living alone, forsaken
by everyone, on the island of Gomera, in the Canaries. On his
sackcloth clothes were written: This is the wretched King of
Andalusia. The Sultan of Fez had caused his eyes to be burned out.

In the churches of Seville, the banners of the Moors had been
replaced by those of Portugal. Elisabeth had married Prince
Afonso; he was older than she, but he was presentable, and the
African gold decorating his clothing said enough about his wealth.
When they returned to Portugal, they made a stop at the monastery

of St. Clare of Coimbra, where they were greeted by a stony-faced lady: Jeanne-la-Beltraneja.

For the monarchs, it was a peaceful year, punctuated by a few periods of intense activity.

It was said that little Juana might be betrothed to Prince Philip of Austria, son of Duke Maximilian, but Isabella put off coming to a decision. Juana was showing disturbing signs of prolonged adolescence. She had a child's face on a woman's body.

The queen could not look into Juana's eyes without a feeling of terror. At times, she saw in them a strange emptiness, an absence of desires, a soulless serenity, but at other times she detected a sudden upsurge of passion. A cold desert, then a raging sea. She dared not consult the astrologers, since one of them had predicted that she would die insane at the head of an empire. Among the people, she was called Juana la Loca: Juana the Mad.

The same astrologer had foretold a short life for Prince Juan. In truth, Juan lived in a world of his own, which could be entered only by those creatures for whom he felt some empathy. One day it might be a poor monk, another day a bird; sometimes his mother, never his father. He devoted himself ardently to passions as fleeting as they were intense, to the exclusion of all else.

When he was alone, he seemed to fade away. He lived only when he was loved. In appearance he was fair-haired and pale. Once Isabella dressed him in gold and white clothes, and cried out when she stood back to look at him. He was the very image of death.

Ferdinand paid attention to nothing except the siege of Granada. His first burst of enthusiasm had given way to a plodding certainty, sometimes tinged with disbelief. Granada was impregnable. A thousand guns could not bring it to its knees. One might as well attack a mountain! What was more, the town seemed to be so well provisioned that it could withstand several months of siege. The Council at Seville decided nonetheless that it would have to be besieged. From the spring of the following year, eighty thousand Christian soldiers would camp at the foot of the Sierra Nevada.

Ferdinand was overjoyed, Isabella less so. Her suspicions were strengthened daily. Ferdinand intended to wage this final war of liberation for his own advantage and for that of Aragon. The slow and difficult process of melting the two great kingdoms into one was not yet complete. Men of distinction in Castile and Aragon argued about honors and rewards, squabbled over questions of precedence. It was no secret to anyone that when he had to resolve a dispute the king openly favored the Aragonese lords, crude though they were.

Clearly Ferdinand was contriving to make Granada an Aragonese victory—with what aim in mind? Isabella took a long time to work it out. If she were out of the way, Aragon would subjugate Castile, crush its aristocratic families. Ferdinand had inherited from his father a calculating mind that was never at rest, a clarity of vision that was able to bring to fruition even the most far-fetched projects. In the same way as King John II of Aragon, the sick old man with the appearance of a blind rat, he was often engaged in very devious schemes.

Isabella resolved to be vigilant all the time. Not the slightest weakness in the unified image they presented to Spain and to the world would be allowed to develop if she could possibly avoid it. They would continue to be the Catholic Monarchs, two heads with the same crown, the most united couple in all Christendom.

She made up her mind to punish the king severely but secretly for the smallest divergences from their agreements, however hard Ferdinand might find those agreements to bear. She forgave him his countless marital infidelities, transgressions she knew of even though he was discreet and clever at smothering any scandal.

In the passages of Cordova or of Seville, Isabella often passed by small children with frizzy black hair, rugged features, swarthy complexions, who looked like the king. She had lost the ability to cry, but she was still capable of feeling a resurgence of pride. So she tolerated Ferdinand's love affairs, but could not accept his treachery when it damaged the equality of Castile and Aragon.

Ferdinand studied Granada. Isabella dreamed about it. She sought out the old ballads of her early youth, and in her mind's eye saw once again the captains seated around her father's table, then her brother Henry returning from an expedition. They didn't discuss Granada as economists or bankers would, but as poets and soldiers of Christ. The simplest stories of their feats of arms would keep the little Isabella from her sleep for hours at a time.

She daydreamed about her childhood love of snow and flowers when she was reviewing the accounts that the secretaries of the royal provincial agencies brought to her, but she could not indulge in the luxury of enjoying those dreams: the soldiers who would be leaving Seville and Cordova in the first days of April could not be fed on flowers and snow.

Isabella's dreams were not only of Granada.

She often saw arriving at the palace of the Duke of Medina-Sidonia a man who made people turn their heads and laugh. He wore the threadbare dress of a pilgrim, clothes whose drabness was taken to indicate poverty in the brilliant Court of the Andalusian Duke. Barely into his forties, he nevertheless had the stooped shoulders of an old, sick man. For him, each passing year felt more like a decade.

⚜

Whenever the chamberlain announced Christopher Columbus, the queen could not repress a feeling of pleasure. She would never refuse to receive him; on the other hand, the king could hardly tolerate his presence.

"He is a braggart and a dreamer," Ferdinand would say. "If it were only up to me, I would long ago have sent him back to King Joao, or—better yet—to his native Italy."

Ferdinand would leave the moment Columbus was announced. He had found out, without being able to prove it, that this character was a converted Jew.

"That may be," Isabella replied. "But what does it matter, since he is now a Catholic beyond reproach? The Prior of La Rabida monastery, Father Perez, commends him most highly."

Columbus would come to solicit a supplementary payment, which the queen never refused him. But he would never leave before unfolding his charts and plans and bringing some new irrefutable evidence of these western isles—Antilea, Cypangu—

that would be found en route to the Indies if only she would charter
a fleet of three or four *caravels*.

What did he ask for himself? To become viceroy of the newly
discovered lands; the title and privileges of grand admiral; a
peerage; and a share of the treasures of which he would gain
possession.

To Isabella, these claims seemed to be exorbitant, but she didn't
bother to contest them, as she felt that Columbus's expedition was
becoming more and more improbable. She could only repeat to him
what he had already been told by Talavera, her confessor, at a
meeting of the council set up to study the explorer's projects:

"I am convinced that there are good grounds on which to justify
your request, my dear Columbus, but this is not the best time to
undertake such an expedition. After Granada has fallen, the council
will reconvene, and then . . ."

"For seven years I have been given the same answer," groaned
Columbus, tears in his eyes. "Seven years, your Majesty . . . I can
wait no more. I offer you an empire in exchange for a few
caravels."

"You know very well that I cannot make a decision by myself."

She let Columbus keep talking, oblivious to the captains and
lords waiting in her anteroom.

"When I was in Lisbon, your Majesty, I came across a
trustworthy pilot, Vasquez de la Frontera. He assured me that he
had been farther out into the Atlantic than any other navigator. He
had to turn back because of floating masses of Sargasso seaweed so
thick that he could not sail through them. Had he been able to keep
going, he would have found Antila, the Island of the Seven Cities,
of that I'm sure. One day, he will again set sail with the Portuguese
caravels, and he will present King Joao with the great empire that
I planned to bring to you."

Columbus pointed out the fabled island on charts dating from
the previous century. Antilia. He circled it lovingly with the tip of
his forefinger.

"A phantom island!" exclaimed Ferdinand. "This man is either
a fraud or a madman."

Afterwards, he laughed about it with his lords, aping the strange Genoese accent.

The end of 1490 brought a fatal blow for Columbus. Talavera announced to him that his proposals had been rejected by the council. At Salamanca University, they merely laughed about it.

"The thing that's missing from your venture," said Talavera, "is a firm basis, a proof—just one—of the existence of these lands. And another thing: even if there were a land beyond the Cape Verde Islands, you would need more than three years' sailing to reach it."

Beaten, despairing, Columbus took the road to Portugal to try one last approach to King Joao. He stopped overnight near the frontier, at the monastery of La Rabida, not far from the port of Palos.

"Don't leave Spain," implored Father Perez. "Be patient for another year or two, refine your plans. I will myself join you in your presentation to the queen when the time comes. Wait, my son. There is a man here who would like to meet you. He has come back from Rome with some new information about the islands. His name is Martin Alfonso Pinzon."

A richly dressed man with an honest, weather-beaten face walked out of the shadows.

"Do you believe that Cypangu can be reached by heading west?" Pinzon asked him point-blank.

"Do I believe it!" the man from Genoa exclaimed.

"Then shake hands. You are my friend. You have come at the right time, Columbus. A few months later, and you wouldn't have found me. I would have sailed for Atilia and Cypangu without you."

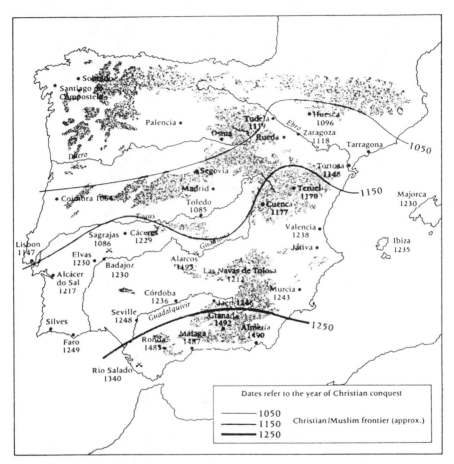

The Shrinking of Moorish Spain

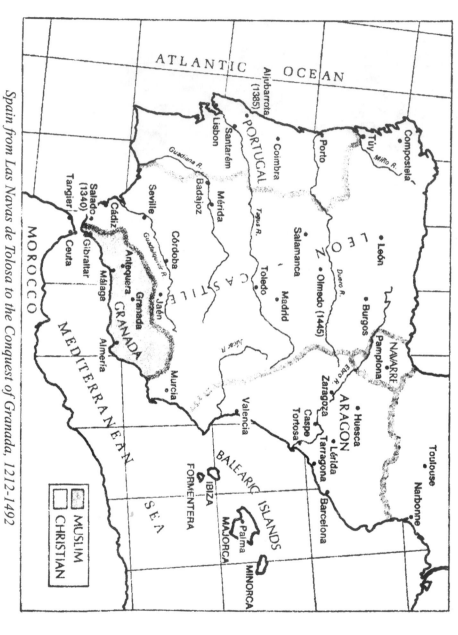

The Ultimate Reconquista

Spain from Las Navas de Tolosa to the Conquest of Granada, 1212-1492

ATLANTIC OCEAN

Aljubarrota (1385)

PORTUGAL
Santarém
Lisbon
Coimbra
Porto
Tüy
Miño R.
Compostela

Guadiana R.

Badajoz
Mérida
Salamanca
León
LEÓN
Duero R.
Burgos
Olmedo (1445)
CASTILE

Salado (1340)
Tangier
Cádiz
Seville
Córdoba
Toledo
Madrid
Guadalquivir R.
Tagus R.

MOROCCO
Ceuta
Gibraltar
Málaga
Antequera
Granada
Jaén
GRANADA
Almería
Murcia

NAVARRE
Pamplona
Zaragoza
Caspe
Tortosa
Ebro R.
ARAGON
Huesca
Lérida
Tarragona
Barcelona

Júcar R.

Valencia

MEDITERRANEAN SEA

BALEARIC
IBIZA
FORMENTERA
ISLANDS
Palma
MAJORCA
MINORCA

Toulouse
Narbonne

MUSLIM
CHRISTIAN

9

The Ultimate Reconquista

Boabdil could read the unmistakable signs of a storm heading toward Granada. He took shelter alone in the depths of a cave, kept his ears covered, and heard only its faint echoes.

The troops of the Catholic Monarchs were tightening their grip on the capital. They could be seen massing in the high valleys of the Alpujarras, up in the lowering rain-clouds. Flashes of light reflected from their lances and shields, and the rumbling of supply wagons and heavy artillery pieces completed the picture. The Moorish warriors fled in panic from the *atalayas* where they had been keeping watch on the narrow passes, or jumped to their deaths from the battlements to avoid capture.

People were still dancing in the *zambra* in the public places of the Albaicin and of the Zaccatin. The *dulzaina*, the mellow flute that sounded like water fountains in the Generalife, could still be heard in the shadows of the souks. At these busy times of the day, it was possible to believe that Granada was not under threat. But this mirage of peace did not deceive Boabdil.

The last caravans of mules and camels climbed up from Motril and then made their way down the Alpujarras. They were loaded with wheat and olives, and led herds of sheep and cattle to provide for a long siege. But Boabdil knew that this siege would not be a long one.

He attended the meetings of his officers more from a sense of duty than from conviction. What was the point of these plans, these defense tactics that the great families of the Abencerages, the Zegris, and the Alabes were putting together in such haste? There was always a hope that the king of Fez and the Sultan Bazajet might come to their aid, but they gave no sign of life. Their indifference was just one more indication of impending defeat.

Boabdil avoided the nagging of his mother and of his wife as though they were the voice of his own conscience. That voice, however, was never silent; it drowned out the growing noise of the storm that he heard in the distance. He sometimes told himself that it would have been simpler and wiser to have kept his word, and to have handed over Granada thirty days after the fall of Baza, Guadix, and Almeria.

He represented for everyone the heart and soul of their resistance. With the help of the Elders, he had succeeded in holding his men together as a sacred union of the last defenders of Islam, and in provoking uprisings in the Moorish sections of the great Christian cities of the south.

No one had found his leadership lacking. No one yet knew that a part of him seriously questioned the outcome of this war. Everyone believed that he was in control of the battle. In Granada, they were telling the story of Sayavedra of Seville. . . .

They were making their way along the Green River, at the bottom of the most threatening and solitary ravine in the Alpujarras Mountains. A dry heat rose from the stones, heated by the May sun. The hoofbeats of the three horses woke echoes in the solitude, and when a small stone was dislodged and rattled down the slope the Christian horsemen stopped, ears cocked.

For three days they had hardly slept. Hunger gnawed at them. Occasionally, they would roast some fat snake they had killed on the bank of the Green River, but their disgust at this dish and their fear of being given away by fire-smoke made them prefer the pangs of hunger.

Returning from patrol in a valley of the Bermeja mountains, they had found their campsite vacant. A Moorish attack had driven away their Christian brothers-in-arms. They had retraced their steps, and since then wandered from valley to valley, hoping soon to reach the coast.

At last they came in sight of a group of cave dwellings hewn out of the red stone. Smoke was rising from a cone-shaped chimney.

Sayavedra favored carrying out a reconnaissance operation. The peasants, be they Moors or Christians, were unlikely to be armed.

"I could swear this is a trap," said Urdiales. "What do you think, Urena?"

Urena felt the same way. Hunger was making his head spin so much that he had already fallen from his horse three times. "I'll follow you," he said.

They started a long, hard climb under a blazing sun, ascending a track more suited to mules than to thoroughbred horses. When they came close to the village, they called out. No one answered.

"Wait for me," said Sayavedra. "I'm going to check whether this village is really inhabited."

He dismounted, went forward rather unsteadily with his sword-belt well adjusted, sword in hand. With only a few steps to go, he stopped and took up his guard. A door had just opened before him, and through it came a man of uncommon height, in the dress of a Spanish soldier, holding an enormous sword.

Sayavedra slid his sword back into its scabbard. "At last—a Christian!"

"Wrong," said the man. "I am a Jew."

Sayavedra frowned. "I have nothing against Jews when they behave in a Christian way."

"That's not the case with me. I was burned in effigy in Seville. Ever since then, whenever I come across a Christian my sword springs from its sheath of its own accord."

The giant moved toward Sayavedra, who retreated while signaling Urdiales and Urena to attack. But at that instant the Jew called out; other doors in the barracks opened, and through them streamed Moorish soldiers dressed for battle.

"Halt!" shouted the Jew. "You are prisoners."

The Christian horsemen were quickly surrounded by a troop of some fifty men, mostly Moors, armed to the teeth with lances and curved knives. One of them pointed at Sayavedra.

"I recognize you, Sayavedra! I was your slave, in Seville! How is your wife, Dona Elvira? Do you like tournaments as much as you

used to? Let me have this man. He will be my slave. I know the way
to make him docile as a lamb. He used it on me. . . ."

Before the Jew could reply, Sayavedra leapt on the Moor,
slashed through his round shield and half-way through his wrist.
The Moor let out a cry of rage and pulled his *alfange* from its
sheath, but had no time to use it. Sayavedra's sword had run
through his chest.

The Christian knight stepped back to face the Moors who were
advancing on him when he felt his throat in the grip of a strong arm.

"Drop your sword, or you're dead!" shouted the Jew.

Sayavedra struggled violently until he was exhausted, ending
up letting go of his weapon, unable to breathe. The Jew had him
tied up and thrown into a shed, where black pigs came to sniff at
him. By crawling on his belly, he was able to reach the doorway
and to see the end of the fight.

Urena defended himself fiercely against a swarm of Moorish
soldiers who literally tore him from his horse. He managed to break
away and get his back against a rock. Protected by his fallen horse,
he fought on for a few brief seconds, finally collapsing with his
head shattered by a knife blow.

Urdiales had taken advantage of an instant of inattention to
break through the Moorish ranks at a ferocious gallop. He hurtled
at breakneck speed down the slope he had climbed with such
difficulty a little while before. Several arrows flew after him, but all
missed. By the time his pursuers had saddled their horses he was far
away.

The Jew came back to Sayavedra, took his weapons, and untied
him.

"What are you going to do with me?" asked the knight.

"It's not up to me to decide your fate. I'm going to have you
taken to Granada, where King Boabdil will do with you whatever
he wants."

Just as Sayavedra was climbing into the saddle to leave the
village, surrounded by ten Moors, the Jew came up to him.

"Sayavedra, has it been long since you saw Queen Isabella?"

"Less than a month ago, I was near her, at Moclin. She and
King Ferdinand were getting ready for their final offensive. She
was involved in it heart and soul, believe me. Thanks to their very

Christian Majesties, in a few months we will be rid of the Moors and the Jews."

The giant's hand tightened on his reins. He spoke simply. "If you should by chance see Queen Isabella again, tell her . . . no, tell her nothing. Forget what I've said."

"I will tell her nothing, for I doubt if I will ever again be allowed to meet my Queen. Farewell."

The Moors and the knight made their way by hidden tracks into Granada. King Boabdil received them as he was climbing out of his bathtub. As soon as he was under the hands of the masseur, he had the prisoner brought before him.

"Sayavedra," said the Little King. "Yes, I know him well. Don Sayavedra of Seville . . . to be seen wherever there was killing and plundering. I could easily find a hundred men in this very town who have a serious complaint against you."

"A hundred—that's not many, your Majesty. I would have hoped that there would be at least a thousand."

The Little King's lips broke into a thin smile. As he squashed a lump of pomade between his hands and smoothed it into his hair, he murmured, "You are more insolent than brave, Sayavedra. But are you really as brave as I've been told?"

"That's not for me to say, but for the hundred men who have grievances against me. Do you want me to put it to the proof?"

"Perhaps." Boabdil's voice was low. He called for a mirror and examined himself for a few moments. "Tell me, Sayavedra, if your God were to let you live for a few more years and to go back to your own country, what would you do if you met me again and I was your prisoner?"

"I would hasten to cast off your bonds and to pay you the proper respects, provided you agreed to embrace the faith of the true God."

"And were I to refuse, Sayavedra?"

"You would pay for that refusal with your head."

Boabdil's thin, dark face lit up. "Very good, sir! That is exactly how you should act if you have the honor of defending your faith. In your place, I would do the same thing."

Sayavedra bowed, smiling.

Boabdil played for a moment with the pompoms of his slippers, and than went on in a low voice, as if speaking with regret. "I acknowledge your courage, Sayavedra, and I would be most distressed if some calamity were to befall you. Take an oath that you will give up your faith, serve my God and myself, and I will make you one of the wealthiest lords in my kingdom. If we have to leave Spain, we can get towns in Africa . . ."

"Stop right there," said Sayavedra. "Have my head cut off, but please spare me these pointless speeches."

"Do you take me for an executioner?"

Boabdil summoned three Sudanese guards, the jet-black *rakkas*—very tall, broad-shouldered, slim-waisted. He pointed them out to Sayavedra.

"You have to fight these men one after the other. If you win all three duels, you will go free."

"I accept—and it is good of you to let me have this chance. But three men? That's not many, and you insult me when you underestimate my capability."

The first *rakka* danced like a dervish all around the Christian, but he had too much agility and not enough strength. Sayavedra turned on the spot, neither advancing nor retreating an inch, and parried the thrusts skillfully. When he saw that his opponent was showing signs of fatigue, he attacked with his other hand and pierced right through the loin of the black, who sank to his knees.

"Congratulations!" exclaimed Boabdil. "Indeed, I'm beginning to believe that I underestimated you. Forgive me. Would you like something to drink?"

"I would not refuse."

Boabdil clapped his hands, and piping hot tea was served. He invited the knight to breathe the perfumed vapor emanating from a delicate silver tripod, and asked if music would disturb him.

"Do whatever you wish," said Sayavedra. "It will not bother me in the least."

Boabdil had musicians brought in. They started playing a lively air on the drum and the guzla, while another *rakka* came from the end of the room and took up his sword. Sayavedra raised his eyes toward the sky, growing pale with the light of dawn. He smelled the fragrance of roses and myrtle that the gusty wind blew from a garden whose greenery he could see through an opening in the marble patio.

He suspected that this would be a more even match. This *rakka* was stronger than the first, and handled his knife with such dexterity that his wrist seemed to be dislocated. His wild leaps were those of a dancer; but fearing the point of Sayavedra's sword, he kept his distance, and his attacks were very cautious.

Sayavedra managed to get his back against a column and to injure his adversary slightly on the thigh. This wound seemed to increase the black's fighting spirit tenfold. As he attacked, he let out loud grunts, and tried to grapple and throw the knight. But Sayavedra seemed to be able to remain upright, as though fixed to the ground, and each grapple ended to his advantage.

Then a misjudged parry almost cost him his life. The *rakka*'s sword, poorly deflected, wounded him in the knee. But a few seconds later, after a fierce clash of steel, the black toppled over, the knight's sword transfixing his throat.

Limping slightly, Sayavedra came back and sat close to the Little King, who had already had ointments and dressings brought in. Teeth clenched, he let them tend to his injury. He had not lost a lot of blood, but the wound was very painful, and he found it difficult to walk.

"If you manage to overcome my third Sudanese guard," Boabdil told him, "not only will I have you released, but you will take with you a fully harnessed horse and a gold-embroidered doublet."

"Freedom will be enough," said the knight.

He rested his leg on the sofa, asked for another cup of tea, and leaned his head back, breathing deeply. His lips moved, and Boabdil was careful not to interrupt what he took to be a prayer. When the Christian had crossed himself, he addressed the king.

"Who is this Jew who captured me?"

"You mean David Ezra?? With just a handful of Jews who had escaped from the Inquisition, he fought alone in the Castilian mountains. On one occasion he joined with a party of Arabs to attack a gold convoy on its way from Ciudad Real to Toledo. Since then, he has fought with us."

"I have never understood why he has engaged in this merciless battle against the Christians. Queen Isabella is his friend. Under her protection, he would have been able to live at court. Today, there is a price on his head. David Ezra is our greatest supporter in the Alpujarras."

Sayavedra didn't seem to hear.

"Are you in a lot of pain? Go—your debt is paid. Tomorrow you can leave Granada."

Sayavedra's lips curled, and Boabdil believed that he was about to be insulted. The knight rose slowly, and the music started again, jangling his nerves with its sharp tones. He took up his position in the middle of the patio, eyes half-closed, and waited.

The last *rakka* leapt on him with such spirit that he was visibly shaken. The exhausted knight took several backward steps before regaining his balance. He had expected a renewed flow of strength: It didn't come. His legs felt like cotton, and his bruised wrist could hardly keep a grip on the heavy sword.

He put his back against a column in the hope that his opponent would tire quickly. He was a very young man, with fast reflexes and a darting glance, accurate in attack. His slender limbs moved with frightening speed in the folds of the *burnous*, which, in the knight's bluffed vision, undulated like waves of brilliant white.

Sayavedra knew that if he lost control of his reflexes for one moment, he was as good as dead. He heard the *rakka*'s hoarse cry before feeling the burning wound in his right side, just above his belt. "Mary, mother of God . . ." breathed the knight.

Again he leaned against the marble column, for longer this time. He felt the stone cool the burning sweat on the back of his neck. He moved just one inch forward, and delivered such a mighty blow with the edge of his sword on the *rakka*'s guard that he let go his scimitar with a grunt.

Down on his knees, the Sudanese picked the weapon up again, and with a swift turning movement scythed the knight's legs from under him. He crashed to the ground, his calf slashed through to the bone.

Before Sayavedra could get back on his feet, the *rakka* whirled his scimitar around and with a precise and powerful blow severed his head from his body.

Boabdil closed his eyes, breathed in the fragrance of burning perfume, and sighed.

Then he made a signal, and the music stopped playing.

᪥

Green River, Green River
Flowing with the color of blood . . .

Isabella was listening to the ballad of "Green River," a song of Sayavedra's exploits.

"Who was Sayavedra?" asked the queen.

Gonzales de Cordova, standing with his hands on the back of Isabella's armchair, bent down to her ear.

"A nobleman of Seville. A prisoner of King Boabdil, he killed two of three black guards in duels, and was himself killed by the third. He had refused to renounce his faith and to betray his king and queen. This happened in early spring."

Sayavedra had become a legend just a few months after his death. Where did the troubadours get the inspiration to write and sing their songs about him? It was as if they had experienced the events they described, as if for them there were no frontiers, no battlements, no obstacles at all.

As soon as a hero fell and breathed his last on Granada's soil, the ballads began. The troubadour was there to record his prayers, his wounds, his challenges, even his last groans as death took him. What wonderful secret did he possess?

The one whom the queen was watching at that very moment, in the remote Alpujarras castle, seemed to be a commonplace sort of individual. He didn't play the guitar very well, but his singing voice had such a ring of truth that the queen could envisage the whirlwind of *jellabas* and *alfanges* around the body stretched out on the patio's marble floor. She suffered each wound inflicted on the Christian Sayavedra, and bowed her head to look at the floor, where she could imagine the steaming pools of blood around the knight's headless body.

Ferdinand seemed to be asleep. Perhaps he really was sleeping, head hidden behind his hand, elbow on an arm of the chair. He was not interested in ballads. He simply lived his own life, and paid with sweat and blood for the heroic reputation that the poets were building around him.

His wound no longer gave him pain, but it annoyed him to think of the wasted time, the enforced immobility. It was no major injury, just a scratch from the blow of a *tabbarzin*, a two-edged battle-ax, which could have torn off his shoulder. But the wound had turned septic, and healing was slow.

No sooner did he arrive at Granada, at the watch-tower, than he sent some army units to guard the narrow passes of the Alpujarras where they opened onto the Granada plain.

Through them, supplies were continuing to get through to the city. He took personal charge of this operation.

League after league, town after town, he had progressed into this wild land and held on strongly.

His declared aim was to break up the resistance system of the mountain dwellers, but Isabella knew that he hoped secretly to lay his hands on the chief of the parties of Moors and Jews who held this region: David Ezra.

He had decided to stop at nothing to bring his plans—declared or secret—to fruition, and poured all his strategic reserves into the effort. Now that he had come this far into the Alpujarras, he could not, would not withdraw.

The country fascinated him. An uncontrollable force urged him forward, prompted the taking of now one hill, now another, this village then that, to storm from one valley to the next. Hills, villages, valleys; endlessly they followed one another, but his hunger for more was never assuaged nor his resolve weakened.

When his troops brought a party of infidels to battle, he would feverishly run his eyes over the ranks of prisoners and the lines of dead. His officers never knew what he was thinking, or what he was looking for with such perseverance.

On one occasion, Isabella had not been able to prevent herself from commenting that he was being rather tactless in this search.

"Ezra is responsible for the deaths of Urena and Sayavedra," Ferdinand replied. "Count Urdiales, who got away, is quite definite. He saw David Ezra. He could pick him out among a thousand others."

"You will never find him again. David will not let himself be captured like a bear."

"That's what you would like to believe. You would be distressed if he fell into my hands."

"Didn't I sign his death warrant?"

"Would you have signed it if he had been a prisoner?"

"You call my honesty into question! That is not worthy of you."

"That's no reply. The truth of the matter is that you still love the Jew. I'm not at all sure that you're not secretly seeing him."

"Ferdinand!"

"I'm sure of nothing more than that you share guilty emotions behind my back . . . forbidden fruit."

Isabella tasted resentment like bile in her mouth. She had to hold herself in check or she would have thrown the names of some of his mistresses in his face. But she knew beforehand what his riposte would be:

"These women are nothing to me. I have even forgotten their names and faces."

And certainly Ferdinand would have been the first king ever to honor his wife with impeccable faithfulness.

Ferdinand went on in a louder voice.

"I will have that Jew's hide! One day soon, I will tie his hands behind his back and lead him to Tomas de Torquemada. He will reserve for him the most refined tortures to make him spit out the venom of his heresy. When his body is in ruin, his soul dead within him, I will have him sent to the stake. And you, Isabella, will sign his death warrant!"

10

January 2, 1492

Long, feverish days went by. Barely recovered from his wound, Ferdinand remounted his horse. But instead of continuing his incursion into the mountains, he left that responsibility with the Duke of Escalona. These preliminaries to the battle had gone on too long. He rejoined the main body of his army, marking time two leagues from Granada.

Before leaving the Alpujarras, he had given orders to the Duke of Escalona to send him news by dispatch messenger every day. In addition, he had assigned to him as a special objective the capture of David Ezra.

The duke was positively disposed to the first order, but he believed that he would have to acknowledge failure in carrying out the second. He had the impression it would be as elusive as the hunting of the unicorn; but these hunts were so bloody, and the quarry so elusive, that he was thinking of calling off the hounds. Then a young peasant from somewhere near Padul confirmed that the Jew had left the mountains and was on his way to Granada.

Every day the Christian camp encroached farther into the olive groves of the *vega*.

This sea of multicolored sails was like an incoming tide, climbing the red-earth hillocks, with no sense of order or symmetry. Without Isabella, Ferdinand was revealed as a mediocre administrator. New arrivals pitched their tents wherever and however they pleased. The best units—especially the cavalry— tried to make their camp as close as possible to the royal tent. This caused problems, and Ferdinand was behaving in character when he avoided making any decisions. Gradually the whole enormous encampment became nothing more than a multicolored assembly of tents set up with a typically Spanish disregard for good order.

And nothing was heard of David Ezra.

This one thought loomed large in Ferdinand's mind. For him, the struggle against Granada was developing into a duel to the death with David Ezra.

At last Isabella arrived. She was horrified at the carelessness that pervaded the camp's organization. But this was Ferdinand's domain; when she tried introducing discipline, the king, gloomier than ever, brushed her aside, wishing to run the whole show.

Tired of unavailing arguments, she made a habit of leaving for long rides around the camp. She found this recreation to be an endless chain of minor joys, and it delighted her. She would dismount to dip her fingers into one of the many streams that brought water to the *vega*, to gaze at the sky through the branches of old olive trees, to pick a nameless flower. Then she would break into short gallops, to please her mare and to enjoy the pleasure that made her horse's neck quiver. She felt the freedom that came from this graceful motion.

Always she had a mild feeling of pain, and felt a lump in her throat on seeing the camp's flags fluttering in the distance, and the thousand towers of Granada's battlements rising before her, its great mosque, the red walls of its palaces. The *vega* was uninhabited, but it seemed to her that behind every bush lurked a Moorish soldier, that even the smallest clump of trees concealed a squadron of *jellabas*.

But all her fear was forgotten when she came to a knoll that she had discovered a few days earlier.

On the outskirts of a deserted village, its walls showing traces of soot, there was an enclosed area on the slopes of a small red-earth hill facing Granada. Names carved on stones indicated the existence of a Christian cemetery from which the corpses had been removed when the village had been abandoned. A copse of laurels crowned the highest point, and Isabella concealed her horse in the middle of them.

Then she stretched out in the sun against one of the tombstones. Disturbed lizards scuttled away. From this vantage point, she could just make out the glittering peaks of the Sierra Nevada and the rooftops of the village to which spring had brought clumps of tall grass and wild stocks. Farther away through the mist she could see the shiny, waving outline of a town, as though viewed through the waters of a fast-running stream.

Isabella let her hand float lazily in the sunshine. She pointed her forefinger at the minaret behind the Bibarambla Gate and her little finger at the Atalaya on top of Mount Elvira. She drummed her fingers on the square towers, pretended to shake the huge green banners with the tip of her fingernail, and felt more like a child than when she used to hear her *duenna*, dona Albonza, tell her the old tales of the times of El Cid and d'Almanzour.

She felt as though Granada was hers. The intensity of her feeling was more than she had dared hope for, more even than when, at Ferdinand's side, she would finally break through its defenses.

For a long time she drifted into a dream of gardens and sparkling waters, passed through slender brick porticos into marble and stucco palaces. Her eyes traced marvelous arabesque decoration, deciphered the infinitely repeated verses of the Koran: *Allah il Allah*, breathed the smell of incense and of the *naranieros* heated by the May sun.

That particular day, tired after a night of watchkeeping, Isabella slid into a deep sleep. There was a halo of sunlight on her brow, and the back of her neck rested against the warm stone.

Dreams of stucco and songs of the *dulzaina* ran through her sleep. She heard the slap of her sandals on the flagstones, and the whinnying of horses that came from she knew not where. Shadows moved in front of her, probably from the cypress trees.

In her dream, she crossed a sun-drenched patio and stopped at the entrance to a room, with a decorated ceiling looking like a chain of mountains viewed upside down from high in the sky. Two dark shapes were moving at the far end of the room, under high recesses in which perfume-burners were smoking. It was then that she recognized King Boabdil, El Rey Chico, and David—David Ezra—as a distant voice came to her: "Isabella . . . Isabella!"

"Isabella!"

She opened her eyes. They hurt in the blazing whiteness of the sky, but she became aware of a man who was leaning over her and gently shaking her arm. She recognized David Ezra, and at first felt no fear, because he seemed to be part of her dream. But the *dulzaina* had faded away, the ceilings of stucco dissolved into the flat sky, and four heads were laughing above her.

Then she screamed.

"Don't be afraid," said David.

He snapped a few words in Arabic, and immediately the four heads, with their wolfish smiles, disappeared.

"How did you find me?" asked Isabella, adjusting her bustier and putting the poppy-red felt cap with a white feather back on her head, which had slipped onto the tombstone.

"This is the fourth day you've come here, isn't it?"

Isabella looked amazed. "How do you know that?"

"Our Moorish knights have extremely acute eyesight. One of them saw you that first day, but ran off when you approached, not knowing that you were alone. I asked him to keep it secret. The next day, I posted guards in one of the houses in the abandoned village. They came back two days later, and observed that you were consistently coming to this rendezvous. But whom were you planning to meet? I thought at once that it couldn't be anyone but me. So here I am."

"You are becoming very foolhardy, David. Do you place so little value on your life, now that your cause is lost?"

"I was always aware that the cause I supported was a lost one," David replied drily, "and I still cling just as much to my life. Every extra day that God allows me to live is a revenge that I take on your glorious husband. Has he given up the hunt? Is the quarry beneath his notice?"

"Ferdinand doesn't give up so easily. If you stay in Granada, he will take you alive and send you to the stake."

"And you will once again sign my death warrant."

"Yes, David."

"I thought that you might still have some affection for me."

"I love you, David, and struggle constantly to be rid of you. My soul will know no peace until you are gone, until there is no more hope that I might meet you again on my way through life. Your existence goes against the ideals to which I am committed: the unity of the Faith, and the unity of Spain. The love I bear for you is an offense against God; the unity of Spain can be no more than a delusion while the queen is in love with a Jew who is an ally of the Moors. Your death will be a terrible blow to me, but it is the price of my dignity."

A gust of wind blew a shower of shriveled leaves from the olive trees.

"On one occasion I believed that everything was over between us, that I detested you," Isabella continued. "Never have I loved you as much. I wished you dead, but at the same time I would have given up everything to have found you again before you joined the rebels.

"And today?"

Isabella turned away.

"Today doesn't count."

"But it certainly does! Time is more pressing than ever. We only have a few minutes together—each one full of so much joy, so much being part of each other! Why this hypocrisy, this side-stepping?"

He had taken her hands and pressed them between his own, covered them with kisses. Isabella didn't stop him. She leaned forward, putting her arms around David's wiry, curly head.

"Today is joined with so many other days, David."

"Today is unique."

He offered his lips to her, and she again pressed toward him, gasping under his lean brown face while one of her hands searched beneath the *jellaba*, caressing his hard skin, his moist armpits. She leaned back, eyes closed, and David followed her down.

She was terrified. In her mind's eye she could visualize the anger of her vengeful God.

The Moors had a deep respect for the privacy of their leader. By the magic of some subtle intuition, they drew away from David and formed themselves into a human wall to protect that privacy.

Isabella was trembling with emotion, and felt as though she was about to faint. She clung tightly to David, and forgot everything—

the increasingly loveless couplings with Ferdinand, the mental struggles against her God—everything.

David was wild with his deep love for her, but he was gentle as his body melted into hers.

On this piece of Andalusian soil, soaked with so much blood, amid the dreadful scenes of war and of death, struggling with all her soul against her awful fear of eternal damnation, Isabella gave herself freely to him, madly, completely.

After one final embrace in this agony of love, they lay holding each other. She began to sob and confessed: "My David, I lost the baby who should have resulted from our night of wonderful passion, in the same way I lost other babies because of my exhausting travels on horseback all over Spain."

David's face was transformed. He wrapped her tightly in his arms. The lowering sky seemed to her to waver and go out of focus. Her body was worn out by too much travel; she held on to David desperately, as though never wanting to let go.

Once more, in the very heart of the country she loved so much, she abandoned herself to David's maleness, letting go of all queenly control. Their deep and utterly complete act of love seemed to last for an eternity.

Suddenly he snapped upright.

"What is it, David?"

"Listen!"

"It's nothing. Two birds arguing."

But at that moment one of the Moorish guards broke in on them, spoke a few rapid Arabic words.

"A Spanish patrol is headed this way," said David. "Don't panic. I have enough time to get away. We will see each other again, won't we?"

"No. Farewell, David."

He leaned forward to kiss her, but she turned away.

"Never again, David."

She watched him as he hurried away, bending under the low branches of the olive trees. He turned before disappearing, and shouted,

"I will be here tomorrow, at the same time."

"Well and good. But you will be risking your life. I will send a patrol to welcome you."

He smiled defiantly, and waved good-bye to Isabella.

The hoofbeats of the little Andalusian horses were replaced by those of the patrol's powerful steeds as shouting burst out behind Isabella. The branches parted, and Gonzales appeared, pale with worry.

He bent down to the queen, and roughly forced her to stand up.

"You're not injured? Did they manhandle you? You know, I warned you. Thank heaven you arc safe and sound, but I shudder to think what might have happened had I not arrived in time."

The queen's face wore a thin smile.

"Yes, Gonzales, dreadful things might have happened. But . . . you're not chasing them?"

"No use," muttered Gonzales. "They are too far away."

The moment she heard that Gonzales had returned with his detachments, Isabella rushed to the doorway of her tent. The captain, still wearing his armored boots, presented himself before her. When he had taken off his plumed helmet to bow to her, she asked,

"So, Gonzales, you surprised them?"

"No, not surprised, exactly. From the way it appeared, they were expecting us."

"At the same place as yesterday?"

"The very same place. Don't you find that odd? But what is even odder is that I noticed among them a man astonishingly like David Ezra, even though he was wearing the battledress of a Moorish soldier. No doubt about it. Same height, same appearance, same walk . . ."

"Really?" the queen stammered. "And there was a fight?"

"There certainly was. We fired several blunderbuss shots, and I saw David Ezra fall."

Gonzales could not fail to notice the way the queen turned pale, and he continued to watch her closely. She lowered her eyes, and handled her rosary with such force that the string broke, scattering black pearls over the carpet.

With an effort, she got the words out. "And . . . is he dead?"

Gonzales stroked his right cheek with the palm of his hand, and smiled enigmatically. "Ahem! To tell the truth, I could be mistaken—there was another soldier almost as tall as Ezra. The Moors put the body on the hindquarters of a horse, and before we even had time to reload our guns they were upon us, yelling like the damned. They hacked a way through our lines and made off at full speed toward Granada."

His voice became graver as he went on.

"We lost one man, your Majesty: the Count of Tendilla's son. A sad business. The king will be very annoyed, particularly if he hears that David Ezra . . ."

The queen interrupted him. "He need not hear, Gonzales. For the sake of our friendship, promise me that you will tell him nothing."

"I promise, your Majesty. For the sake of our friendship."

That evening, Isabella stayed up very late. The night was stormy and oppressive, and seemed to hold the camp in its grasp. The tents were covered with red dust blown from the hills, and distant thunder rumbled around the Alpujarras.

It was near midnight when the queen dismissed the three men with whom she had conversed for a long time: Friar Talavera, her confessor; Cabrera, the Master of the Household; and the monk Diego Deza, her children's private tutor.

The temperature inside the tent was unbearable. Despite the gauze netting that shielded the entrance, mosquitoes whirled around making their irritating noise, attracted by the light from the big candles. It was as much as she could do to try to kill them with well-aimed blows. She was a dreadful sight, with her blisters, her red dusty footmarks, the sweat she felt dripping from her brow and stinging her eyes.

"Is there anything you need, your Majesty?"

Isabella turned around, and a flash of lightning revealed a vague form behind the mosquito net. Dona Beatrix de Babadilla, Cabrera's wife, had come as she did every evening to learn what the queen wanted, and to talk with her if Isabella felt like it.

This evening, the queen was weary; she sent Beatrix away. She undressed, keeping on only a fine silk shift that completely hid her arms and legs. Then she rubbed her face with citronella oil, to keep away the mosquitoes.

"I'm not disturbing you?"

Before the queen had time to reply, Ferdinand entered the room and sat down on a wooden stool. Isabella smiled. He was dressed in the Moorish style, like many of the lords living in camp, wrapped in a dazzling white *jellaba* of flowing material.

"I have doubled the patrols," he said. "The darkness seems to encourage raids. Yesterday evening, our supply of weapons were looted—I don't want that to happen again."

"I'm sure." The queen sighed.

She filled two tumblers with warm and sickly sweet barley water, and offered one to Ferdinand. He pulled a face.

"Do you think we're going to have a storm?" Isabella asked.

Ferdinand shrugged. Most of the streams that ran through the *vega* were dry, and horses had to be taken to the Genil River to find water.

"A storm would be welcome," he said.

A loud discord of guitar strings angrily plucked, a few shouts, followed by silence. The camp was jolted out of its sleep, and then subsided into silence.

"The men are on edge," said Ferdinand. "I've never seen them like this. Tomorrow I will give them a few bulls to kill. That will take their mind off things."

"It's a costly way of distracting them. The last time, we lost a dozen horses, and one of our captains was badly gored."

"Would you rather the men squabbled among themselves?"

The wild guitar call sounded again.

Ferdinand stood up and moved close to Isabella, sitting on her narrow camp bed with her hands squeezed between her legs. He sat down next to her. Isabella breathed in the sharp smell of his sweat, and felt his damp hand on her shoulder.

"I would like to stay with you this evening, Isabella."

"I'm very tired."

He smiled thinly.

"What are you smiling at?"

"If we go on living separately, how will anyone be able to say that we are the closest-knit couple in Spain and in Christendom? The beautiful fairy-story will be no more! We will be seen as two business partners. How sad. . . . Do you remember that night at Duenas, near Valladolid, when we met for the first time? We hardly dared say hello, we were so overcome by each other."

"I remember," Isabella cut in sharply.

Suddenly she sat up very straight. A woman's scream pierced the night, coming from the direction of the French quarter.

"It's nothing," said Ferdinand. "Just a camp-follower playing coy."

"But I have forbidden . . ."

"We can't expect the Frenchmen to live like monks."

"The French will abide by the camp rules, or else."

"You are very tense."

"I tell you again, I'm tired."

Ferdinand rose to his feet.

"Very well then, I'll go. I will see you on parade tomorrow morning."

Ferdinand left. The queen threw herself on the bed, dazed with fatigue. The woman's cry rang out three more times, and Isabella felt the sound drill into her brain, as if it were she herself screaming.

What woman was Ferdinand going to rouse? The little Jewess from Toledo, Mincia de la Torre, Beatrice Pacheco, some servant girl? Whenever he came near her, Isabella imagined that she could smell on him the fragrance of these women who followed him like some hideous string of pearls.

She tossed and turned for a few minutes, sinking into a restless sleep full of women's screams and the throbbing of a guitar, and then snapped awake as she remembered that she had not said her evening prayer.

She fumbled her way out of bed, found the flint lighter, and relit the candle.

Suddenly she felt two hands pressing on her shoulders from behind, and let out a small cry.

"Ferdinand, I've already told you . . ."

"I'm not Ferdinand."

"David!"

She had recognized him in the darkness by the muffled sound of his voice, the pressure of his hands. She gasped for breath.

"You're mad, David. You cannot stay here. Get out!"

"I need to see you again, Isabella. Let me stay with you for a few moments. Just a few."

"You will get yourself caught. Ferdinand has doubled the patrols."

"I really don't care. I haven't been living since that day we met again on the *vega*. The evening when the Moors came to rob your supply store, I was with them. While they loaded the mules, I came to your tent, but didn't dare enter. Two other occasions I tried to get into the camp, but had to turn back when sentries spotted me."

"You talk only about yourself, your great adventures, the risks you run. But me, David, me—don't you think that I risk anything? What would happen if you were found here, in my tent, in the middle of the night?" She spoke harshly.

"This is the last time I will bother you," said David. "You will not see me again. If you hear any news of me in the future, it will be to say that your men have captured me in Granada, or that I have died on the battlements of that city."

"Well, that will be that! I don't want to hear of you ever again. It will be better for both of us. And now, go!"

He pulled her against him, and she had the sensation of standing against the trunk of a sturdy, deep-rooted tree, safe from all dangers, all fears. It was no use repeating to herself that she must throw him out, that they were on a powder-keg ready to explode—she could not muster the strength to push him away.

The woman was crying now, her voice sometimes rising to a high-pitched scream. She too wanted to scream, but David smothered the cry on her lips. She heard him whispering, as though he was talking to himself, "Let me stay. I love you. I'm exhausted with loving you."

She pulled herself away from him, went to the door of the tent and watched the comings and going of some knights who could not get to sleep. A distant fire glowed redly on Mount Elivra, above Granada. Another burned in the foothills of the Sierra Nevada, where lightning flashes revealed snow. She let the corner of the gauze flap fall.

"You can leave now. The right-hand lane will take you to the French encampment. The password is 'El Zagal is dead.'"

"I know it. Farewell, Isabella."

"Farewell."

As soon as the black silk marotta he was wearing was lost to sight, she leaned her back against the central tent pole, eyes closed, biting her lip, waiting for the faintest shout, the least sound of a galloping horse. She kept repeating "El Zagal is dead" as if the password, like a prayer for help, would ensure that David would have a clear run out of the camp.

After a few minutes she moved away from the post and, with a trembling hand, lit a candle beside Borgia's ivory crucifix. She began to pray.

The wind had risen again, raising clouds of dust in the lanes between the rows of tents, and rattled around the flapping canvas of the camp. Its noise mingled in Isabella's mind with the droning of her prayer. With no apparent effort she made up a long monologue in which the words Madre de Dios were repeated mechanically.

"Give me the strength to wish him dead. Kill him in me, and then there will be no more problems. Let me have no remorse, Madre de Dios, let David's death be no more to me than that of the bull that will fight in the ring tomorrow. . . ."

A gust of wind blew the gauze curtain over the fluttering candle flame. It quickly caught fire, scattering sparks on the rug, which itself started to burn in several places.

"You know what I have suffered because of him, and that it is only memory that ties me to him, Madre de Dios . . ."

The canvas flaps were starting to burn when a guard sounded the alarm. Isabella screamed, burst through the wall of flame, and found herself in the open air, in the middle of a worried group. Ferdinand had just left his tent, almost naked, shield in hand, sword by his side.

"Sound the alarm! The Moors are here!"

He was told that this was not the work of the Moors, that the fire had started in the queen's tent for some unknown reason.

Terror-stricken people threw themselves out of the neighboring tents, now beginning to take fire. The Duchess Pacheco only just had time to throw a coat over herself; Beatrix de Bobadilla bore traces of soot on her bare shoulders. Isabella, trembling, took charge of the situation. She organized a bucket chain, but this quickly proved quite inadequate for the job. After a few minutes there was no more water, so the fire grew, leaping wildly from one tent to the next, burning the flags, crackling viciously as it spread, throwing up columns of sparks that themselves started new fires.

Desperate measures had to be taken. The farthest tents were folded and carried away from the blaze. The horses were becoming nervous and threatened to break their tethers, so they were led away. Supplies from the dumps were carried off to safety.

The Christian camp burned all night under a sky heavy with the storm that did not break.

"We will build a town!" Isabella had said.

The idea came to her when she saw the Christian camp burning and the Moors attacking in the *vega*.

A town. A town built of wood, surrounded with mighty ramparts, resembling a galley sailing through olive-grove seas to the island of Granada.

Isabella had already named the town: Santa Fe, the city of Holy Faith.

She spent the following days in the mountains, looking for the most dense forests. Plans were drawn up in less than a week. The defensive system was established. Streets were to cross each other at right angles. Two sturdy towers were set on the central avenue, which was aligned in the direction of Granada.

In Granada, the fire was the cause of uproarious merriment. From the battlements of Bibarambla the men howled with glee to see the Christians laboriously dragging timber from the mountains in the oppressive August heat. Occasionally Boabdil would unleash his cavalry against the ant-like columns, making their way up and down the hills. He would count the severed heads that his captains brought back to him.

But gradually their hilarity gave way to anxiety, and anxiety to dread. The surveyors' lines that indicated the foundations of the new city could be seen from Bibarambla's towers. Santa Fe was rising from the plains before their very eyes.

Each soldier became transformed into a carpenter, a quarryman, a builder. But at the least alarm he would drop pick or trowel and become a soldier once more.

Sleeves rolled up, surrounded by a team of architects, Isabella directed the work. In the evenings, exhausted, she would go back to her tent and her camp bed, covered from head to foot in yellowish-brown dust. The children laughed to see her brush this dust off in a cloud that stung nose and throat.

At the end of the three months, the town was complete. There were great celebrations; tournaments were held. At the mass held to dedicate the church, the officers were crammed in under vaults that still smelled of green wood and fresh plaster.

October brought rain. In the Christian camp, a deep sense of boredom developed. The siege of Granada got under way again with a few individual exploits that were endlessly discussed; they achieved nothing except a heightened desire for combat.

One day, a man dressed all in black came to call upon the queen. He put his black gloves on his black hat and took off his cape, the color of night. Isabella had the feeling that grave words were about to be spoken, and in this she was not mistaken. The man brought bad news: the death of Afonso, Elisabeth's husband.

Hunting in the forest of Montijo, his horse had bolted. A branch struck his forehead and unseated him, but one of his feet remained trapped in the stirrup. The horse had continued galloping until exhausted, dragging the rider behind him. When the prince was found, he was unrecognizable.

Elisabeth had nearly died of grief. She spoke of joining the convent of la Beltraneja. She spoke of dying.

For many days, Isabella's dreams were punctuated with black mares wildly galloping through forests on which fell a rain of blood.

This continued until the day another messenger presented himself to their Majesties. A Moor, dressed completely in white, who wore on his turban a chain of fine pearls and feathery plumes. He put one hand on his dazzling *jellaba*, and bowed.

His name was Abdul Kacim. He came to convey King Boabdil's greetings to the royal couple, and to bring an offer of peace. They agreed on a sixty-day truce. Boabdil put forward a sixteen-point peace plan. Ferdinand and Isabella countered with a different fifteen-article draft treaty.

During the two months of truce, there were incessant comings and goings between the gates of Bibarambla and the fortress of Santa Fe. The journey was made for the sake of a comma. One badly translated word threw the whole issue into question. Ferdinand threatened to bombard the tower of Comares if Boabdil did not add ten hostages to the number proposed by the Moorish King. He showed Abdul Kacim the door because Boabdil demanded forty thousand pieces of gold for giving up the Alhambra, instead of the thirty thousand previously agreed. In the rains of that October and November, the plumes on the captains' helmets, Christians and Moors alike, took on a woeful appearance as they traveled between Santa Fe and Granada.

Isabella and Ferdinand were beginning to despair of ever concluding the negotiations. Then one bright morning early in January they saw, through the mists of the River Genil, a most unusual procession coming toward Santa Fe.

Abdul Kacim, whose plumes they immediately recognized, was at its head. Midget grooms led by the bridle two magnificent Andalusian horses caparisoned in silk and with amazingly luxurious harness. Behind them, heads bowed, came a file of young Moorish noblemen and women, sons and daughters of Granada's aristocracy—the hostages.

The Catholic Monarchs had the gates opened and great numbers of banners hoisted. They came forward to meet the ambassador. Abdul Kacim fingered a few of the pearls on his endless chain, as a courteous pause before declaring:

"My master, King Boabdil, begs to be your servant."

"Does he agree to sign the peace agreement?" asked Ferdinand.

Abdulkacim bowed low. One of his plumes brushed lightly over Ferdinand's knee.

"Here is a letter from my master, your Majesty, and here by way of a gift are two horses, the finest examples of our bloodlines, completely caparisoned and harnessed."

The queen smiled while Ferdinand, frowning, opened the letter that the ambassador had handed to him.

"Good God! Kacim, you are right—Boabdil agrees to our terms."

He read the letter again, examining the seal as if to be sure nobody had tampered with it. He was tense, and this seemed to communicate itself to his horse, which pranced from one hoof to the other. All at once, he turned to his companions—Gonzales de Cordova, the Marquis of Medina-Sidonia, the Count of Cabra, and the great financier Luis de Santagel—waved the letter above his head, and shouted loudly:

"Peace, gentlemen! Granada is ours!"

A clamor of voices greeted this news. Ferdinand turned his back on the astonished Abdul Kacim, and set off toward Santa Fe, followed by his escort.

Isabella was left alone in front of the ambassador. She dismounted, and tried to hide the expression of joy on her face. But her lips were quivering as she whispered,

"Most noble Lord, please forgive our joy. Spain has waited eight hundred years for this moment. Thanks to your king's wisdom, the moment has come not on the field of battle but through negotiation. I shudder to think how many lives would have been lost in this last stage of the reconquest."

Abdul Kacim, vexed by Ferdinand's attitude, kept his reply short. In an icy voice, he said,

"May the wisdom of your husband be equal to that of my king. We will not then regret having put our confidence in your Majesties."

They had only just left when the thunder of cannon could be heard rolling as far as the foothills of the Sierra Nevada. Soon after, the bells of Santa Fe could be heard pealing all over the *vega*.

❧

Ferdinand walked around Isabella.

"No," he said, "not today. Not mourning clothes. It doesn't make sense to dwell on the past at a time when Spain has just made such a great leap into the future. I would like to see you dressed in brilliant fashion."

He went to the wardrobe where the queen hung her robes, rummaged around, and threw on the bed what he considered to be her most gorgeous things.

"I could well imagine the red robe going with this ermine-trimmed violet cape . . . oh, yes . . ."

The queen smiled. "Let me make my own choice, with the help of my ladies-in-waiting."

"Today, I want you to be the most beautiful woman in the whole kingdom! I want people to say that my wife is as young as Spain—and just as proud and radiant. I want no sign of sadness to be visible on your face. Isabella, are you happy?"

Isabella nodded. Then Ferdinand did what he had not done for a long time: he took Isabella in his arms, kissed her on the lips, and covered her face with more swift little kisses. Each kiss helped her to put out of her mind the picture of a young knight, handsome as a god, being dragged through the undergrowth at Montijo by the stirrup of a bolting horse.

Each kiss also dimmed the thought of the twenty-year-old widow, face drowned in sorrow, confined in a Santa Fe cell and deaf to the joyful volleys of blunderbuss and artillery, to the unceasing bells, to the celebrations of the soldiers going arm-in-arm round the streets of the town.

The kisses also helped her forget the fire that had engulfed the canvas city like a rising tide of flame. Her presentiments of defeat and death were themselves fading.

Isabella was conscious that the joy whose taste she had forgotten was being reborn. They were tied together, Ferdinand and

Isabella, like the bundle of arrows they had taken as their insignia. The earth no longer shook beneath their feet. Spain was no more a hundredheaded monster rolling in its own blood and excrement, gripped by anarchy and madness, drunk with its own destruction. The country was coming back to life under the peaceful yoke of its monarchs. It was marching forward along a pathway of light to meet its own destiny.

"You are crying!" Ferdinand exclaimed.

Why couldn't he understand that she was crying tears of joy?

Ferdinand turned toward the ladies in waiting: Beatrix de Bobadilla, Mincia de la Torre, Duchess Pacheco. They quickly pushed their handkerchiefs back into their waistbands.

"Not a tear!" he shouted. "Everyone must be joyful!"

⚜

The January morning was unseasonably bright. Small pink clouds hung over the blue foothills of the Alpujarras. To the south, the snows of the Sierra Nevada climbed in dazzling waves to the sky.

Some two miles from Santa Fe, Ferdinand had drawn up his entire army in perfect formation. Every banner was flying from the top of its flagpole or from the knights' lances, which were decorated with cocks' feathers and with foxes' tails. Eighty thousand men! And not a sound.

They were ready for the queen, who was dressed in a deep purple robe and a red cape, embroidered with gold and silver braid, and trimmed with ermine. She wore the silver diadem of Castile on her forehead, and golden spurs were fastened above her damascened leather shoes. Ferdinand had every reason in the world to look satisfied; the queen had surprised him with her smile of pride when she saw him.

The king had followed up on his intention of showing himself to Boabdil in all his splendor. Aragon's golden crown was set on his dark hair, now shot through with just a shade of silver. He wore a bright red velvet doublet, decorated with an enormous solid gold chain embellished with the red cross of the Order of Santiago. Mouse-gray leather breeches, and boots of supple leather adorned

Muhammad XI, Abu Abdullah, known to Christians as Boabdil, emerges from his citadel to hand besiegers the keys to his capital in The Surrender of Granada to Ferdinand, 1492, a painting by El Pradilla that occupies an honored place in the Palacio Senado in Madrid.

with pearl buttons. The royal couple was followed by Prince Juan and Princess Juana.

Monsignor Mendoza, Primate of All Spain, and a humble monk, Ximenes Cisneros, whose eyes shone with the light of the Faith, and high functionaries of the crown, were standing behind them, preceding the great captains with their impassive faces.

The queen lifted her gloved hand.

"Look who's coming. I think I can see the Moorish King."

"I'm sure you're right," said Ferdinand.

Boabdil was accompanied by only fifty knights. Nothing in his bearing or dress indicated any desire to impress; on the contrary, he was dressed very simply, without precious stones or plumes. Boabdil walked slowly, as if he wanted to delay for as long as possible the moment when he would have to kneel before the monarchs and pronounce the words that kept reverberating in his brain:

"My property and my life are at your disposal. I am yours. This capital is your city, this country your kingdom."

He had spoken in so quiet a voice that he was unsure whether the monarchs had heard him. Nothing could have made him kneel: his knees refused to bend. But when, lifting his head, he saw Isabella's beaming smile, and Ferdinand's, too, with its stamp of majesty, he did what he had vowed not to do: he went up to them and took the king's hand to kiss it.

Ferdinand quickly pulled his hand away, dismounted from his horse, and then the eight thousand men of the Catholic Monarchs' army saw an amazing sight. King don Ferdinand hugged the Moorish King Boabdil. Not one veteran of the Andalusian campaigns, none of these one-eyed, one-armed, one-legged men was affronted by this gesture. Even the old Count of Cabra was seen wiping tears from his eyes with the back of his hand.

It had taken eight centuries of battle, hundreds of thousands of human lives, wealth beyond measure, to get to this kiss of peace. A kingdom was collapsing, and a young and united Spain was ready finally to make it disappear—without violence, simply with overwhelming peaceful strength. Boabdil sobbed on Ferdinand's breast, which made him feel very uncomfortable.

"Forgive your servant," said the Little King. "Please understand that the sacrifice I'm making excuses this moment of weakness."

"We will follow you," said Ferdinand.

The eighty thousand men of the Christian army stepped off as one, in a blur of moving steel composed of the flashes of weapons, helmets, and shields. The monarchs rode behind Boabdil. They passed close to the little village where Isabella had met David Ezra a few months earlier; the grass had turned yellow, and one of the roofs had collapsed under the weight of winter snow.

The queen's gaze wandered over these ruins, which prompted her to think about David. Was he still in Granada? Had he joined forces with the partisan bands who fought on in the Alpujarras? Was he dead? No—he couldn't be dead. Word would have gotten around.

They were getting nearer to Granada. The sharp teeth of its battlements began to stand out, the impregnable fortifications of the Alhambra could be seen ranged in lines up the hills, the slender buildings of the Albaicin came into view. Ochre and white merged in delicate harmonies.

Isabella experienced a few moments of intense emotion. In her imagination, she was following the little Isabella of Medina del Campo and of Segovia, who had taken her by the hand and was leading her toward the town. It looked as unreal as Christopher Columbus's Isle of Seven Cities.

They were closer than two miles away from Granada's first line of defenses when Boabdil stopped and raised his hand. Immediately the gates opened, and a crowd of men rushed forward on foot, surrounded by Moorish guards. Ferdinand felt a lump in his throat when these men broke ranks and ran, laughing, toward the Christians.

Boabdil turned around.

"These are your men. In accordance with our agreements, they are free. As you see, they have been properly treated."

The liberated prisoners, shouting excitedly, were greeted by roars from the entire army. Some of them came to kneel before their monarchs. Others ran to their regiments and vanished into the ranks, which opened to receive them. Battle songs broke out.

Finally, the Moorish notable came out from Granada, bearing the keys to the main gate. Boabdil took them, and entrusted them to Ferdinand. He passed them on to Isabella, who put them into the hands of Prince don Juan. Highly embarrassed, he gave them to the Count of Tendilla.

"Sire, permit me to go and raise the cross on the Tower of Comares," asked the Primate of all Spain.

"That could be dangerous," Boabdil commented.

In fact, the fortress, dominated by the tall Tower of Comares where the green standard of the Prophet flew, was far from calm. In the alleyways of Bibarambla, the crowd was gathering in ominous silence.

"Go," said the king. "But take some men with you."

He called from the ranks about ten knights known for their coolness. The Cardinal took the time to buckle on a sword-belt, and set off at the head of the small group.

When the Moors saw the Christians coming toward them, insults and threats broke out. Mendoza's horse had to force its way through a mass of humanity that was becoming ever more dense and excited. To let just a handful of men take a town like Granada, that was provocation indeed! An old man stepped in front of the cardinal and hit his horse on the nose with a stick. The animal reared up, whinnying.

The cardinal kept on going without veering to the right or to the left. He clasped tight to his chest the precious relics: the silver cross of Pope Sixtus, the banners of Santiago, and of the Catholic Monarchs. A party of Moorish soldiers threatened to run him through; he stopped, calmly watched their menacing gestures. As he started moving again, their lances were pulled back.

As they climbed in the shade of tall trees toward the Gate of Justice, an arrow lodged in the fleshly part of his shoulder. Without stopping or looking to either side, he deliberately pulled it out. He had only one fear: that the Alhambra's gates might be closed. They were open.

He made his way across the slopes and the fortress courtyards, and reached the Tower of Comares with no further mishap.

Hitching his horse to a ring, he brushed aside the *rakka* who tried to bar his way, drew his sword, and leapt up the Tower's stairway.

When he reached the top, he paused to catch his breath and to let his pulse return to normal. His wound was hurting, and the blood was flowing freely under his clothes—he felt its warmth right down to his belt.

Beyond the city's exterior houses, beyond the battlements where a few sentries were still keeping watch, he could make out a moving mass that was the Christian army, and heard the thunder of the *"Te Deum"* swelling over the massed regiments. Then he crossed himself, and set about completing his task.

Mendoza replaced the standard of the Moorish Kings with those of the Catholic Monarchs and of Santiago. He tied the heavy silver cross of Pope Sixtus to the top of the flagpole. The flags snapped in the fresh cold wind from the Sierra Nevada. At that moment the cardinal heard from far away in the *vega* eighty thousand soldiers' voices carried to him on the wind. He knelt and began to pray.

"I can't see a thing," said Ferdinand.

Princess Juana, who had slipped between the two sovereigns, let out a cry.

"They must have killed him, Mother! These pagans are quite capable. . . ."

Isabella interrupted her. "Idiot! Hold your tongue."

The little girl stopped talking. Both her hands were on her face, holding back the cry she felt rising in her throat. It was a cry of joy.

"I see him now, Mother. Yes, it's him, Mendoza! He's lowering the flag of Granada, and hoisting ours."

It was no use blinking—Ferdinand could see nothing of what Juana was reporting, even though the air was clear as crystal. Nor could Isabella. Tears were misting her eyes and blurring her vision of the battlements.

"Are you sure?" she asked.

"Oh, yes, Mother! There's no mistake—the flags are flapping in the wind, and the sun is making the cross sparkle."

"My God!" the queen whispered. "My God, thank you for letting us give you this kingdom."

She got down from her horse, and came toward the king, who was dismounting at the same time. She took him by the hand, and both fell to their knees.

The powerful voice of Ximenes Cisneros began singing behind them. Gonzales took up the hymn of thanksgiving, then the lord, and finally the whole army.

Only the Little King remained standing, head bowed. If the wind from the sierra had not flapped the corners of his cape, he could have been mistaken for a statue of white marble.

❧

The Christians waited for a few days before moving into Granada. As soon as the last of the forts that were part of its defenses had been taken, they decided to make an impressively solemn entry and to do it with a splendor never before seen.

Along the monarchs' route, the Christians in Granada had set up altars made from the myrtle, orange, and eucalyptus trees that kept the streets so fragrant. Isabella and Ferdinand went through the town on foot, stopping at each altar to offer up a brief prayer.

The crowd was fairly sparse. The Moors had stayed in their homes, closing the doors and shutters, or had taken refuge in the mosques and bolted the doors from inside. Boabdil, alone except for his mother, the old Queen Aicha, his wife, and his son, wandered around the deserted rooms of the Alhambra whose rich tapestries, precious objects, and rare furniture had been taken away.

"Stay," Isabella said to him. "There is plenty of time for you to make a decision."

"No, your Majesty. I must leave Granada. I cannot live in this town—it shouts of my defeat and my cowardice. For me and mine, it would be worse than prison."

"You know that you have only to make out a country from your old kingdom to be able to live there in peace?"

"I thank you for your generosity, your Majesty. But any city in Spain would be a prison for me."

"Where will you go?"

"Africa, your Majesty. That is my true kingdom."

Boabdil and his retinue left Granada early one January morning, ten days after the surrender of the city.

Isabella and Ferdinand, accompanied by the prince and princess, went with him as far as the Genil Gate. At the urging of the old queen, the *Rey Chico* had agreed to stay for a while in one of his old estates in the Alpujarras, between Padul and Motril.

Boabdil behaved with great dignity. When he came in sight of Padul, he reined in his horse on a low hill, leapt to the ground, and went on alone to an embankment. From there he could get a view of Granada through the layers of mist that the morning sun's yellow light was dispersing.

He stayed for a moment, motionless, his throat filled with the bitterness of tears, gazing at the town that had seen both his splendor and his misery. He felt that there was nothing left for him but to die.

Without his being aware of it, his mother, together with a few officers, came up to him. She tugged at his sleeve. Boabdil turned around, leaned on her shoulder, and burst into tears.

"Cry, my child," said the queen, "cry like a woman over this city that you didn't know how to defend like a man . . ."

Portrait of Christobal Colom, Spain, 16th century, unknown painter
Author's family patrimony

11

A Beggar Called Columbus

She knew that he could not have left Granada. Perhaps he was dead. Sometimes she actually wished he were dead, but at once regretted the thought. And all these possibilities would start up once more in her brain. "Do you know David Ezra? Have you heard anything about him? When did you last see him?"

She put the same questions to government ministers and donkey-drivers, to Boabdil's captains, and to water-carriers. She would interrupt children at play, give out a handful of coins, pat the backs of heads.

A lot of people had known the Jew. After he came back from the Bermejas mountains and the Green River, he had been seen fighting in Granada. They remembered his broad, powerful shoulders, his youthful appearance, his smile. A minister of state had often seen him with the king; a donkey-driver remembered spotting him leading an armed band; children knew a song about him.

Then one day the Jew had disappeared. The people Isabella talked to made a gesture of dismissal. *Pffft* . . . gone.

David could not have left Granada. He was certainly in hiding there. Isabella vowed to herself that she would find him. She poured gold into spies' moneybags, promised double to whoever could get onto the Jew's trail . . . and a fortune to he who could bring him back.

Fifteen "David Ezras" were brought to the queen—none of them the real one. In the end, she had to give up. A whole regiment of Swiss guards in full dress uniform could have been hidden in the Albaicin quarter alone, a beehive riddled with galleries, souks, underground passages, cellars. The Christian soldiers only went there armed to the teeth and in groups, their blunder-busses ready to spit flame. Anyone who lost his way never reappeared; at best his body might be found in the River Darro. There were more Moorish partisans in the Albaicin than in the Alpujaras and the Filabres combined.

Moreover, this searching was becoming dangerous for the queen.

Ferdinand made the observation one day that she was wasting her time. His smile was enough to tell her that he was aware of what was going on. One of Isabella's spies must have talked.

"You still love him as much, this Jew?"

"You may think whatever you like. But you are mistaken. I just want to be certain, whatever that certainty might be."

"If David is alive, we will find him. Two months from now, he will be groaning in a Triana jail. I will get his conversion before having him taken to the stake by Torquemada—and this time, not just in effigy. You know, I have to confess something. If Ezra renounces the Mosaic law, if he recants his Jewish heresy, everything will be possible: There won't be a Jew from Barcelona to Motril who will be able to refuse conversion."

"You will never get him to recant."

"Perhaps. But the game is exciting. I will be there each time the question is put to him. I will count his groans of pain."

"He will not groan."

"Really?"

Isabella shuddered. The steely eyes remained fixed on her, studying her, noticing the slightest weakening, the least tightening of her facial muscles.

"What makes you think David will be in your clutches two months from now?"

"All the Jews in the kingdom of Granada must leave Spain by March. All! Unless they accept baptism. You know my plan."

"I understand it, Ferdinand, and you know that to me it seems to be dangerous. The kingdom of Granada owes much of its prosperity to them. They hold considerable wealth, and . . ."

Ferdinand interrupted her. "They will leave Granada without their gold. Now more than ever, their wealth is an affront to the poverty of the royal treasury. Their gold belongs to Spain."

"Get rid of the Jews, and it won't be long before you see Greeks, Levantines, Genoese, even more greedy and grasping, and much less clever in astronomy, medicine, and history."

"No matter! Our treasure chests will be full."

"So you have no fear of God's judgment! It would be better if you accepted the offer that I proposed to the Jewish banker who came to see you two days ago. Take the five hundred thousand gold coins that he offers you, and leave the Jews in peace. Talavera will take the responsibility of turning them into good Christians."

Ferdinand leapt to his feet.

"Bargain with them? Never! Tomas de Torquemada, our Grand Inquisitor, was present when this Jew came to find me. He handed me the crucifix, and said, 'Sell them this Christ—the same as you are doing already? Such a thought is unworthy of you, Isabella. If you support that idea, people will think that you are protecting the Jews. I wonder, by the way, if that isn't what's at the back of your mind—your acceptance of the Inquisition has always been tinged with disgust! You are only grudgingly present at the *autos-da-fe*; and this Ezra, this rebel, this soldier of Satan, whom you are trying to save . . .'"

"Ferdinand!"

"Do you take me for a child, Isabella? My father, King John, taught me to be wary of my immediate circle, even of my own family. None of your thoughts, none of your actions escape my notice. I know that at this moment you detest me and love the Jew. There's no use hiding your face with your hands."

Isabella felt the world crumbling around her. She could not bear David being absent, nor the knowledge that only chance, or his own initiative, could bring them together again. And she knew that if he did appear before her once more, she would try to tear him out of her consciousness as though he were part of herself.

Although he was away, she imagined him to be all around her. When he was with her, she saw only a reflection of him. They would never again meet in a simple relationship, not through this maze of contradictory emotions. Even as she thought about this, she imagined David with such intensity that he seemed to come alive in the palms of her hands. She heard herself say a prayer that sounded as though it was coming from outside herself.

Then she heard Ferdinand's voice breaking into her thoughts:

"Ezra isn't the sort of man who could spend a long time in hiding. He will mingle with the Jews who leave Granada, he will try to go with them to Portugal, to Africa, but we will stop him. Because he's still alive, isn't he, still in Granada? You know it, you feel it?"

"Yes. David is alive."

At the close of the month of March following the fall of Granada, the queen knew that she was pregnant.

This news put the king into an excellent frame of mind. The future of the dynasty rested with Juan; but, at fourteen, the prince of Castile had scarcely more maturity than at the age when he and his sister Juana were playing with dolls. He had developed no interests other than looking after his appearance, watching the light entertainments put on by strolling players, close friendships, and passionate love affairs with the equerries and young ladies of the court.

He was fair-haired, pale-looking, and of such delicate health that the slightest vexation was enough to make him sick. The queen saw in him the living image of her brother Henry, both physically and morally, and nothing led her to suppose that he would have any more brilliant a future. And so the evidence of her pregnancy and the hope of a male heir to the throne gave her, as well as the king, profound joy.

"So, your Majesty, you refuse?"

In Columbus's voice was such a tone of distress that Isabella was moved by it. She felt pity for this man dressed like a beggar, carrying in his pouch wads of greasy paper mixed with crusts of bread—sketches of a world that was the product of his fevered imagination. The westerly route to the Indies, Antilia, the Isle of Seven Cities, Zipangu . . .

"Yes, we refuse," said Ferdinand, "and I advise you not to bother us again. We've had enough of your wasting our time with your shameless pestering."

"But I bring you an empire, gold—mountains of gold! What I ask in return is nothing . . ."

"What empire? What gold?" shouted Ferdinand. "Bring me one grain of proof of what you have told us, and I am ready to help you."

Quickly, Columbus rummaged in his pouch with suppressed frenzy. Ferdinand stopped him.

"No use! Your scribblings are not proof, not even a hypothesis. Besides, the academics at the University of Salamanca are quite positive: Beyond the known islands are nothing but sea, emptiness, and danger."

"Beyond those islands," replied the beggar, "there are . . ."

"You are becoming a bore! And what's more, your demands are outrageous. A noble title, the rank of admiral, an appointment as viceroy? What more do you want, Jew?"

"One tenth of the wealth of the lands conquered by your Majesties." Columbus spoke very calmly.

The beggar turned his large watery eyes to the queen. Isabella smiled at him, and immediately reproached herself for having done so. Columbus was no longer funny. A few months earlier, he had amused them and given them some ideas to dream about. Now, he was sad, whining, short-tempered. Moreover, it was said that he was living with a young woman from a class of people with fairly loose moral standards.

Isabella spoke non-commitally.

"Our treasury is exhausted, Columbus, exhausted by the war in Granada. Our treasurer, Luis de Santangel, told you so—and he is one who likes and supports you . . ."

Columbus sighed faintly and shook his head. The queen wore round her neck a medallion that could have been sold to supply enough flour for three *caravels* for a voyage of several months. The two pearls that adorned the king's shoes represented a month's pay for a hundred seamen, including the officers. . . . He bowed, and left. Ferdinand's voice struck him like a whip on the back of his neck—"Adios!"

Three men were waiting in the antechamber. Luis de Santangel, Juan Cabrero, the king's private secretary, and Diego Deza, the monk who was private tutor to the prince and Princess of Castile. Columbus saw them, and shook his head. Anger and despondency were mingled in the pitiable expression on his face. He dropped on to a bench and began to sob.

"The *caravels* are ready, moored in the port of Palos. They only need to be fitted out, to get permission to load, and a few guarantees. To fail, so close to our goal! The king threw me out— me, Christopher Columbus! He humiliated me, trampled all over me with his sarcasm, insulted . . ."

"What did the queen say?" asked Santangel.

"The queen . . . the queen . . ." stammered the unhappy man. "What would you want her to say? She seemed to be convinced a few months ago, but suddenly I realized that she has lost interest. All she could do was offer me words of pity . . . of pity!"

"That's the end of that, then," sighed Friar Deza.

"We have done all that we could," added Cabrero, his hand on the beggar's shoulder.

"No!" said Luis de Santangel.

All three looked at him.

"No!" continued the treasurer. "We haven't explored every possible avenue. Columbus, do you still have confidence in me?"

Columbus didn't seem to hear. His dreams in ruins, he was crying, face buried in his hands.

"Let me talk with the queen. She will be alone in a few minutes. I will make one last attempt. If I don't succeed, I will have earned the contempt you will have for me—the faith that I have in you will not have been strong enough for me to persuade dona Isabella to share that faith."

Columbus waited an hour, and then rose. He had not said a word since Santangel had left. His eyes were red, and the lines in his cheeks shone with tears. He checked that his pouch was still slung from his shoulder, and walked like an old man across the antechamber.

"Where are you going?" asked the friar.

Columbus didn't reply.

"Wait for us in the garden!" Cabrero called after him.

Columbus turned around, and shook his head.

"Luis promised to be brief," said Deza, who was beginning to lose patience.

"I'm going to take a nap," said Juan Cabrero. "Wake me up if anything happens."

Luis was fighting for his convictions with all the force he could muster. When the queen had heard the reason for his request for an audience, she almost lost her temper and sent him away. But Santangel had begged with such persuasiveness for the right to be heard that she finally relented.

He really had a fight on his hands, to overcome first the queen's hostility, and then her indifference. He made her recognize that if the worlds that Columbus so believed in were nothing more than a fanciful dream, the privileges he demanded with such persistence would remain, by the same token, a dead issue. The monarchs would risk nothing.

"And how would the expenses of the expedition be met?"

"I will take care of them," Santangel assured her.

The words just slipped out, but they had such an impact on the queen that he did not regret saying them. What did it matter how he planned to fulfill such a risky commitment, if it helped to make the queen yield!

She yielded.

"We have yet to convince the king," said Santangel.

"I will make that my business. I have given in too much and too often to don Ferdinand on equally important matters—he will not refuse me this favor. Go quickly and let Columbus know that I will be waiting to see him early tomorrow. And make him understand that he should not appear before me dressed like a tramp."

Feeling unsteady with joy, Luis de Santangel made a dash for the antechamber and shook Deza and Cabrero, who were leaning against each other, asleep.

"Where did Columbus go?"

"He's waiting for us in the courtyard."

The treasurer leapt down the stairs, ran through the courtyards and the galleries, jumped on a horse, flew to the Santa Fe parade ground, rushed back to the palace, questioned the guards. They had seen some sort of beggar leave town and set off in a northwesterly direction about two hours earlier.

Without dismounting, Santangel went back to his two friends.

"Follow me! We must find him before nightfall!"

The three riders headed at full speed into the *vega* and galloped several leagues toward Moclin. They reached the Rio Cubillas, on the lower slopes of the Sierra Elvira and crossed by an ancient bridge, clogged with sheep and turkeys. On the far side they could see the beggar, leaning against the wall of an old mosque in the sunshine. He seemed to be asleep, with his mule tied up beside him. Santangel dismounted.

"Colombus! Wake up!"

"What do you want with me?" were the beggar's first words. "Where am I?"

"You are at Pinos Puente. You must come with us to Granada."

"Never!" the beggar roared.

"Don't be ridiculous. I have managed to persuade the queen. She expects you tomorrow."

"No! She will only tell me that she hasn't been able to reach a decision. Anyway, they are expecting me at Palos."

"Then why are you taking the Moclin road?"

Columbus was stubborn. He stayed seated, gray with dust, forehead on his bent knees, hugging his pouch to his stomach. At each comment from Santangel, Deza, or Cabrero, he shook his head obstinately. When one of them got too close to him, he recoiled like a hunted animal.

"Help me," said Santangel.

They managed to force him onto his mule. He mumbled some words into his beard that Santangel couldn't make out.

"What are you trying to say, Columbus?"

"I'm telling you that I don't even have one penny to go to the barber's shop."

⚜

All Castile, all Spain, was beginning to tremble.

It only needed a red-coated *alguazil*, a police constable, to make a public announcement in the towns and villages, to flourish and read the royal proclamation, for a palpable shudder to sweep through the populace. Little groups of urchins gathered in the alleys, shouting,

"The monarchs are driving out the Jews! In three months, there will not be one unconverted Jew left in Spain!"

In those few moments, it seemed as though a dreadful fire had started raging through the streets and houses. In the towns, the Jews locked themselves into their ghettoes and blocked up their windows. There they heard with terror the mutterings of the excited populace, the noise they knew usually heralded a massacre.

They were being driven out! What would become of them? That uncle in Cyprus, the cousins in Algeria—would they make them welcome? Poor as church mice, they will leave for the ports of Andalusia or the Levant. The monarchs had ordered them to turn over their gold to the public funds.

They were being driven out! Why? They had been forced out of Egypt. Now they were being thrown out of Spain, where some families had settled more than a thousand years before. Would they be able to find ships? And how would they pay for the voyage? All the Jaces, the Abners, the Levys of Spain who were afraid to seek permission to stay began making preparations. They sold their estates and their businesses at ridiculously low prices.

And the great exodus began.

Who would have imagined that there were so many unconverted Jews in Spain? In the old kingdom of Granada, 200,000 of them set off for southern ports, on their way to Africa. During the whole three months, that number would rise to more than 800,000.

The roads were jammed with great wagonloads of pathetic belongings and with an unending stream of exhausted people straggling in the spring heat. The dust raised by all this movement

The King Ferdinand and Queen Isabella issued a writ that decreed the expulsion of all Jews from Spain.

only settled at night, settled back on the track worn down to its rocky bed by the wheels, the clogs, the feet of the refugees.

Highwaymen had a field day: they attacked and robbed with ease. They stormed down from the mountains in bands, intercepted the fleeing streams of people, and returned to their lairs, as often as not without having had to use a weapon.

When arrested by police, the Jews were hardly any safer. Mightn't they swallow gold coins cut into small pieces? The constables had no hesitation in killing suspects to search their entrails. The women were humiliated at finding their dirty hands all over their bodies.

Even in the middle of such misery, Israel sang. The rabbis who walked at the head of their flocks chanted old Hebrew melodies that told of the hope of the Promised Land, unendingly frustrated, unendingly revived.

In the evenings, sitting around great fires, they recalled the ordeals of the lost tribe wandering in the Egyptian desert. Everyone acknowledged that their ancestors' lot had been even harder to bear than their own. They kissed the ground when they saw the sea appear in the distance at Palos, Malaga, or Valencia, where Ferdinand's ships were waiting.

Not long before the end of May, the Jews who were coming from Caceres to board ship at Palos encountered a strange company.

A man who seemed to be in a hurry was walking at the head of fifteen or so soldiers who carried a standard bearing the five anchors of the Admiral of the High Seas.

Now and again he turned around to speed them up. When he caught up with the straggling Jewish crowd, he raised his hand in greeting, but kept his eyes fixed on the ground. The Jews pulled to the side of the road to let the Grand Admiral's convoy go past. They inquired of the driver of the last vehicle as to the name of this great personage.

"He is the famous Christopher Columbus. In a few months, he plans to set sail for the Indies by the westerly route."

"Christopher Columbus," the Jews murmured.

Columbus was one of theirs, they knew, a *converso*. He was on the road to glory, they to misery. Through the golden dust rising from the track, they watched for a long time as the great Columbus's procession headed into the distance. When they started on their way once more, the road seemed longer and rougher.

"What are you hiding in these bags?"

"Bread and dried meat," replied the Jew.

The *alguazil* mopped his brow, drank a mouthful of sherry from his flask, and his attitude became more threatening. He seized the old man by his shirt collar and shouted in his face.

"And your gold, Judas, where have you hidden it?"

"I have no gold—you know that the monarchs have forbidden us to bring any. Besides, I'm only a poor Granada cobbler, and . . ."

There was violent shoving behind the pair, who were stopped in the entrance to the port of Palos. Shouting broke out. People were getting impatient.

The *alguazil* took the old man aside, still holding him at arm's length. He shook him like a tree.

"If you tell me where your gold is hidden, I will let you through. You will have no problems, I will keep my mouth shut. In your bags? In your clothes? In your belly? You've swallowed it, right, Jew-pig?"

"I swear that I have no gold! I am . . ."

". . . penniless! They all say that. Don't force me to hurt you. Admit . . ."

The *alguazil* threw the old man onto a bank of earth between two empty warehouses, drew a knife, and held it to his throat.

"Stop!" The voice came from behind him.

The *alguazil* turned around sharply. He turned very pale when he caught sight of the giant who was quietly approaching him, smiling through his blond beard.

"You are wasting your time. Abraham Mardoch has not one gram of gold."

"Who is this?" the *alguazil* demanded of the old Jew.

"My son."

The constable turned to the giant. "What do you want?"

"I want you to leave this man alone. Give me your knife."

The colossus, still smiling, held out his hand. The *alguazil* struck at him with all his strength, but the blade was lost in the folds of the Jew's billowing shirt. The giant grabbed his wrist, effortlessly pulled him closer and, with a violent blow, stretched him out in the dust without a sound.

"We are done for!" groaned the old man. "Get away quickly, or you will be recognized and thrown in jail!"

"I don't want to leave you, Rabbi Abraham."

"It's not me who's at risk. Go, go—otherwise you're as good as dead—so close to your goal! Go, and may God protect you."

The giant had only just turned around when he caught sight of two more *alguazils* heading his way. He quickly retrieved the knife, slid it into his belt, leapt behind the wooded warehouse buildings, and started to run through the port. He jostled past excited groups of people, jumped over heaps of baggage, at such a speed that the two *alguazils* who were running after him soon lost track.

Even so, he did not slacken his pace, but continued running. When he saw another police patrol coming from the opposite direction, he altered his course and ran into a huge stone building in the center of the port—the one place he should have kept clear of.

He found himself in a dark corridor giving onto rooms from which came the sound of conversation. He had reached the end of the corridor when a voice called out:

"Hey, you there, where are you going? What do you want?"

The Jew coolly turned around and stood towering in front of the squat, bearded doorkeeper.

"I am trying to find out the name of a man for whom I have an important message. Would you believe, I've forgotten it on my way here. Let's see, now . . ."

He drew back a curtain and looked into a narrow room filled with charts and globes, compasses and sextants, smelling of parchment and old leather.

"Let's see, now, who is that balding man with the hooked nose and stooped shoulders?"

"That is the famous lord don Christopher Columbus, Castilian Grand Admiral of the High Seas."

"Christopher Columbus! He's the very man I'm looking for. Please let him know that I've arrived."

The doorkeeper studied the shabbily dressed man in front of him with some defiance. He pulled a face.

"Your weapon! Leave it on the table. What name shall I say?"

"Tell him that I am here on behalf of Queen dona Isabella."

The admiral barely lifted his eyes to look at the newcomer. He toyed with the compass while he listened distractedly to the Jew's stumbling introduction of himself. Suddenly he gave a start.

"What's that you said?"

"I said that I am called David Ezra, my lord."

"David Ezra . . . David Ezra . . . that name sounds familiar. King don Ferdinand was talking about you on one occasion with some of his lords—and not very favorably, I might add."

"I am Jewish. And I refuse to be baptized. They were hunting for me, so I fled."

"And they are still looking for you?"

"More than ever. Even as we speak, the *alguazils* are scouring the port to find me."

"And you've come to me to find refuge?" cried Columbus. "As if I didn't have enough problems. What do you want of me? What can I do for you?"

"Let me embark in one of your ships bound for the Indies."

Columbus screwed up his tired eyes. His big nose betokened his intelligence; now, all the wrinkles around it deepened.

"The Indies . . . Ezra, do you believe we can get there?"

David lowered his head and pounded a clenched fist into his open palm.

"I believe that there is somewhere in this world where men are something other than wolves, desperately trying to destroy and devour each other. I would do anything to discover such a place. I am afraid of nothing and of no one and, when I commit myself to a person or to a cause, my own life doesn't count. Take me on, my lord Columbus—you won't regret it."

"What you are forgetting, Ezra, is that we are not going on board until August. What will you do between now and then? I can't keep you in my sea chest, you know!"

"I left Granada dressed as a mule driver. I can get away with equally surprising things."

"Do you know what risks I run by protecting you? It could mean the end of everything I've worked for over the last sixteen years. Sixteen years, do you hear me? There is no man alive who would do such a stupid thing."

"If Jews will not come to the aid of Jews, where are we all heading, to what eternity of misery?"

"I am not Jewish!" screamed the admiral. "We are all Christians in my family. When I was a child, I used to sing in church, in Genoa! Jewish! Where did you hear such nonsense?"

"Very well." David sighed. "You can hand me over to the police. But I will just mention that you and your family were born in Felanitz in Mallorca before you became 'pure' *converso* Christian and moved to Genoa to escape the Inquisition."

At this, David really believed that the admiral was going to choke. He watched him raise his fist and smack it down on a chart criss-crossed with red and blue lines, where islands and continents were outlined in yellow and green dots. The blow threw up a cloud of fine, sweet-smelling dust.

"Hand you over to the police? Do you know to whom you are speaking, you idiot? On the cross of Christ, I would rather that my ships never left this port . . ."

Painting of Christopher Columbus, Modern, Spanish
Property of the author

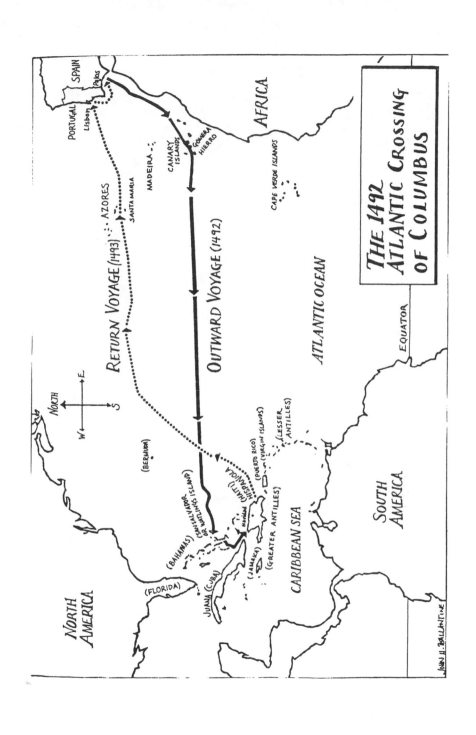

THE 1492 ATLANTIC CROSSING OF COLUMBUS

SPAIN
Palos
PORTUGAL
Lisbon
MADEIRA
CANARY ISLANDS
GOMERA
HIERRO
CAPE VERDE ISLANDS
AFRICA

RETURN VOYAGE (1493)
AZORES
SANTA MARIA

OUTWARD VOYAGE (1492)

ATLANTIC OCEAN

EQUATOR

NORTH
S E
W

(BERMUDA)

NORTH AMERICA

(FLORIDA)

JUANA (CUBA)
(BAHAMAS)
SAN SALVADOR OR WATLINGS ISLAND
(JAMAICA)
(GREATER ANTILLES)
Navidad
HISPANIOLA
(HAITI)
(PUERTO RICO)
(VIRGIN ISLANDS)
(LESSER ANTILLES)

CARIBBEAN SEA

SOUTH AMERICA

JOHN H. BALLANTINE

12

Calamities and the New World

For the Catholic Monarchs, 1492 was a year of high hopes. It was as if Columbus, by sailing away to find the eastern isles, had given greater significance to the conquest of Granada. It was as though he had been given the mission of bringing to continents as yet unknown the news of this triumph, a triumph that was reverberating around all Christendom.

The little kingdom of Navarre, always hovering between France and Spain, was imperceptibly becoming closer to the monarchs.

When Isabella and Ferdinand looked at Portugal, they saw nothing but grounds for rejoicing. They were counting the days to the marriage of their older daughter Isabel, widow of Prince Afonso, to the new King, don Emmanuel. Isabel had consented—unenthusiastically, but without strong objection—to cease wearing mourning dress, and to trample underfoot the bitter memories of lost love.

Little was needed for the monarchs to rule over a totally united Spain: just the counties of Cerdagne and Roussillon, sharing the capital of Perpignan.

Spain was expanding like a purse full of gold. Her internal boundaries were disappearing, and her frontiers were her coastline.

With the expulsion of the Jews, the concept of "pure blood" was becoming a reality. One single faith was being achieved under the bloody banners of Torquemada and of Ximenes de Cisneros, now known as the "Third Monarch."

One night, Ferdinand had a dream that was so vivid he fell out of bed, bathed in sweat. He woke with a splitting headache, as if a

The enforced baptism of the Moors of Granada in 1499: a detail from the Capilla Real, Granada, High Altar

too-heavy crown was weighing down on him. Shivering, he tried to recall his dream:

Columbus had just disembarked. He had brought back for him new lands, exotic animals, and gold, gold, gold—gold flowing like a river from his pockets, his sleeves, his mouth. Ferdinand was perched on a throne, high as a mountain, from which he could see a vast empire laid out beneath him. His kingdom was spreading rapidly to the east and to the west. The seas were not barriers, but highways leading to his distant possessions. Austria and Italy were under his dominion. Austria . . . Italy . . .

Ferdinand had gone back to sleep with those names on his lips.

A few days after that episode, he sent one of his most skilled diplomats, Juan Manuel, to the Emperor Maximilian. His mission was to expedite the double union he had developed. Prince Juan was to marry Marguerite of Austria, and Princess Juana would wed Archduke Philippe-le-Beau. If this double marriage worked the way the King of Spain envisaged, the Habsburg empire would fall under Spanish rule.

Ferdinand's plan was a very clever one, and Isabella could only agree with it. If Juan were to die without an heir, the right of succession to Castile and Aragon, which he would inherit from his mother and father, would go to Isabel, or failing that, to Juana. Moreover, in marrying Juana, Archduke Philippe would bring with him the Habsburg empire and the Houses of Burgundy and Austria. Ferdinand told his ambassador to make sure Emperor Maximilian understood that his states could be taken over by the Spanish crown, while Spain itself was not at risk of being absorbed into Austria.

It was an audacious plan, but Juan Manuel succeeded beyond their wildest dreams.

Boabdil had finally decided to leave Spain with his family, his personal black *rakka* guards, and his innumerable retainers. His small kingdom in the Alpujarras—a castle and some villages—was no longer enough for him, and the methods Ximenes was using to convert his fellow Muslims were repellent to him.

The Inquisition, originally against the Jews, was extended to the Muslims of all of Spain to the limit of the year 1500 to be fully executed.

He sold the few acres of land under his control to King Ferdinand for 800,000 ducats and went to Africa. Here, in an engagement against other tribesmen, he fell, his chest pierced by the thrust of a lance. His body was not recovered until the next day, half eaten by hyenas . . . but they had spared his face.

Ferdinand told Isabella about his dream.

"It is not right for you to believe your dreams,"

the queen told him. "Accept what God gives you, follow the path He has set out before you, but do not seek to see beyond that. Who knows when you might be no more, or what traps might be lying in wait for you? God will provide for our greatness, just as He has provided for our military successes. But He doesn't like our forecasting His intentions, or taking his generosity for granted."

Isabella knew how useless it was to talk this way. Ferdinand listened only to his ambitions: this voice, which was not God's voice, spoke to him of world domination. Sometimes he would repeat these words as if he were still dreaming. Isabella pretended not to hear him, and Ferdinand would appear to be shocked. He liked to think that his wife was a mirror of his smallest wishes, of his most fanciful ambitions.

Isabella no longer heard him. An inner voice told her that such a wealth of favors would be followed by sad tomorrows. She watched Juan playing in the courtyard and wondered, what would happen if he were taken from us? Juan was their only male heir. He was no healthier than their other children, Juana, and the last two, Maria and Catalina.

How could it have been otherwise? The queen had endured difficult pregnancies. Life had not been easy for her, nor had she taken the care of herself that she should. And what did she have to show for it? Her people's adoration? She felt herself to be distant from that adoration, vague, lacking enthusiasm. A sort of cloud was carrying her, but that could very easily give way.

Ferdinand's love? She didn't believe in it any more. The radiant couple of Valladolid, the outlawed newlyweds, rich only in their love and in their hope, had become a mundane married pair, with their full share of storms and compromises.

The affection of her children? Sickly, raised in a court of monks and soldiers, they had grown up almost as though they were in hiding. Their exteriors were that of thorny plants: the gentle, loving side of their natures had turned inward, making them egoistic.

Isabella kept some happy memories. David. The very name threw her soul into confusion. If she spoke the word, she would not be capable of rational thought guided by the logic and wisdom that were among her major attributes. Everything else would become unclear, and only David's face would remain in focus.

Was he dead? If so, she was amazed that no one had found his body. Exiled? She was forced to admit that he could have left Granada. Whatever might have happened to him, she had crossed out his name to no avail; her balance, her rationality were lost. She would have turned him away if he had come to her again, and yet his absence gave her a feeling of irreparable loss.

⁂

"God does not like our forecasting His intentions, or taking His generosity for granted . . ." She had repeated those words to Ferdinand many times, but he had paid no attention to the warning. And this is how God struck.

The bells of Barcelona were tolling midday when Ferdinand decided to end the tribunal session. As soon as the great iron door leading to a sunlit Plaza del Rey had been opened, the crowd surged noisily through it. It was a fine December morning, and a sea breeze, laden with the smell of tar, was blowing.

Ferdinand left last, with his treasurer, Luis de Santangel. Santangel went on talking, and Ferdinand was listening and nodding his head.

"Come with me to the Palace," said the king. "We will have plenty of time to discuss our concerns."

They reached the bottom of the steps leading to the square as the bells' vibrations were dying away, among the ceaseless talk of judges and people. Ferdinand signaled to his equerry to bring his horse. Just as he set foot on the very last step, a youth holding a sword rushed out from behind a pillar, leapt at the king, and struck him a terrible blow in the back with all his might.

The king did not fall at once. He got as far as his horse, to have something to hold on to, and only then did he turn to see his assailant, a swarthy little peasant on whom he had imposed a fine for some offense involving cattle theft.

Ferdinand pointed at the wretched man who, a moment later, was buried under a mass of people. He allowed them to tie him up without resisting.

When the king was picked up, he seemed to be dead. The blade had made a deep gash from the top of his head to his shoulder, half severing an ear. His golden chain had prevented the blade from going farther.

Isabella leapt up and threw herself toward the window. The crowd was shouting, "the king is dead!" and the square seethed with people rushing in every direction. Someone came up from behind the queen to support her, whispering words she did not hear. The room was suddenly full of lamenting monks and knights. Juana was crying, sitting next to Juan, who was stroking Catalina's head with the palm of his hand to keep her from moaning.

The queen managed to reach the courtyard, leapt on a horse, and forced a path through the crowd to the Plaza del Rey.

The king had been laid out on the steps, his head resting on a saddle. He was not dead, but seemed to be very close to it. When Isabella bent over him, he did not open his eyes. A doctor who had obeyed the emergency summons gently moved the queen to one side, put a plaster on the profusely bleeding wound with an air of confidence, and called for a stretcher.

"Has the culprit been arrested?" asked the queen. Santangel pointed at a group standing behind her.

The queen turned to see in what guise God had appeared.

Ferdinand healed slowly. The wound became infected several times, and, when it looked as though he was on the road to recovery, a sharp bout of fever would set him back into an uncertain state.

The queen had him taken to the monastery of San Geronimo de la Mata, not far from Barcelona, set in a solitude of stone and greenery. The spring was balmy and fragrant with all the flowers of the mountain. Isabella only left his side to go to the chapel, where she lost herself in endless prayers.

An unforeseen incident took place that disturbed the king's healing process—the return of Columbus. He had disembarked on March 15 in the little port of Palos. Ferdinand heard the news while, leaning on the queen's arm, he was taking his first steps in the myrtle walk at San Geronimo.

"Now you can see that God has not abandoned us,"
he said, smiling through his unkempt beard.

"We must write at once to Columbus, ask him to come and tell us about his voyage. I am eager to see the color of the gold from Antilla and Cipangu . . ."

❧

"He's coming! Make way, make way! Here's the Grand Admiral!"

Mounted *alguazils* charged in a whirl of red and gold brocade to make way through the throng in front of the royal tribune. Here, under an immense green velvet canopy supported by small wreathed columns, the Catholic Monarchs were waiting for the admiral.

When the constables had opened up a passage wide enough for the two leading coaches, a mighty murmuring rose from the square, and the bells of San Jaime, San Justo, Santa Maria del Mar, and the cathedral all started to swing at the same moment. A fanfare sounded from the trumpeters in their yellow-striped red jerkins, drawn up in a line on top of the palace battlements.

Prince Juan, who took precedence over all the great men of Spain ranged on each side of the tribunal, went up a few steps toward the queen. She smiled at him, and asked,

"Do you see the admiral coming, my angel?"

Juan nodded. He had just spotted a rider mounted on a dark chestnut horse. Behind him came the five-anchored banner.

Isabella nearly stood up, and the sword of Justice that she was carrying fell off her knees. She felt more emotional than she liked to admit, even to herself, and the beating of her heart was painful. With a sense of shame she remembered that this man was the beggar to whom she had given a handful of coins so that he could present himself at court properly dressed. Today, this same man was bringing her a world: She would now have to beg him to go back to sea, so that he could add to the territories of Christ and of Christendom.

She felt very small in front of this giant who had enough faith to believe in his dreams, and enough courage to make them come true. What had she herself done? What had she achieved, compared to Columbus? Her own accomplishments had been limited by what she thought to be possible. Columbus, on the other hand, had undertaken what no man before him had dared—and there he was, just a few steps away.

Ferdinand rose and went to meet him just as if the admiral had been the Emperor Maximilian of Austria, or King Charles VIII of France.

Columbus had assumed the airs and graces of a great lord. After kissing the monarchs' hands, he sat down beside them on a stool placed close to the royal chairs for his benefit. He dominated the crowd of courtiers with a majesty that could have been taken for haughtiness had it not been entirely natural to him.

Hardly had he sat down when he gave a signal, and the Court was stupefied to see two half-naked, copper-colored men come forward. They bore two caskets, which they placed on the knees of the king and queen. The queen's box contained an enormous emerald; its solid-gold setting was engraved with strange designs. The king's revealed a life-size mask of gold set with precious stones for eyes, which seemed to be alive. The king and the queen both gasped.

"These two slaves are yours also,"

said Columbus. The queen frowned, and thanked him coldly. Even though the emerald delighted her, she found it difficult to understand how the generosity of the Viceroy of the West Indies could be sullied with such tactlessness. Before he left, Columbus had promised her that he would not introduce slavery into the Isles. They had taken a lot of trouble to eliminate it from Spain.

"Are they baptized?" she asked.

Columbus looked offended.

"They certainly are, your Majesty! The same as all those you see passing in front of you. These people are amenable by nature."

Columbus had very cleverly collected together anything that would surprise, interest, or intrigue. The splendor of multicolored birds, the exotic animals in their cages, the odd appearance of the Indians' style of dress, all this held the monarchs and the court spellbound. The spectators of this parade seemed to be in a kind of waking dream. It seemed to them that they had entered a world that had no connection with everyday reality.

"I had intended . . ." said Columbus, as the spectacle drew to its conclusion with a performance by bare-breasted dancing girls,

"I had intended to bring back one of the extraordinary creatures from the province of Cibao who are born, boys and girls alike, with a tail. Unfortunately, I didn't have time."

Ferdinand and Isabella gazed open-mouthed. There were no limits to the possible. They were now prepared to believe anything Columbus told them, whereas some months earlier they had doubted the feasibility of his plans.

Ferdinand turned toward the Viceroy of the Indies, Grand Admiral of the High Seas.

"When do you expect to sail again, my dear Columbus?"

The response of the Grand Admiral chilled him.

"I don't yet know. There are so many projects clamoring for my attention."

More than anything, Ferdinand was afraid that Columbus might respond favorably to the King of Portugal's offers. While the Grand Admiral was at Court, the king made sure that he was treated splendidly. He even went so far as to have the servants taste his food in front of him, so that he would have no fear of being poisoned.

He was authorized to lodge at any of the castles belonging to the Spanish crown, together with five retainers, and would be charged only for food. He was granted permission to incorporate the lion and the castle into his personal coat of arms, usually a royal prerogative. He was showered with gold. He was accorded all the benefits he had asked for, and even some he had never dared claim. With not the slightest scruples, he pocketed the ten thousand *maravedis*, which by royal decree were to go to the first sailor to sight land.

When it was decided that Columbus would go on a new expedition to the Indies, it was not with just three poor ships, but with seventeen *caravel*s. The second departure would be not from the little port of Palos, but from Cadiz.

By mid-September the armada and its fifteen hundred passengers was ready for Columbus. They set sail for the Canaries on the 25th.

⚜

"God doesn't like our forecasting his intentions," Isabella repeated.

With humility, she accepted the power and wealth that seemed to Ferdinand to be in the natural way of things. The Catholic Monarchs never ceased in word, thought, and deed, to serve God. God rewarded them; better than that, he gave them strength for new challenges. According to Ferdinand, it was not proper to scorn such generosity.

Ferdinand talked about these new worlds, whose discovery had been begun by Columbus, with such enthusiasm and conviction that the queen became a little scared. She was not yet prepared for such ambitions. The goals she had set for herself—the unity of Spain and of the Faith—were enough for her. Those distant horizons where Ferdinand's aspirations were forever roaming seemed to her to be nothing but a bottomless abyss. She thought to herself, "The greater will be the fall."

"Let me through!" shouted the queen.

With difficulty, she made her way through the crowd besieging the Episcopal palace of Toledo, shoving past black-capped students in pointed hats, cowled pilgrims, monks in their blue habits. She struggled along like the humblest of women in the middle of this throng where no one knew her.

Archbishop Mendoza was dying.

Could it be that he was already dead? All alone, she had dismounted and run to the palace, where the Toledo crowd was gathering in the ice-cold rain. A woman laughed in her face. A lost child became tangled in her robe, and clung to her belt. She had to see the cardinal before he died.

She ran like a mad woman. All the gates were open. She followed in the wake of black robes, in the smell of burnt tallow.

The cardinal lay on his bed, eyes closed, his beautiful plump hands resting on the sheet.

"Your Eminence, it is I, the queen. Can you hear me? I rushed here the very moment I heard that you had fallen ill."

Bowed heads were raised. The queen could now see pallid faces appearing in the candlelight, golden crosses gleaming, gems sparkling on hands joined in prayer. A voice whispered,

"His Eminence cannot hear you, your Majesty."

The queen's brow dropped to the back of the hand resting on the sheet. Mendoza was so bound up with her own life that it seemed as though part of that life had just been taken from her. She could remember him as a young bishop, just twenty-six years old, when she had been a mere child at the Court of Castile. Years later, he had fought for her against the usurper, Jeanne-la-Beltraneja.

He was sometimes rough and very candid, sometimes clever and affable. He was a classic example of the great warrior-prelate in an age when Christ needed such men for his Kingdom. The queen had been his dear child. He had shown her how great was her royal mission. He had been her most clear-sighted advisor, her severest confessor.

He had been the only one to whom she had ever dared speak of David Ezra, that evening long ago in the cloisters and gardens of Santa Cruz, just a few steps from where she was kneeling now.

The queen would have liked to have joined her prayers with those being murmured around her, but the words would not come out. She could not accept that this tall figure, still warm, stretched out on the bed, was a corpse. She felt herself to be linked with him in a kind of half-light that was neither life nor death, and in which they could resume the conversation that had been broken off.

Voluntas Dei . . . Missus a Deo. . . .

The French King Charles VIII's banners bearing these words were surging back toward the north of Italy. The king's pre-emptive "crusade" against the Moors who were threatening the peninsula, and against the anarchy that was splitting the little Italian republics, was broken off.

Gonzales de Cordova, the Catholic Monarchs' most valiant officer, the "Great Captain," had just come ashore in Calabria and Apulia. In the middle of a torrid summer, with forced marches along the worst mountain roads, he advanced on Naples at the head of his formidable Spanish infantry. He finally entered the town early in 1496. A few days later, he sent the crown of Naples to the monarchs.

All of fifteenth-century Italy shone from the gold and the jewels in that crown. Ferdinand looked at it for a long time and fondled it, stroked it with the ends of his mustache, lifted it up to the sun, put it on his head, invited Isabella to wear it. He played with it like a child. He played with it so much and so well that it ended up slipping from his fingers and rolling under a piece of furniture. The king had to get down on his knees to retrieve it.

❦

"We have driven the French from Italy," wrote Maximilian.

"Now we should think about getting our children married."

"Poor, dear Maximilian," said Ferdinand.

"He has just offered us the Habsburg empire in a golden basket. And he presses us to accept. How could we insult him by refusing?"

He winked at the queen before going on.

"Does God suggest that we should refuse, Isabella?"

Prince Don Juan
Son of Queen Isabella and King Ferdinand

Original painting and frame, circa 1495
Property of the author's family for centuries

13

My Life is On the Sea

The Church of the Assumption was scented with the last flowers of the season. Isabella blinked as she left it to go down to the port, leaning on Ferdinand's arm.

The sea shone in the cool September morning. Over the waterside houses of the Cantabrian port of Laredo could be seen the distant Gulf of Santona. In the luminous mist the slow movement of sails created a decorative frieze.

They walked down between rows of fishermen dressed in their best clothes, bowing as the monarchs passed by. At the end of the sun-filled street, the port had a dramatic impact on the senses. A hundred-and-thirty vessels were moored side by side along the quays, and already the twenty-five thousand troops who were to escort Princess Juana to Flanders had begun embarking amid the din of shouted orders and shrill whistles.

Isabella and Ferdinand stopped under a canopy facing the sea. It had been erected specially to shield them from sun and wind so they could watch the embarkation without discomfort or fatigue.

Juana came up to the queen. Her eyes were red, and she was biting her lips nervously.

"Have you been crying again?" asked the queen.

"I don't want to go, Mother. As soon as I arrive, I won't even wait to see Philippe—I will ask Enriquez to take me back on board. I don't want to live in the Emperor's Court. I don't want to leave Spain."

Isabella caressed the princess's feverish cheek. She ignored the great sobs that she felt rising in Juana's throat. It was at least the hundredth time she had heard Juana saying these words. She smiled.

"You will come back to us, my child. Philippe will be the best husband in the world for you."

Juana pushed the queen's hand away petulantly. Her mother didn't love her. With this unconcerned hand, she had forced her elder sister Elisabeth to marry Afonso of Portugal and then, after his death, Emmanuel. When the armada returned in a few months' time, this same cold hand would welcome little Princess Marguerite, sister of her fiancé, Philippe of Austria, and urge her on Juan.

Whenever this hand, which had engineered these royal unions, touched her hair or her face, Juana wanted to bite it. She was not surprised by this sort of detached coldness on the part of her father; he was swayed neither by pity nor by feelings. But her mother, her mother . . .

Juana threw an imploring look at her brother Juan, who was hiding behind the queen's shoulder. Juan came to her as though he had understood her call for help. They embraced each other, and, hand in hand, they waited for the preparations to be completed.

Three men came forward to the monarchs.

"Admiral Enriquez," said the queen, "I entrust the princess into your care. Keep her entertained. Don't let her be alone for more than a few minutes. As you know, a mere nothing can upset or irritate her. There's no denying that you have a difficult job. But you can delegate to her duenna, her tutor, and her confessor."

She added, in a quieter voice,

"I don't want any harm to befall Juana, you understand?"

Enriquez bowed.

The king addressed the other two men.

"Bernat de Villamari, Pedro Navarro, keep a very close watch when you are off the French coast. If at all possible, run from any risk of action, and don't get into a position where battle is forced upon you."

The deputy admiral and the privateer bowed in their turn.

"Sire," said Villamari, "we are ready in all respects. We will set sail with the first breath of wind."

Isabella turned her gaze toward the flagship that would take away the seventeen-year-old fianceé. The Spanish colors floated from the crow's nest. Up in the rigging, the sailors, looking like great birds, signaled with their caps held at arm's length and broke into rough sea shanties. The mouths of cannon poked out from the red-and-gold tapestries that streamed from the deck right down to the waterline.

Isabella held the cold and numb princess in her arms. She knew her daughter was shying away from the thought of leaving.

"What's the matter, Juana?"

"You don't love me, Mother."

"I am on your side."

"If I remain in Maximilian's Court, my first priority will be to forget you, you and Father."

Indifferently, Juana allowed the king to embrace her, and then decisively walked to the gangway, holding on to Juan's hand.

"What's the matter with her?" asked Ferdinand.

"It's nothing," sighed Isabella. "She is learning how to be a queen."

⚜

Enriquez's fleet had sailed from Laredo at the end of September. October went by with no news. It was now early November, and each day the queen put the same question to her secretary, Juan de Coloma.

"Well, Coloma?"

"Nothing—still nothing, your Majesty."

Cordon House, at Burgos, where Isabella was awaiting news from Flanders, was sinister. Pigeons no longer flew in the deserted courtyard. Monks and captains stealthily passed through the dim rooms and walked along galleries chilled by icy drafts. It was as though the vast residence had been built to house a corpse. The inhabitants took care not talk to too loudly, or to wear bright-colored clothes.

❦

Ferdinand had come back from Perpignan, where the Franco-Spanish war had flared up again following the Italian episode. He was growing older. The war was wearing him out. When Isabella saw him dismount from his horse, chilled to the bone, shoulders stooped, white hair floating down to the collar of his riding coat, she could not repress a shudder. What she read in the king's features was the end of her own youth: he was like a mirror for her, a mirror that she dared not look into.

"Still nothing, Isabella?"

She shook her head. They dined in silence by the light of great candelabra, their backs warmed by the glowing copper braziers. Nothing was going well. Bad news from the New World; they were waiting to call Columbus to account for his deplorable maladministration.

Navarre was imperceptibly slipping back into French control. The counties were the scene of a merciless war. In Naples, Gonzales was taking things far too easily, and playing the part of an absolute monarch.

And still no news from Flanders . . .

Juan had stayed in Laredo, disregarding the weather of the Cantabrian coast. Ferdinand and Isabella had not been able to persuade him to come back with them to the heart of old Castile, where the winter was milder, the winds less blustery. The prince had decided to wait there for the *caravels* that would bring his betrothed, Princess Marguerite of Austria.

Every morning, as soon as the noises of the awakening port got him out of bed, he hurried down to the jetty, climbed the ladder to the watch tower, and stayed there motionless for many hours, watching the sea. The lookout would try to dissuade him from staying there any longer: the sea was too rough, he would say, the winds from the wrong direction. Juan would sit out of the wind, in the setting sun, frozen to the marrow and burdened with anxiety.

He caught a dry cough that moved into his chest. One evening, he threw up a mouthful of blood. The next day, he was not allowed to go out, and he stayed fretting at the window, from where he had a view of the sea, swept by violent rain squalls.

He wrote to his parents.

"The doctor is a spiteful man. He has forbidden me to go down to the jetty, even though my life is on the sea. Remember that, I beg of you."

"Well, Coloma?"

"I have some news that will gladden your heart: Grand Admiral Columbus has returned to Burgos. He would like to see you. I believe that he has some important information for you."

⚜

Christopher Columbus had come ashore one June morning at Cadiz, some months previously. A few weeks earlier had seen the arrival of two senior officers the monarchs had dispatched to find out just how well-founded certain accusations were that had been made against him. For the most part, these accusations proved to be justified.

Friar Buil and don Margarite were of one voice: Columbus was acting as a tyrant. He was revealed as being tactless—cruel, even—to the Indians. With his two brothers, Bartholomew and Diego, his abuse of power was threatening to cause dissension among the white settlers on the island of Hispaniola. He was practicing slavery, but not only with prisoners of war, as provided by law. In addition, he was held responsible for the massacre of forty colonists who had been left behind at La Navidad when he left for the first time, and who had been wiped out by the native kings Coanobo and Maireni.

Columbus hastened to follow the investigators back to Spain. The marvels he brought back in his *caravels*—Indians, gold masks, parrots—were every bit as good as those the people of Seville and Madrid had so much admired a few months earlier. But Columbus himself had changed a great deal.

He bowed before the queen, who gave a start. She had not heard him come in; her thoughts were at sea, between the Isle of Wight and the Spanish coast.

Columbus wore a Franciscan robe, held in at the waist by a frayed cord, a wooden figure of Christ on his chest. The queen had no doubt that this apparent humility was largely a pretense. The Grand Admiral had planned to head off the monarchs' anger by presenting himself as a humble figure.

The monarchs were not deceived by this tactic. However, neither Ferdinand nor Isabella had any intention of being hostile to Columbus; they simply wanted to warn him about his excesses.

After lamenting about how ungrateful people were about what he had accomplished, and kissing the monarchs' knees, Columbus's self-confidence quickly reasserted itself. Had he not captured the dreadful King Coanobo, discovered nearly four hundred new islands, and christened them "The Queen's Garden," establishing the new town named "Isabella"?

He had heard it said that the discovery of the New World was a fraud. From a casket, he casually picked out gold nuggets as big as hazelnuts, solid gold masks, and a necklace that drew from the queen a gasp of astonishment; it weighed six hundred *castillan*.

"It is yours, your Majesty."

Columbus had very quickly regained the friendship and the confidence of the monarchs. They had reprimanded him, to which he had responded contritely, and then they had confirmed him in his responsibilities, with a few changes.

Since this first audience after his return, Columbus had but one ambition: to get back to sea with more *caravels* and even more impressive forces.

"I heard," said Columbus, "that King don Fernando was away this morning, so I hurried here at once. What I have to tell you should be told in private. It is sad news, your Majesty. It concerns David Ezra."

The queen sprang upright, suddenly very pale. She coughed quietly, and then regained her composure.

"Indeed, I know David Ezra very well. You know that he had a price on his head."

"He won't be giving you any more problems. I have come to let you know that he is dead."

Columbus looked at the queen surreptitiously. He could read in her expression her feelings of deep distress.

"Really? How did you find out . . . ?"

"Ezra came on board secretly in Palos, when I first sailed. It wasn't until we landed on Hispaniola that I learned who he was. I would willingly have clapped him in irons, if only I hadn't needed every one of my men, without exception. You know that because of the loss of the *Pinta*, one of my *caravels*, I had to leave about forty men in the fort of La Navidad when we set sail for the return voyage. And you know what became of those forty men: they were attacked by Indians, and not one survived. David was among them. You would be right in thinking that he would not have returned to Spain even if he had to, by facing Coanabo's Indians himself."

"And . . . while you were together, did David talk about me?"

"Not once. He was a solitary man, and only spoke when it was absolutely necessary. I believe, however, that under that rough exterior was a good heart."

"David was the best of men,"

sighed the queen, her voice barely audible.

"I never saw him do a mean thing. He was as open and honest as the day is long."

She threw out her chest, the tone of her voice hardening. "But he fought against our Lord's commandments. The Devil had got into his spirit, and there was no way to get him out." In a lower voice, she added,

"For me, his death is a deliverance."

Columbus would have liked to learn more, but the queen ended the conversation.

"Leave me now, please,"

she said, after a few moments' pause.

"I need rest. For weeks I have awaited news of our armada, and this waiting is making me ill."

"If it pleases your Majesty, I would like to put my modest abilities at your disposal. I will try to find out why it is so late, and perhaps make a forecast of the date it will arrive."

"You could do that, Admiral?"

"I said that I would try, your Majesty . . ."

"A letter from our Grand Admiral Columbus,"
said Ferdinand. The queen's heart beat very fast while the king
tore off the seal. The letter had been dispatched from Laredo.
Columbus made some comments about wind direction, and about
the probable whereabouts of the armada. He ended:

"Wednesday, it will be off the Isle of Wight. Provided the
Admiral does not elect to call in there, the ships will reach Laredo
sometime on Monday.

"If this forecast turns out to be wrong, then the art of navigation
has no meaning."

Ferdinand read the letter again. It prompted him to say,

"This man is either mad, or a genius. But, by God, if he is right,
we can refuse him nothing."

Columbus was right.

Never had Ferdinand and Isabella seen such an expression on
Prince Juan's face. He didn't have to say it out loud—the joy
stirring within him was quite obvious, lending a new liveliness to
all of his movements and gestures, bringing a fire to his eyes that a
few tears only served to enhance.

He had not yet spoken more than ten words to Marguerite: she
spoke only Austrian, and he knew nothing but Spanish. He was
dying with desire to look at her, but dared not stare. The first
glance, however, had been enough to reassure him. Marguerite was
exactly what he had been waiting for. She had a serious little face,
rather impassive perhaps, but her eyes glowed with love for this
Spanish prince of whom she had dreamed, even though she only
knew him by an indistinct likeness on a medallion that Deza, Juan's
private tutor, had surreptitiously slipped into the young princess's
hand.

Juan and Marguerite found themselves alone on the quay, near
a group of seamen who addressed tactful greetings to them. Juan
lowered his head, bit his lip, and said quickly,

"I thought that you would never arrive."

Marguerite looked at him with her blue eyes and shook her head to indicate that she didn't understand. But when the prince covered his face with a corner of his cape to stifle the terrible coughing fit that shook his whole body, she took his hand and secretly caressed it.

The love Juan bore for Marguerite was a little frightening to the queen. Juan did not truly know how to love. He gave in to the least of his passions with such violent abandon that nothing else had meaning for him. He would forget himself to the point where both his reason and his health were threatened. And Marguerite had quickly become for him no ordinary passion.

He could not bear to be away from her for more than an hour. He clung to her like a desperate man. Several times he had woken in the middle of the night and knocked on the princess's door. She would sleepily let him into her room, to lie on the counterpane and to talk to her until they drifted innocently off to sleep.

During the day, he never left her side. When they went into the town, they were warmly greeted. They were beautiful in their youth and in the love that shone from them.

On one occasion the queen reproached her son for forming an attachment that she judged to be too self-centered and dangerous to his well-being. To her astonishment, she saw Juan's hackles rise; he turned pale, and she heard him utter some hurtful words:

"You are jealous of Marguerite, Mother. It's quite obvious. You are delaying our marriage because you detest my betrothed."

"My poor child, how you misunderstand me . . ."

"But I understand you all too well. I am learning to know you. You are taking revenge on me because you have not been happy with the king, you . . ."

The queen's hand struck his face before she even realized what she was doing. Juan stepped back. His face went green and blotchy, his lips moved but produced no sound.

"Forgive me," said the queen. "I acted without thinking. Please understand that I have nothing against Marguerite. I want nothing more than your happiness, the happiness of both of you. But this happiness is jeopardizing your health. The doctors . . ."

"I don't care what the doctors say."

Juan spoke through clenched teeth.

He turned to leave the room. Two steps from the door, he clutched at the curtain, and slowly slid to the floor.

The king felt that the two young people should be married.

"As soon as they are wed, they will lose their affection for each other."

He was used to pointing this out, to counter Isabella's objections to the marriage. Bitterly, she reflected that he spoke from experience.

She finally gave in, and the ceremony was scheduled to take place in March of the following year: 1497. The monarchs wanted a truly magnificent wedding: It was to be more lavish than anything yet seen. Juan seemed to be overflowing with happiness, but he was only a shadow of his former self. The previous winter had undermined his strength. A terrible joy was consuming him.

Friar Deza, Juana's tutor, sent a letter that threw a shadow over these thrilling days. All was not well between Juana and Philippe: He was unstable; she, jealous. Regrettable scenes had flared up in Maximilian's Court. Juana was adapting badly to her new role. Philippe was still behaving like a young boy.

Juan and Marguerite's honeymoon did not last long.

They had gone to spend April in Granada, and had chosen to live in the Generalife. The gardens became their own little world. They roamed around them without ever being bored. In the evening they would linger by the windows that looked over the Albaicin, listening to the Moors as they sang on the roofs and in the small meadows by the Daro.

The Andalusian spring delighted the princess. The air still had the flavor of snow, and green fruit grew plump on the branches of orange and lemon trees. Water from the mountains flowed down the gutters beside the steps, and into the canals that criss-crossed this paradise. The slightest ray of sunshine was enough to persuade myrtles and laurels to give off their fragrance.

One day, she suggested to the prince that they go bathe in a lake. They frolicked, got drenched in the fountains, and stretched themselves out to dry on the warm marble flagstones.

That evening, a fever sent Juan to bed earlier than usual. Dreadful coughing spasms ended his sleep; he woke up with his mouth full of blood.

On the direct advice of the doctors, the queen considered separating the young couple. Very diplomatically, she tried to get Marguerite to listen to reason, but the effort only drew bitter replies from her. Ferdinand, convinced though he was of the need to slow down this harmful passion, had no more success.

Better times came with the summer. The prince and the princess stayed in Madrid during the hottest period. Occasionally they would go to the ring to see a bullfight; Juan could not stand the sight of this entertainment, but Marguerite was delighted by it.

Twice they were invited to take their place in the royal tribunal for an *auto-da-fe*, where some models made of wood and fabric were burned, as well as some important Jews accused of having broken Christ's laws after having been submissive to them.

For the king and queen this was a routine spectacle that had almost ceased to cause them any emotion. But it was not the same for Juan, who only accompanied Marguerite because he refused to be separated from her. He endured, teeth clenched, the sight of the first *auto-da-fe*; but at the second two guards had to half-carry him, knees sagging, to the coach, which brought him back to the palace.

The doctors' views hardened. If the young couple were not separated, they could no longer be held accountable for Juan's health. But it was obvious that this was a last, desperate measure, and it offered only a small chance of saving him.

"Impossible!" said Isabella, with a sigh. "I have tried, but in vain. Besides, God wanted this union. It is not up to me to break it."

She knew now that the prince would not recover. He was slowly fading away. He sought to use the small pleasures of court life as a way of delaying his fate. For a whole month, he asked hourly for more joy, more fulfillment to be given him that he had ever had before. All the poets and musicians of Spain were gathered together at the court, and festival followed festival, the brilliant entertainment lasting until dawn.

Juan and Marguerite stayed together now more than ever: she was full of life, and he was already the image of death. When the queen and the two little princesses, Maria and Catalina, saw them on the dance floor, wearing the same velvet, the same satin, each a reflection of the other, tears sprang to their eyes: the queen because she saw the shadow of death on her son, the princesses because they saw an aura of beauty and youth surrounding their brother.

The dog days of August persuaded the young couple to seek solitude in the Sierra Guadarrama. They found refuge in a little retreat, glittering with whiteness, and perfumed by all the flowers of the mountain.

They spent long periods stretched out side by side on the only bed. From the window of their room, they had a view of distant mountains stretching to the horizon in the direction of Segovia. The mountains changed color and shape every hour of the day. Evening signaled its arrival with streaks of blue mist and a softening of the faraway outlines.

One September morning, Marguerite got out of bed first, opened the window, and breathed in air that was crisper than usual. It had snowed on the forests, and in the far distance the peaks of Navacerrada were sharply profiled, all white against an azure sky.

Marguerite shivered, and hastily closed the window again.

A few hours later, they prepared to leave.

Early in September, the queen had gone to Portugal without the king to meet the young King Emmanuel, whom Isabel was to marry.

She left Ferdinand at Juan's bedside. The prince had taken to his bed when he arrived at Salamanca, and the doctors doubted if he would see the year out. In all the churches of Spain, masses were being said for his recovery. Ordinary women included his name in their prayers. Each morning, heaps of flowers were placed on the palace steps.

"Go without me," said Ferdinand. "You mustn't keep King Emmanuel waiting. I shall stay here with Juan."

Elisabeth had patiently overcome the grief caused by the death of her first husband. Nearly six years had gone by since the day that a bolting horse had dragged the prince's body through the forest. The young widow with the sad expression had learned to live again, and to free herself from the chains of that memory. Now twenty-five, she was at the peak of her beauty, and the queen saw in the princess her own lost youth.

The betrothed couple were to meet at Alcantara, a town on the left bank of the Tagus, on the frontier between the two nations. The queen and the princess stopped for prayer at Garrovillas. Isabel went on ahead to the Rock of Alcantara, towering over the river. She sounded like a child again when she turned back to the queen and shouted, "Mother! Mother! I have seen the king's standards. Here he is, coming to meet us . . ."

Juan died only a few days after returning to Salamanca. He was sleeping hand in hand with Marguerite . . . she only realized he was dead when she woke and felt in her palm a hand of stone.

Hardly was the funeral over when Ferdinand left Salamanca for Alcantara, where the queen was waiting for him. He arrived in the midst of great celebrations. Portuguese and Spanish flags flew together over the church of Santa Maria de Almocobar and on all the main buildings. The Tagus was packed with beautifully decorated small craft, and the Roman bridge was garlanded with flowers and foliage.

Queen Isabella was radiant, as was Elisabeth. It was difficult for Ferdinand to recognize his daughter in this resplendent bride-to-be, whose hand Emmanuel was holding.

"How is Juan?" asked the queen.

Ferdinand could not bring himself to tell her the truth. He lived with this secret in his heart through the days of jubilation that led up to the departure of Elisabeth and Manuel for Lisbon.

Juan's death sounded the knell for many great hopes. With the Monarch's son gone, the fate of their dynasty would lie with the children of Elisabeth and of Juana. They would have to begin all over again. Would the benefits to be gained be worth it, with the fatigue and the beginnings of old age that Ferdinand and Isabella already felt weighing on them?

A monarch's job is never done. He cannot have certainty about either the stability of the throne or what will happen to it after his passing. A twenty-year-old prince dies, and everything is at once called into question.

It was not until they were returning that Ferdinand confessed to Isabella that their son had died. They were not far from Canaveral, in a wilderness of rock and water on the banks of the Tagus, its current carrying living trees down in its reddish mud.

"I know," she said. "The moment you arrived, I understood. . . ."

Marguerite did not linger in the Spanish Court after Juan's death.

For some days, she seemed to live only for her memories. Her father, the Emperor Maximilian, and her mother, Mary of Burgundy, summoned her back to Germany. She wondered to whom she would now be offered as a prospective bride. She had been promised to Charles of France before marrying Juan; her father could be relied on to not leave so young and pretty an heiress unemployed for long. Seventeen! And with expectations!

Marguerite wiped away her last tears, and found herself humming while fastening her trunks. She was not unhappy to leave the palace of Madrid. Everything there was so dark and gloomy; the only inhabitants seemed to be cardinals, monks, and soldiers.

King don Ferdinand seemed to be unaware of her, but she felt sure he held himself largely responsible for his son's death. The queen, on the other hand, was less tightly self-controlled; she would hold Marguerite's hands and talk about her beloved son. But besides Juan, the only name on her lips was that of the Lord. She spoke as though she was personally the Primate of Spain.

14

The Island of Seven Cities

Columbus was preparing for his third voyage to the New World. Everything was going too slowly for his liking. He was consumed with impatience. This time, he was sure he would bring back much gold—where there were parrots, dark-skinned men, and great rivers, the explorers were sure there would be gold. They would push on farther to the west and find great numbers of islands on their way to the continent they dreamed of. Perhaps they would discover the legendary Island of Seven Cities, or perhaps even Paradise on earth.

These were the dreams that preoccupied him one day early in March as he sailed down the estuary of the Guadalquivir, bound for Sancular de Barrameda.

He had rented a small boat to avoid the fatigue of the road journey. *Ganaderias* of bulls and wild horses roamed over the flat *dehesas* that bordered the river; in his mind's eye, he saw not these, but the islands of his dreams.

If instead of limited allowances he had been given really generous grants, and if at every stage he had not come across stupid or ill-intentioned people who delayed progress, he would already have gotten to Cipangu. By now, he would have beaten a path through worlds unknown, to the capital of the Great Khan.

Six *caravels* were waiting at Sanlucar, crewed by two-hundred men. The moment Columbus came on board, they weighed anchor. He had just received news that rebellion was brewing in the New World.

Dona Beatrix de Bobadilla lost one of her shoes, hopped a few steps to retrieve it, and blushed under the mocking gaze of the sentry standing guard at the entrance to the courtroom, from which she could hear snatches of conversation. She straightened up; the hurt showed in her face as she put her hand on her painful side.

The monk who had become Grand Inquisitor after Tomas de Torquemada's death was Lucero, and it was his voice that now reached her ears. It was extraordinarily dry and clear, like his personality. He was a thin and swarthy man, known as "The Dark One."

Isabella's controlled voice replied to him. Dona Beatrix smiled; the queen was still holding out. For three years she had been fighting against Lucero, against the king, against the other Inquisitors. With scornful disregard for promises and agreements, they had decided to set up an Inquisition tribunal in Granada. The Moors had been converted, but were gradually slipping back to their old religion.

"Let us light some fires!" proclaimed Lucero. A few examples would be sufficient to bring the pagans back to Christianity.

"Light some fires," the queen shot back, "and you will see the Moorish rebels hiding out in the Alpujarras and the Filabres mountains take up arms again, and go on the offensive."

Dona Beatrix, her ear glued to the door, trembled with rage as she listened to Lucero. She almost forgot why she had come.

Dona Beatrix altered her plan, and ran to the home of dona Mincia de la Torre, another of the queen's ladies-in-waiting. She found her in the inner courtyard, busily picking flowers with the help of a gardener. Gesturing rapidly with her hands, she whispered a few words in dona Mincia's ear.

"Are you sure?" asked dona Mincia.

"It is only a rumor, but I believe it to be true."

"Let us go and tell Beatrice Pacheco. She should be in the library."

Dona Mincia put her flowers down on the box hedge, and the two ladies hurried away through galleries and corridors.

"I know already," said Beatrice Pacheco, closing the heavy Salamanca Bible that she had been leafing through. She rose slowly.

"Our duty is to inform the queen and the king, even if the rumor turns out to be unfounded. Do you know this pilgrim who has arrived from Lisbon?"

Neither of them had heard of him before he appeared at the palace in his soaking wet pilgrim's clothes and started to chat with the servants in the dining hall of the travelers' quarters. He was some sort of low-ranking lord from the Gredos mountains. But there was such conviction in his words that it was difficult not to believe them.

"The audience will soon be over," said Dona Beatrice.

"Let us go and see the queen."

They found an animated group outside the courtroom. Lucero was beaming and chattering away in his dry voice, but the queen's head was bent, and she was not talking. Dona Beatrice shivered involuntarily: the queen had lost.

"Which of us is going to talk to her?" she asked.

"Let me," said dona Beatrice Pacheco.

She went up to the queen, and they both left the group. The queen placed her hand on the lady-in-waiting's forearm. As the duchess spoke, the queen's expression changed. She leaned against a column; her whole body was shaking. Dona Beatrice Pacheco had to hold her up to prevent her from collapsing on the flagstones.

The news was confirmed that evening. Little Queen Elisabeth had just died while bringing her first child into the world.

The boy, Miguel, was alive.

꧁꧂

"Will there ever be an end to the problems in Granada?" asked Isabella. "These latest expeditions have cost hundreds of dead."

The troops Ferdinand had sent to put down the Moors and Jews who held the Alpujarras and the high valleys of the Filabres had been decimated. The terrain was dangerous, a wilderness of mountains and valleys, deserted and dry. It was ideal country for the raiding parties sent out by the defenders.

The queen had been right, and Ferdinand had finally come to understand that, a little late in the day. The problems would never be ended as long as the Inquisition attempted to convert the Moors by threatening them with the dungeon and the stake. This situation was now a fact, and it was too late for the monarchs to reverse it.

"We are not the rulers of Spain," Isabella went on, bitterness in her voice.

"The real rulers are Deza, Ximenes, and Lucero. They impose upon us their views about everything. They have subjugated the Holy Church; they are in the process of subjugating us. With each heretic they send to the stake, they burn a little more of our authority.

"They have respect for nothing. Agreements don't count with them, and our wishes are totally disregarded. Not content with hunting down the Moors of Granada, they are even attacking the family of our archbishop, Monsignor Talavera. Which informer talked to them of heresy, to make them suspect this honorable family of converted Jews?"

Ferdinand shrugged, a gesture of impotence. He was watching the shadows lengthen on the floor, and keeping his shadow out of them as though they were a tide of mud.

"Suspicion is falling even on those close to us, with the excuse that many of those we love and cherish are of Jewish origin. Even you, Ferdinand, will not be immune to their accusations. They will manage to detect in you a few drops of Jewish blood, inherited from the maternal line of your family."

"The 'pure blood,'" Ferdinand whispered. Isabella could not tell whether he was expressing hope or regret.

Isabella realized that 'pure blood' was a dangerous, impossible dream. No blood is ever 'pure.' One pure blood line, one pure religion, these were the things she used to believe in. She had given the Inquisitors encouragement, as long as they did not use the cross as a weapon. She had signed the decree for the expulsion of the Jews.

But she rationalized that such decrees were not of themselves inhumane. The inhumanity lay in the way they were enforced. It seemed the Inquisitors were always right, and it was they, in the end, who triumphed.

Ferdinand slowly stood up, and, with effort, stretched his limbs. He had put on weight these last few years, and his joints had grown stiffer, to the point where he was occasionally aware of some lack of mobility.

"The Inquisition," he said indifferently, "has become a state within the state. But what of it? History will not hold us responsible for the abuses that are being committed."

"Do you really believe what you have just said?" asked Isabella. Ferdinand looked around himself distractedly, as though he had just awoken.

"I don't understand anything any more. All these problems . . ."

All these problems of race and religion were quite beyond him. He had enough confidence in Isabella to leave her to deal with them. What interested him was the conquest of new lands. He had just divided up the kingdom of Naples with Charles of France. The war in Rousillon was going well, and he was still waiting to see what would happen in Navarre.

Even though his dreams of reigning over all Europe had come to a sudden end with the death of Juan, he still had high hopes of Portugal. Prince Miguel had cost his mother her life, but one day he would be King of Portugal, and the dynasty founded by Ferdinand and Isabella would rule the whole peninsula.

In the spring, they had been to Lisbon to see their grandson. He was slight and fair-haired. Only a few months old, he had a lively expression on his face, but seemed unable to move. It was as though the future man was still asleep in the motionless child's body. He had been born prematurely, and there was anguished concern about whether he would survive.

Whenever Ferdinand thought of the lands that Columbus and his captains were winning for Spain on the other side of the Atlantic his sense of space changed. The distance between one room and another, one house and another, one town and another became completely unimportant. The blood ran more quickly in his veins, and his strength was renewed.

Columbus wrote long letters whose enthusiasm amused the monarchs. He wrote about everything with such emphasis and innocence, they had to smile. He had just discovered the mouth of a great river that, according to him, could well be one of the four great rivers of Paradise. And, while investigating a stretch of coastline, he had found limitless beds of pearl oysters.

Unfortunately, he still showed himself to be a very poor administrator. One of his deputies, Roldan, had mutinied. Columbus behaved toward the Indians with such cruelty that it roused the indignation of the monks whose task it was to convert them. The natives proved to be bad workers; to make them obedient, the admiral enslaved them and threatened them with hanging.

Columbus was falling into disfavor at the Spanish Court. Some of the notables had no hesitation in spitting on the footprints of the admiral's two sons, Diego and Hernando, looking on them as Jews.

Then Fonseca, the New World's *charge d'affaires* at court, revealed to the monarchs that Columbus was planning to make the Genoese benefactors of his discoveries. Worried, Ferdinand and Isabella sent a new investigator to the West Indies, Francisco Bobadilla, a knight of the order of Calatrava. They vested in him the full power of their authority.

"Act moderately and wisely,"

Isabella said to him, as the wind filled the sails of the *caravel* flying the Castilian flag.

⚜

The century was drawing to a close. The greatness of Spain only became apparent after very difficult times. Commerce declined following the massive exodus of the Jews and the threats made by Lucero against the *conversos*. The rich farmlands of

Granada, Malaga, and Almeria, gradually abandoned by the Moors who went back to Africa, became a landscape of wild grass and deserted villages.

Beneath all this misery, however, could be discerned a new spirit of freedom. Anarchy had come to an end. Under the law of the *cuadrilleros* of Santa Hermandad, the countryside was regaining its peacefulness, and the roads their safety. Spain was awakening to its destiny.

One rainy evening a cry was heard coming from the queen's rooms. Prince Miguel was dead. The queen and the king were the only ones to cry over the grandson in whom such great hopes had been placed.

But had Miguel ever really lived?

⚜

Columbus pushed the captain of the *Gorda*, Andres Martin, roughly aside, and, his chains clinking, stood up straight.

"No, Andres," he said. "I want the people of Cadiz to bear witness to my misery, and I want my shame to be borne by the monarchs. Leave my chains locked."

"Don Cristobal, you're not going to . . ."

". . . go through the town in shackles? Who's going to stop me?"

"But I have to stay by your side."

"So, you'll have to come with me!"

Andres Martin sighed, and put away his key. It was difficult to disregard an order from Columbus, even though he had fifty pounds of iron on his body. He had never been able to think of him as an ordinary prisoner, no more than his brother Bartholomew, that proud and arrogant adventurer.

"Very well," said the captain.

"That's not everything, my good Andres. I would like you to do me another service. I wrote this letter for the monarchs while we were at sea—it must be sent before Bobadilla's. I insist that my defense should be read before the accusing document of that wretched individual. I want my innocence to be proclaimed to my sovereigns before their judgment is warped by his infamous accusation . . ."

Columbus went through Cadiz with his head held high, between two *alguazils* more ashamed than he. He attracted crowds of passersby, shouting his name and that of his accuser at every cross-street. By the time he arrived at the chief magistrate's palace he was leading a procession of indignant followers.

Columbus and his brother slept in beds provided by the magistrate. The next morning, mounted on donkeys as a calculated symbol of their humility, and still wearing the same shackles, they set out for the Catholic Monarchs in Granada. In each of the Andalusian villages they went through, Columbus displayed his chains. He swore that he would stay in them until justice had been done, and that if necessary he would take them with him to his tomb.

With the villages behind them, the odd procession now headed into mountainous country. Bartholomew saw his brother slump down on his horse and weep convulsively, grieving over his lost glory and his jeopardized fortune.

"Just because I had a few Indians executed, just because I was anxious that nothing should slow down the progress we were making in bringing religion to those savages, I am humiliated, hunted, destroyed!"

The monarchs were startled when they saw Columbus arrive in the very heart of the Alhambra, barefoot, dragging a ball and chain, and shackled to Bartholomew. The admiral had somewhat overestimated his stamina; he had gone on foot all the way between the Bibarambla Gate and the Gate of Justice, so his exhaustion was not feigned, as he had planned.

The queen came forward to meet him, pressed this old white-haired man with torn clothes into her arms, wiped his moist eyes, his sweaty, dusty face. Ferdinand remained behind the queen, frowning.

"There you are, Andres! You may now release me."

He turned back to the queen.

"If you only knew, your Majesty, of what abuses of authority I am accused."

"I know, my friend."

Columbus sighed with relief—his letter had arrived. As he came in under the high white-and-gold ceilings of the Alhambra, his shoulders slumped.

The queen remembered Columbus in Seville, amid a dazzling array of pennons, surrounded by Indians and parrots . . . Columbus at Burgos, dressed in the cowled robe of the Franciscan order, the signs of his impending downfall already evident in his expression and in his bearing . . . And now, here he was, conqueror of the ocean, Viceroy of the New World, Grand Admiral of the High Seas, don Christopher Columbus, the most magnificent lord—crushed with grief, shame, and sorrow!

Isabella did not doubt for one moment that this ordeal had been sent by God to punish the navigator's overarching ambition.

"It is God's will," she said to Ferdinand.

"Yes," he replied. "God's will."

Then, in a silent afterthought to himself,

if this is God's will, what sins will we blamed for?

Princess Maria left the monarchs to go to Portugal, where she was to marry the prince. Then it was Catalina's turn: the Prince of Wales claimed his betrothed. Isabella and Ferdinand were alone once more.

Death and departure had created a vacuum around them. They were waited on by faceless servants whom they no longer recognized, strange and indifferent. Their world became one of anonymous uniforms. They looked in vain for new objects for their affections. They were too familiar to each other, their own reactions too predictable, for them to take comfort from shared tenderness in this solitary existence.

It was at this time that Juana and Philippe announced that they would visit.

All the bells of Flanders had just greeted the birth of their first child, a boy, Carlos, the future Charles V of Spain, when they decided to present their heir at the Spanish Court. Spain, after all, was a part of his birthright.

Isabella became feverishly busy. What gifts would be suitable for her grandson? Was he fair, was he dark? Philippe asserted that Charles was a Habsburg—that protuberant lower lip, those steely eyes. Juana called him Carlos, and saw in him the looks of Ferdinand. But what did it matter—the queen's anxious waiting made these idle conjectures completely unimportant.

She was sure that he would become a great king, that he would complete the work Ferdinand had begun: the creation of a great Roman-German empire that had been the dream of all the kings of western Christendom since Charlemagne.

Juana had changed a great deal. Under her heavy dark brocaded robes, glittering with reflected light, she looked like a badly painted and skeletal wooden doll. Her eyes were too deep-set, and looked like unnaturally brilliant black pearls set in their sockets. Isabella thought she looked ill, and was terrified.

"Don't concern yourself about my health," Juana said stiffly. "You would be better advised to take a look at yourself, Mother. You have grown outrageously fat . . . and all those white hairs . . . have you had much worry of late?"

Without waiting for a reply, Juana turned back to the cradle where an emperor was sleeping in his baby clothes, and began talking to him in a soft voice.

Juana had returned to her old ways without a break. She gave orders to domestic staff and government ministers alike, as though she had been away for only a few days. She was amazed that the queen accepted among her husband's personal staff these *senorinas* who looked much too passionate for her liking. In the Flemish Court, Juana got rid of those young misses who were overzealous in serving the Archduke Philippe.

"I know," said the queen. "It is said that you won't change, even in the face of ridicule, and that your jealousy has caused many upsetting scenes."

"What do I care about such malicious gossip!" Juana shot back. "I love Philippe, and I look after him."

It was not long before Isabella realized that Juana was not exaggerating.

Ferdinand and Philippe set off one day to hunt wild bulls on the plains of Murcia, leaving their wives in Granada. Philippe took such pleasure in their activity that he begged the king to postpone their return. They stayed three days longer than planned. When they came back, they saw Juana mounting a horse.

"Where are you going?" asked Philippe.

"I am going to sail back home. You have made me look like a fool. We will see each other again in Gand."

Powerless, sick with shame, Isabella and Ferdinand witnessed the dreadful scene that ensued. Philippe broke away from the squabble. He was holding his head in both hands as he left.

"Don't you think you went a bit far?" Ferdinand asked the archduchess.

"You were with him in Murcia, among all those whores! Father, you are as worthless as he is."

Similar violent scenes erupted over nothing. The atmosphere in the palace became unbearable, so much so that one day Philippe made up his mind to leave. Alone. And without a word of farewell for the Archduchess.

Juana unemotionally accepted this affront, and then, some hours after Philippe had left, started to weep and wail. She had a horse saddled so she could ride after him. Isabella managed to hold her back: Juana was pregnant, and to have behaved so unwisely could have been fatal for her.

Two months later, Juana gave birth to another boy. He was christened Ferdinand.

That night, Juana was delirious. Her cries woke the entire palace. "Philippe! Philippe!" Wide awake, she ran along dark passageways, banged on all the doors, screamed her husband's name, and finally collapsed, moaning.

The archduke wrote to her:

"I am waiting for you." She ripped the letter up with her teeth, kissed the torn pieces, had her bags packed, and left the palace that very day.

Silence and peace suddenly fell again on the Monarchs.

"Sooner or later they will go their separate ways," sighed Isabella.

Ferdinand made no comment. He bent down to pick up a colored ribbon, used to tie on little Carlos's bonnet. He crumpled it in his hand for a moment before slipping it in his pocket.

⚜

"No, Columbus, you are not going back to Hispaniola, and we are not going with you to liberate Jerusalem."

Free Jerusalem from the Turkish yoke! That was Columbus's new dream. He had just published the *Book of Prophecies*, and he insisted on presenting it personally to the Catholic Monarchs. In it, he explained that the end of the world was approaching, that Jerusalem would once again be in Christian hands, and that the New World would also be Christian. Isabella and Ferdinand listened to him patiently as he expounded his daring ideas.

Ferdinand fell asleep in the middle of one of St. Augustine's prophecies, and he was awoken with a start by a shout from the admiral.

"Allow me to set off again!" Columbus begged.

"For where?" Ferdinand had lost the thread of all these plans.

"For Hispaniola."

"Once more I tell you—that's impossible. Would you like the title of Marquis to be conferred upon you here in Spain? I am prepared to grant you that."

Columbus straightened up as if he had been whipped. A marquisate in Spain! He who had discovered more continents . . . He rubbed his big nose, and returned to the attack.

"So you agree with that wretched Francisco de Bobadilla, who dared raise his hand against me."

Ferdinand sighed wearily. Isabella interrupted, saying gently,

"Have you forgotten that we have relieved you of your responsibilities?"

Columbus was not disheartened. If he didn't set out again, foreign explorers would lay hold of all the lands yet to be discovered. Already, it was a stampede. The ocean was being crisscrossed by the wakes of Portuguese, French, Genoese, and English *caravel*s. All the western nations were rushing for the New World. Alvarez de Cabral had acquired Brazil for King Emmanuel . . .

"You cannot go back there, Columbus," the queen said softly.

"But if I promised not to land in Hispaniola? If I limited myself to the search for the Island of Seven Cities, and the strait—it exists, of that I'm sure—which would open the way to a new ocean?"

"No!" the queen replied patiently.

Ferdinand showed a spark of interest. "A strait, you said?"

The Monarchs listened as the navigator explained. Beyond these scattered islands was another ocean. The Indians were quite positive about that. Another ocean . . . The monarchs were still visionaries. Columbus left once again, carrying his burden of unfulfilled dreams with him. But he came back the next day.

At last, Isabella said to him,

"It's agreed, then—you will set off again. But take care not to land on Hispaniola. If you do, you will completely lose our confidence."

And so it was that Christopher Columbus sailed on his fourth voyage.

Medina del Campo

15

Snow in Medina

Isabella very often pondered the meaning of greatness. On those frequent occasions when weariness overcame her, it was indeed her main subject of meditation.

Spain was great, as were its monarchs. Had they succeeded in only one-third of what they had actually achieved—and that was but a small part of what they had promised themselves—their reign would still have been glorious. Spain was great, and had become aware of her destiny; she was full of buoyant, well-founded optimism. A nation that had been nothing but chaos a few decades earlier had now taken shape in the powerful hands of the monarchs.

Isabella did not have to think back very far to call up scenes of misery and anarchy: the main roads infested by highwaymen, the Courts dominated by high-ranking brigands. A strong escort used to be needed to go from one town to the next, and the fear of poison was never out of mind when dining at the royal table.

Today, Spain breathed more easily. The Santa Hermandad policed the main roads, and there were no more mysterious deaths at Court. The flight of large numbers of Jews and Moors had at one time jeopardized commerce and agriculture, but they had since taken on a new vigor. The orchards of Valencia and Murcia were verdant with new plantations, and the *vega* of Granada was again opening up to the plough. Springtime in Spain no longer triggered the hellish cycle of civil war.

Spain was truly being remade in the hands of the monarchs. But this complete and harmonious union of its provinces was the color of blood and ashes. What is greatness? Isabella mused, kneeling on the small cushion, facing Borgia's ivory cross and David's Jewish lamp. The blood was that of the Moors, and that which had flowed in the Roussillon, the "Cemetery of the French," in the Italian mountains, in the virgin forests of the New World, in the rebellious Alpugarras. The ashes were those of Jews and Moors burnt in the public squares.

What is greatness? Must it always co-exist with evil? Isabella put the question to God, but God did not reply. She tried to take Him by surprise in the middle of the night, when she imagined Him to be beside her. She looked for Him in the cold light of a midwinter dawn, and in the heat of the summer days when everyone in town, from the highest to the most humble, was fast asleep, but God seemed to hide His face from her. She proclaimed that she was mistress of her own destiny, and God did not rebuke her. She cast herself down, and God did not come to lift her up. She was an old woman begging for help, and God did not take pity on her.

"If God doesn't answer you,"

her confessor, Ximenes Cisneros, told her, "it is because you have his approval. It is because he judges that you are strong enough to bear the burden of greatness."

"What is greatness?" Isabella only felt great when that question was not on her lips, together with the taste of blood and ashes. But at the times when she felt the repeated question growing more persistent, she seemed to step outside her personality, to see herself as simply a human frame of confined and painful flesh, no more than a mere shadow of her greatness.

Calamity came in the form of a ship flying the Flemish standard, which one day arrived at Laredo. It carried a message from Philippe le Beau, Archduke of Austria.

Juana's excessive jealousy had at last wearied the prince. He had decided on a separation. Thus collapsed the Catholic Monarchs' dream: the foundation of a great western empire, which Ferdinand saw as the starting point of worldwide domination.

It was a fatal blow for them both. They took to their beds, sick with anguish, their strength sapped by so much useless struggle.

The queen's room was in the main building of the castle of Medina del Campo, facing south; the king's was on the other side. They communicated by messages passed orally by their servants, by the ladies-in-waiting, or scribbled in little notes when they felt better. Then once more there would be silence, and the servants and the ladies said at the bedside of the king or of the queen,

"Her Majesty asks to be excused. She slept very badly last night, and she is so tired that she is staying in bed."

"Beatrix, I beg of you to read to me again the passage in Columbus's letter where he tells of the storm that he rode out in the Carribean Sea."

Dona Beatrix made herself comfortable at the queen's bedside. Her large frame made her armchair creak. She adjusted her spectacles, leafed through the heavy bundle of papers, brought the sheet into the light, and again began to read.

"The wind prevented us from making headway, and we were unable to hold our course any longer. It bottled me up in a sea which seemed to have turned to blood, boiling like kettle on a hot stove. None of us had ever seen such a terrible sea. Day and night, it burned like a furnace. The sky was aflame with lightning flashes, so much so that I was continually looking up to see if my masts and sails had been carried away . . . ."

Isabella closed her eyes. Her pale and swollen fingers drummed on the sheet, keeping time with the sentences. Outside, the July sun hung motionless in the sky. The *meseta* was white and gold with ripe wheat as far as the eye could see. But in the humble brick-vaulted square room, dona Beatrix's narration brought the storms to life. Storms like those which had disturbed the queen's sleep when she heard the news of the divorce of Philippe and Juana.

"The Indians, dona Beatrix. What does he say about the Indians?"

"Two Indians took me to Carambaru. The people go naked, with a golden mirror hung from their necks. These mirrors they would neither sell nor offer in barter . . . In the province of Ciguare, there is unlimited gold: the natives wear coral on their heads, and very thick gold bracelets on their wrists and ankles. . . . As soon as they arrived, the Indians sent me two heavily made-up young girls, the older was not yet eleven, the younger seven. But both were so uninhibited (here, dona Beatrix coughed and paused for a moment) . . . that prostitutes could not have done better. . . ."

Columbus stumbled from misfortune to catastrophe. Storms again beat down on his disaster-prone ships, and the rivers where he sought shelter washed them back out to sea. Food and fresh water were running low. The sailors said confession to one another as each new disaster struck.

This long and woeful letter had been written early in June in a Jamaican anchorage, on board one of his ships so full of worms that it was like a honeycomb. The stifling oppressiveness of the virgin forest surrounded them with mists like the smoke from many fires. Indians came out in boats to prowl around his ship. Through the porthole of his cabin, where he lay motionless with gout and exhaustion, the admiral saw through the dissipating mists carved tombs, big as houses, silhouetted against the golden mountains.

The queen went peacefully to sleep before dona Beatrix had finished reading. Her fingers still lay rigid on the sheet. Dona Beatrix replaced the sheets of paper. Drops of sea water had smudged the words and dotted the writing with little gray stars. She looked at the queen; what she saw was such a perfect imitation of death that she had to prevent herself from disturbing what was only a deep sleep.

"Dona Beatrix, I talked in my sleep, didn't I?"

The fat lady shrugged, and blushed slightly.

"Come on, tell me the truth. I talked. I mentioned names. Whose?"

"You talked about don Ferdinand, yes . . . and also of Christopher Columbus. . . ."

"Is that all?"

Dona Beatrix averted her gaze.

"I think that you also mentioned the name David . . . David Amra or Ezra, I didn't catch it clearly. Isn't that the name of the son of your father's doctor?"

"Yes," said the queen, carelessly. "A childhood memory that came back to me, I don't know why. Can we ever really know why we dream of something that we have long since forgotten?"

Isabella blinked. A cold tear had been gathering in a corner of her eye for a few moments; it gave her an uncomfortable feeling.

"David Ezra! It seems as if he died only this morning. But how many years has it been, dona Beatrix? The Indians laid siege to La Navidad, then they set fire to the fortifications. David died pierced with many arrows, like Saint Sebastian. God will have received him into heaven, don't you think, dona Beatrix?"

"Of course. Don't upset yourself any more. Try to get back to sleep."

"I am not sleepy now. Listen, dona Beatrix. I have to tell you a secret. Even the king does not know it, just the blessed Archbishop Mendoza, whom God has in His holy keeping. . . ."

The lady leaned forward, her face alive with curiosity. Isabella went on.

"What am I doing? I am saying such foolish things, can't you understand that?"

Dona Beatrix looked very frustrated.

"You are right," said the queen. "I'm going to try to sleep."

Her eyes were swollen by sickness, by hardship, by the long nights of prayer. She was constantly troubled by the ever-present image of a good-looking baby boy, the first curly hair on his head. This baby she had given into the care of a young priest belonging to her entourage. The priest was a cousin of Gonzales, from a family of *conversos*, and he was a secret friend of David's.

This image blocked out her vision of God. Where and with whom was the fruit of her true love? God seemed to have been on her side. Ferdinand's extended absences, during which he was totally absorbed in his own needs for conflict and for so many fleeting romantic adventures, had created a situation in which her pregnancy could pass unnoticed by him. Ferdinand was feared and respected, but not loved. Isabella was always able to rely on the complete devotion of those closest to her.

Where was her baby? Was he still here, in the Old World? Or perhaps he might be in the New World, that earthly paradise so well described by Columbus!

In fact, this son would outlive his father, David, far from a Spain soaked with so much murderously shed blood. In Hispaniola he never spoke, of course, of his origins—under a common Spanish surname, his descendants lived in peace as Christians. In the eighteenth century, by pure chance, a priest of the Inquisition discovered some documents. Himself originally from a *converso* family, he never mentioned the discovery—the old documents, buried within thousands of old manuscripts, passed unnoticed through the centuries.*

Eyes half closed, Isabella dreamed of a glorious future. Then she gradually slipped into a peaceful and sound sleep.

The king was on the mend. News from Gand was reassuring; the announcement of the divorce between Philippe and Juana had been premature. Juana had promised to lavish on her husband a less tyrannical affection. She had even agreed to spend some time away from him, and by this means they had arrived at a new harmony in their relationship.

One question tortured the king: was Juana really insane? The Spanish people, especially the students, made up songs about her, called her *la loca*, Juana the Mad. But people are too much influenced by outward appearances.

Ferdinand had started to get out of bed. His first visit was to the queen. He was shocked to see her as she was, after so many long weeks apart. Dropsy had swollen her limbs, and her face was bloated like a watermelon. What was worse, she no longer seemed to be completely lucid.

Ferdinand cut short their conversation and limped back to his room, with a sturdy black servant supporting each arm.

*Documents in the "secret parts" of the Inquisition files in the Alcazar cattle, Segovia, Spain.

The first rain squalls swept across the massive brick walls of Medina del Campo. The *meseta* took on the color of old bone. The cawing of the crows around the castle keep became less insistent.

Early in November, it was announced that Christopher Columbus's *caravels* had come alongside at Sanlucar, at the mouth of the Guadalquivir. The admiral made his way to Seville. He had returned gouty, exhausted, disappointed, but that was only to be expected. After years of waiting and misery, the Mallorcan weaver's son had reached the peak of his glory. Then, year by year, he had slid down the far side of this mountain that he had so laboriously climbed.

He wrote to the monarchs:

"It is my cruel fate that I have hardly profited from my twenty years of service in the midst of so many hardships and dangers. Today, I own not one stone in Castile. If I want to eat or sleep, I have nothing except an inn or a tavern. Most of the time, I don't have enough money to pay my way. . . ."

That is only to be expected, Isabella thought. Then she told her secretary,

"Write to Columbus, and ask him to come and see me as soon as he is fit to travel." She continued, more quietly, "But tell him not to wait too long if he wishes to find me still alive."

Toward mid-November, snow started to fall. Enormous copper braziers were brought into the queen's room to maintain a constant temperature. From time to time, the knights came to visit: Medina-Sidonia, Gardenas, Tendilla, Cabra, and many others. They walked around the queen's bed, stood against the canopy posts, and looked silently at the queen before leaving. Ximenes Cisneros had installed himself in a nearby room, accompanied by Franciscans, awaiting the moment he dreaded.

The white light reflected from the snow scarcely penetrated the queen's swollen eyelids, but in her mind's eye she could sense the shining radiance. She lived through these last days of November in this same whiteness. It seemed to lift from her the burden of all remorse, all blemishes. She would go to her death as though she were escaping from herself through the window that opened on the snows of the *meseta*. The air around her crackled like ice. She was sinking into a cold purity that was turning her into a statue.

One morning she whispered,

"I wish to see Columbus. Tell him to come quickly."

It was dawn on November 26 of the year 1504. The secretary inscribed the date on the letterhead that he addressed to the Admiral. An hour later, a rider galloped off into the snow.

Where was Ferdinand? He came and went, flitting like a shadow through unending passages and ice-cold galleries, stopping to turn and shudder whenever the chapel bell tolled the hour. He could not bring himself to watch Isabella dying, and he reproached himself bitterly for such weakness. She was so much joined to him that a part of him would die as well. He was waiting for someone to come and tell him, "Sire, the queen is dead."

He had a horse saddled up, and set off, intending to go across country for a short ride. But in fact he rode all around the fortress without going too far away, conscious of the least noise that echoed in the freezing air.

Ximenes slowly straightened up, completed the prayer for the dead, and crossed himself before kneeling in front of the ivory crucifix. When he had given her extreme unction, the queen, in a last burst of modesty, had refused to have her feet uncovered.

Dona Beatrix and dona Mincia de la Torre pestered the doctor. Perhaps the queen was not dead. Why was he just standing there among the bishops, pretending to be important, instead of listening for a heartbeat? The doctor leaned over the queen's stiff body, confirmed that she was still living, and came back to talk in a low voice with the Bishop of Medina.

"What is the king doing?" asked dona Beatrix.

"Look!" said dona Mincia.

They pressed their foreheads against the window panes.

Motionless in the snow, a man on horseback was looking toward the castle.

The king reigned in his horse, and turned around quickly. He heard the sound of hoofbeats crossing the bridge. His heart beat faster.

He started riding in the direction of the fortress, to meet the dark shape coming toward him. He spurred his horse into a trot, then into a full gallop. His cloak blew away, but he did not turn to pick it up.

Just a few yards from the man, he suddenly stopped his horse, which reared up at the pain of the bit. It was Diego, the queen's page, Columbus's son.

"Sire," said Diego, "please come with me to the castle."

The snow had started to fall again. Through the frigid air, the chapel bell could be heard tolling continuously.

"Is the queen dead?" asked Ferdinand.

"Sire, God has received her."

Epilogue

The end of the reign of Ferdinand and his queen was dramatic. Isabella was gathered unto God, as she had wished, and was quickly forgotten in the tormented upheaval that was Spain. She was laid to rest in her carved stone sarcophagus in Granada, the city that had filled her dreams. When Ferdinand joined her, his coffin was similarly carved from stone and placed beside hers, but, ironically, the images of their faces were turned away from each other, symbolic of their life and of their reign.

They were together, as together they had created their own vision of a Spain that would last for centuries. They had shared a love together, although in many ways Isabella's love for Ferdinand was stronger than his for her. But in the end, in spite of that love, they were separated in death by an invisible wall that would be between them for all eternity.

Spain was on its way to becoming what Charles V, Ferdinand's own grandson, would call "the country on whose empire the sun would never set." But the only lasting legacy the Catholic Monarchs bequeathed to their country was the malevolent horror of the Inquisition. It is no longer a secret that Ferdinand, on the false pretext of his religious faith, lusted so much for gold and silver that he used the Inquisition as a dreadful instrument of plunder.

History will record him without doubt as the worst anti-Semite the world has ever known, because the results of his actions were not limited to his reign, but continued for centuries.

Sangre pura—'pure blood'—would become the watchword for everyone and everything in all-powerful Spain. To be honest, it is important to mention that the Inquisition, its total intolerance, was instinctively accepted by the Spaniards. It is an old fact that the Spaniards have intolerance in their blood (so *sangre pura*). It was not really Catholicism that made Spaniards intolerant, but Spaniards who made Catholicism intolerant. The leaders of the Inquisition (Spaniards) naturally developed that horrible tendency.

This nation that grew, gradually but steadily, under their heirs, especially Charles I or Charles V, would become a vast empire. *Sangre pura,* the guiding principle under the flag that to this day is known in Spain as "blood and gold," an immense enterprise would unfold. For God and king, the *conquistadors* would invade all of South and Central America. This limitless new world, this enormous unspoiled continent, was to become life itself for these *conquistadors*. The word *conquistadors* is itself most appropriate; it describes their role as adventurers, with neither faith nor conscience, under the protecting armor of the flag.

Under this pretext Spain would plunder, burn, torture, and vandalize an entire continent for the next three-hundred years. The Church—strong in its support for the Inquisition—the king, all the civil servants, all the officers, all the captains General, would behave in the same way.

Nowadays, it is popular wisdom to talk of the grandeur of all these conquests, the opening up of the New World. It is true that these discoveries and explorations brought a part of old Europe into a new world and left the Spanish language as a unifying heritage.

But the horrific excesses of the Inquisition (with the sometimes sick rationale that they were designed to bring people to the one true God) were in reality nothing more than looting on a grand scale. The magnificent civilizations in South and Central America were virtually wiped from the surface of the earth. Spanish galleons ploughed the seas, carrying back to Spain their cargoes of untold treasure. Contrary to what might be imagined, the effect was dramatic and disastrous.

The primary results of the reign of Isabella and Ferdinand, the Catholic Monarchs, were the brutalities of the Inquisition and the occupation of Granada, which led to the diaspora—the flight across the Mediterranean and on into Europe of the majority of Spain's Jews, poor, barefoot, and miserable. It is difficult to estimate, but probably some 800,000 Jews fled Spain in less than a hundred years. Back in medieval Spain and Portugal, to which they traced their origins, these sephardic Jews had considered themselves the elite, the nobility of Jewry. They still do. In Iberia, the sephardim were not only the bankers and financial advisors to the royal courts; they were also Spain's scientists, physicians, jurists, philosophers, and poets.

The sultan of Turkey, when he heard that Ferdinand and Isabella had ordered the Jews expelled, commented,

"The King of Spain must have lost his mind. He is expelling his best subjects."

He sent his boats to transport the Jews into Turkey. The Jews were expelled and Spain has never been the same.

This diaspora took from Spain thousands of active, productive, valuable, talented people. Those Jews who remained in Spain as converts had a difficult life: fearing discovery that they had originally been of the Jewish faith, they had to become more Catholic than the Catholics to reinforce their status as *conversos*. The old traditions, all their heritage of a golden age dating back to the Middle Ages, gradually faded away.

A similar diaspora, one to which shamefully little attention is paid, scattered the Muslim population of Spain. The vanquished Moors of Granada returned to Africa and settled in Morocco and Algeria. They brought some of their culture and infused it into cities such as Fez and others along the coast. Through it all, however, the ancient Arab soul kept a feeling of bitterness that, even after all these centuries, is as strong as ever. For this Muslim population that had been part of Spain for seven-hundred years, longer than any other civilization at that time in Europe, there would remain nothing but dreams of the Andalusia, the second paradise lost.

These Arabs were gradually submerged into the spreading masses of the Ottoman Empire, which was beginning to emerge and become increasingly powerful. The Jews, 'displaced persons' as they would now be called, settled in North Africa, in the south of France, in Venice, in Rome, in the Southern Balkans, in Germany, in the Ottoman Empire, and eventually made their way to Holland and England. The most desperate got as far as Poland and Russia.

The origins of anti-Semitism, and the reasons why it took root in these eras, are no longer a mystery. The Spanish diaspora was the cause.

This diaspora continued in the seventeenth and eighteenth centuries. The *conversos* were increasingly hunted down by the Inquisition, which had become as powerful as Isabella had foreseen. The majority of these *conversos* were forced to renounce their country and to emigrate even farther afield. Some even arrived in 1620 in what would become New York, in the New World. But that is another story.

The forced conversion of the Jews and the Moriscos by the cruel Inquisition was even judged by a famous French cardinal. Cardinal Richelieu said,

"This most barbarous act, in the annals of mankind, was a folly as well as a crime."

The great reign of Isabella the Catholic would bequeath to those who followed the new empire of South and Central America, stretching as far as the Pacific, a spreading of culture, the terrible influence of the Church, and the creation of a New World.

All the centuries that have led to our own time carry the ineradicable mark of these great events. Without Isabella, and without Ferdinand's greed and lack of intelligence, the world would have been a very different place. But that also is another story.

However, in the course of these tumultuous centuries, a profound reaction took shape and gathered strength. Contrary to what might have been reasonably foreseen, Spain did not grow wealthy. She plundered an entire continent, brought back untold riches, but what remained at the dawn of the twentieth century? Virtually nothing.

All the sons of families had left to make their fortune in the New World—to plunder, to settle, to take back to Spain silver and gold, *objects d'art*, jewels. But Spain had lost the habit of intelligent effort. Its work ethic, its sense of the magnificent, which had created its earlier turbulent glory, had faded away.

The nation, enriched by gold, unnoticed by the rest of Europe, very gently drifted into a half sleep. It slowly lapsed back into an agricultural society, and created an aristocracy that was at once proud, arrogant, pretentious, and brutal—all faults acquired in and nurtured by the New World.

When Central and South America shook off their chains in the latter part of the nineteenth century, and broke up into a multitude of independent countries linked only by the Spanish language, Spain was once more alone; small, poor, low in the ranking of European countries.

Some kings—Charles III, for example—tried, in spite of everything, to keep alive the old Spanish dream. But this was not enough. Europe developed at an astonishing pace in the nineteenth century, but it was not until the twentieth century that Spain followed, slowly and painfully. She escaped the First World War, only to be sucked into the horror of a civil conflict that had its origin in the old ways of destructive thought: for God and king, for money and glory.

Communism, with its war-cry of liberating the country, would have been the worst of governments. Generalissimo Franco established a 'reign' that was to some extent successful in keeping the lid on all the old instincts of Spain.

From this point on, Europe and the world developed very rapidly. Since Franco, Spain—perhaps repentant of its old excesses rooted in dreams of blood and gold—has been devoting its efforts to becoming an integral part of the new civilization, a civilization that she purported to represent without exhibiting its qualities.

One of the ironies of recent Spanish history is that, unknown to almost everyone, the Inquisition remained in legal existence until January 31, 1989. Not until then—nearly five hundred years after its brutalities began—was the news quietly released that the Cortes had voted for dissolution of the "Holy Inquisition," and that the new king, Juan Carlos I, had signed it into law.

On March 31, 1992, five-hundred years after the signing of the Edict of Expulsion against the Moors and the Jews, a ceremony was held in the first synagogue to be rebuilt in Madrid since that time. In his speech, the President of the State of Israel made a moving plea for a consensus. His Majesty, Juan Carlos I, replied by talking about "the vicissitudes of history." He did not condemn or even mention the infamous Edict.

All the fights and horrible acts of Ferdinand's life brought exactly the opposite of his dreams. He was the last King of Spain of Spanish blood and roots. Instead of conquering an empire for his blood and descendants, his kingdom and the incredible empire of the New World passed to foreign families. The Austrian Habsburg Dynasty and the French Bourbon Dynasty have ruled Spain for the last five-hundred years, up to today.

So much blood, so many crimes, so much cruelty for nothing! History has its own revenge. To build his dreams of power and for his thirst of gold, Ferdinand also instigated the Inquisition. The Inquisition led to oppression, bigotry, and anti-intellectualism. It stifled the Renaissance in Spain, and operated with a dreadful sadism and intolerance that scarred Spain in the eyes of the American continent, and indeed of the whole world.

Today, the ancient aggressive instincts still exist. As an old Spaniard, it is my most profound wish that modern Spain attempt to erase that *legenda negra*, that dark legend. Then, lovely Queen Isabella, at rest in her sarcophagus of carved stone, will perhaps dream of her great and beautiful Spain . . . and of her great and beautiful love, David Ezra.

Isabella and Ferdinand in their tomb in Granada.

Isabella

Documentation

The Study of

the Dynasties's Trees

confirm that

Queen Isabella

and her husband

King Ferdinand

"The Catholic Kings"

were born Jewish even being of the Catholic religion.

After the year 1496 the Inquisition's action created the spread of the conversion in all the Spanish population and especially in the Aristocracy.

The Castilian Succession

- The Jewish Blood

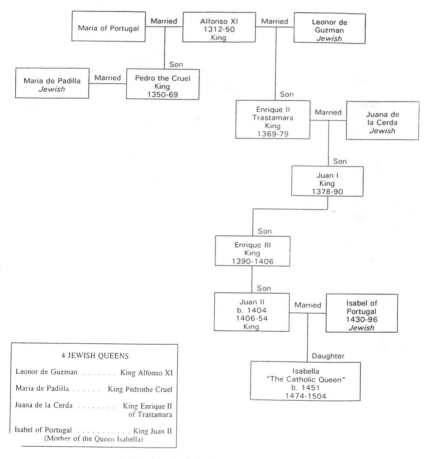

	4 JEWISH QUEENS	
Leonor de Guzman	King Alfonso XI	
Maria de Padilla	King Pedro the Cruel	
Juana de la Cerda	King Enrique II of Trastamara	
Isabel of Portugal	King Juan II (Mother of the Queen Isabella)	

* When the mother is Jewish, her children are Jewish.
(Bible. Religion - Blood's genes)

The Aragonese Succession

- The Jewish Blood

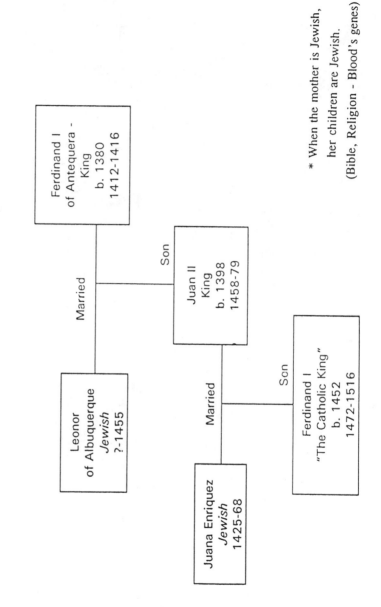

Ferdinand I
of Antequera -
King
b. 1380
1412-1416

Leonor
of Albuquerque
Jewish
?-1455

Married

Son

Juan II
King
b. 1398
1458-79

Juana Enriquez
Jewish
1425-68

Married

Son

Ferdinand I
"The Catholic King"
b. 1452
1472-1516

* When the mother is Jewish,
her children are Jewish.
(Bible, Religion - Blood's genes)

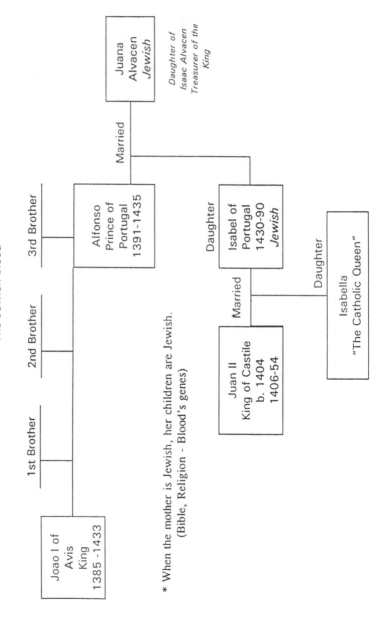

The Portugese Succession

The Jewish Blood

Joao I of
Avis
King
1385 -1433

1st Brother   2nd Brother   3rd Brother

Alfonso
Prince of
Portugal
1391-1435

Married

Juana
Alvacen
Jewish

*Daughter of
Isaac Alvacen
Treasurer of the
King*

Daughter

Isabel of
Portugal
1430-90
Jewish

Married

Juan II
King of Castile
b. 1404
1406-54

Daughter

Isabella
"The Catholic Queen"

* When the mother is Jewish, her children are Jewish.
(Bible, Religion - Blood's genes)

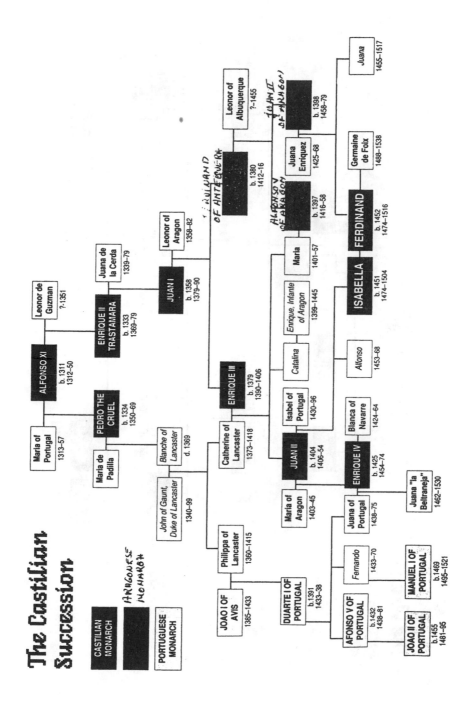

The Castilian Succession

CASTILIAN MONARCH

ARAGONESE MONARCH

PORTUGUESE MONARCH

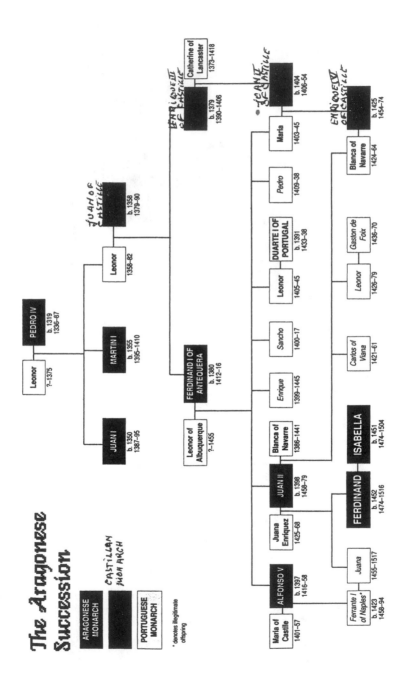

The Aragonese Succession

ARAGONESE MONARCH

CASTILLAN MONARCH

PORTUGUESE MONARCH

* denotes illegitimate offspring

Leonor
?–1375

PEDRO IV
b. 1319
1336–87

JUAN I
b. 1350
1387–95

MARTIN I
b. 1355
1395–1410

Leonor
1358–82

JUAN I OF CASTILLE
b. 1358
1379–90

Leonor of Albuquerque
?–1455

FERDINAND I OF ANTEQUERA
b. 1380
1412–16

ENRIQUE III OF CASTILLE
b. 1379
1390–1406

Catherine of Lancaster
1373–1418

JUAN II OF CASTILLE
b. 1404
1406–54

Maria
1403–45

Pedro
1409–38

Leonor
1405–45

DUARTE I OF PORTUGAL
b. 1391
1433–38

Sancho
1400–17

Enrique
1399–1445

Blanca of Navarre
1386–1441

JUAN II
b. 1398
1458–79

Juana Enriquez
1425–68

ALFONSO V
b. 1397
1416–58

Maria of Castile
1401–57

ENRIQUE IV OF CASTILLE
b. 1425
1454–74

Blanca of Navarre
1424–64

Gaston de Foix
1436–70

Leonor
1426–79

Carlos of Viana
1421–61

ISABELLA
b. 1451
1474–1504

FERDINAND
b. 1452
1474–1516

Juana
1455–1517

Ferrante I of Naples*
b. 1423
1458–94

The Descendants of Isabella and Ferdinand

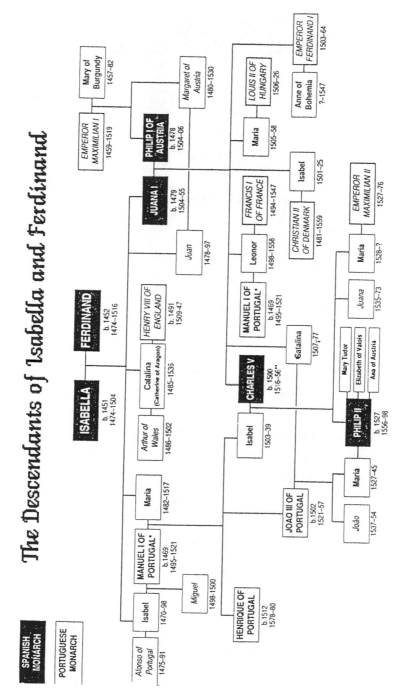

SPANISH MONARCH

PORTUGUESE MONARCH

Alonso of Portugal 1475–91

Isabel b. 1470–98

Miguel 1498–1500

MANUEL I OF PORTUGAL* b. 1469 1495–1521

HENRIQUE OF PORTUGAL b. 1512 1578–80

Maria 1482–1517

JOAO III OF PORTUGAL b. 1502 1521–57

João 1537–54

Maria 1527–45

ISABELLA b. 1451 1474–1504

FERDINAND b. 1452 1474–1516

Arthur of Wales 1486–1502

Catalina (Catherine of Aragon) 1485–1535

HENRY VIII OF ENGLAND b. 1491 1509–47

Isabel 1503–39

CHARLES V b. 1500 1516–56**

Catalina 1507–77

MANUEL I OF PORTUGAL* b. 1469 1495–1521

Leonor 1498–1558

FRANCIS I OF FRANCE 1494–1547

Juan 1478–97

JUANA I b. 1479 1504–55

PHILIP I OF AUSTRIA b. 1478 1504–06

EMPEROR MAXIMILIAN I 1459–1519

Mary of Burgundy 1457–82

Margaret of Austria 1480–1530

PHILIP II b. 1527 1556–98

Mary Tudor
Elizabeth of Valois
Ana of Austria

Maria 1527–45

Juana 1535–73

Maria 1528–?

EMPEROR MAXIMILIAN II 1527–76

CHRISTIAN II OF DENMARK 1481–1559

Isabel 1501–25

Maria 1505–58

LOUIS II OF HUNGARY 1506–26

Anne of Bohemia ?–1547

EMPEROR FERDINAND I 1503–64

* Manuel I of Portugal married three descendants of Isabella and Ferdinand.
** Charles I, king of Spain (1516–56), and Charles V, Holy Roman Emperor (1519–58)

Christobal Colom

Christobal Colom

was born on the Island of Mallorca (Baleares) in the small village of Felanitx.

Since the 16th - 17th century the small town is called uptoday = Felanitx - Porto Colom.

His parents were Jewish.

They converted to the Catholic religion (conversos) when Christobal was five years old - This is the origin of his first - name - Christobal.

The birth certificate and the document of conversion had been - for centuries - uptoday - in the Archives of the Catholic Bishop of Palma de Mallorca - in the old cathedral.

In the Mallorca population, the name Colom is hold - uptoday - by few hundred families, all from Jewish origin. They converted to catholicism, in the course of the last centuries, under the action of the Inquisition.

The family escaped to Genoa - Italy - when Christobal was seven years old to avoid the Inquisition's persecutions.

Christobal Colom's Log Books (his tree trips) were written = one page in Spanish one page in Ladino. (The normal language of the Jewish - Spanish's population for centuries).

Christobal Colom

The "Archives of the Indies," on Seville's Avenida Quiepo de Llano, is the principal historical repository for Spain's exploration and conquest of the New World.

On shelves of Cuban mahogany and inside centuries-old chests, some four-hundred-thousand documents are ranked and filed. Of course there are, too, the charts, account books, logs, letters, and memoirs of Christopher Columbus.

"The admiral of the ocean sea" was a Jew. His Spanish name, Colon, was one from the Hebrew Spanish tradition; his father was a weaver, one of the few trades open to Jews. His mother, Susanna Fonterossa, was the daughter of Jacobo Fonterossa and the granddaughter of Abraham Fonterossa. They were old Jewish families from Mallorca. Today, this name still exists as a *converso's* name—so mother and grandmother being Jewish, Christobal Colon (his real name) was also Jewish.

In one of his letters found in the "Archives," he wrote:
"I am not the first admiral of my family. Let them find me whatever name they want and please, for when all is done, David, that most prudent king of Jerusalem; I am a servant of the same Lord who raised him to such a dignity."
Nothing can be so clear!
In his ship's log, supposedly lost (according to the legal history) but, available today, in the library of the "Dukes of Alba," in Madrid, Columbus makes frequent references to the Hebrew Bible, to Jerusalem, to Moses, David, Abraham, Sarah, and Isaac. He computes the age of the world according to the Jewish calendar— and from the destruction of the second temple, so according, to the Jews, to his present days, being the year of the birth of "Our Lord 1481"—he notes 1413 years.

In discussing the mines of the New World, he observes:
"Our Lord, who rescued Daniel and the three children, is present with the same wisdom as he had then."
In his Last Will and Testament Columbus asks that:

"one-tenth of his income be given to the poor; that a dowry be provided for poor girls in such a way that they do not notice whence it comes."

That is a characteristically anonymous technique of Jewish philanthropy.

In preparation of his first trip to Lisbon, Columbus consulted the famous Jew, Joseph Vecinto, and Martin Behaim Zacoto, the writer of the famous *Astronomical Tables*, endorsed his proposed Atlantic expedition. Born Jewish, in Mallorca, he had an easy access to all the maps from the famous Mallorcan cartographers, and with no possibility of financing his trip in Lisbon, Columbus moved to Spain. Then appeared "The Italian Genova's Origin." He created it as a legal facade to avoid the Inquisition.

A great part of his crew were Jewish *conversos*: Alfonso De LaCalle; Rodrigo Sanchez De Segovia, a surgeon, relative of Aragon's treasurer Gabriel Sanchez; Maestro Bernard of Tortosa, another surgeon who had only recently had escaped the Inquisition; and Luis de Torres, a Jew who had accepted baptism just in time to sign on with Columbus's fleet.

Christobal Colon finished his life horribly poor—abandoned by everybody that was involved in the actions of the Inquisition—and for centuries the Spanish (legal) history focused on the *conquistadors* and not on Columbus.

Why have all these facts never been mentioned? Because the Catholic Inquisition, and at this time, the Catholic Monarchs, were very uncomfortable with them.

The bureaucratically powerful Inquisition was able to hide all these facts inside thousands of documents. For centuries, nobody had the opportunity and "the right" to go inside the "classified archives."

The Italian facade was maintained—after so many centuries and with the general tendency towards racism in the west, it was very difficult to transform the "legal history"—so the Italian's original version of history was maintained.

Notes

I. Reference pages 171-172

Autodafe Sevilla. Real historical facts described "in horrible details" in the documents of the Inquisition Holy Office Archives in Sevilla. Not opened to normal public.

II. Reference page 290

Son from David Ezra. The document mentioning him (seems to have been dictated by Isabella) is in the Royal Archives in the Alcazar Castle of Segovia inside a great lot of documents referring to the Inquisition. Start page 226.

III. The Isabella and Ferdinand family trees. Facts from all the official documents in the Spanish Archives.

IV. Christobal Colom. West Indies documents in the "enormous" lot of documents, not in table of contents and not normally open to the public. A lot of archivists today are young Catholic priests.